Improving Criminal Justice Workplaces is a very innovative and novel book, which seeks to improve criminal justice workplace practice by translating research into policy, but also to help develop best practice work environments. This is a must-read for those concerned with workplaces in the criminal justice field.

Sir Cary Cooper, *50th Anniversary Professor of Organisational Psychology and Health, Manchester Business School, University of Manchester, UK*

This book addresses issues which, for many years, have been recognised as having a major effect on the functioning of criminal justice organisations. The authors provide a comprehensive and informative review of theory and research on these issues, along with practical suggestions on how to improve the work environment of these organisations. The book offers an extremely valuable synthesis of research and practice for both researchers and practitioners in this field.

Michael O'Driscoll, *Professor of Psychology, University of Waikato, New Zealand*

More than ever the criminal justice sector is in the focus of public attention. So the time is ripe for a state-of-the-art overview that might serve as a basis for evidence-based change and intervention. This volume not only provides a detailed analysis of criminal justice workplaces from an organizational psychological point of view, but it also offers tools, solutions and best practices to improve those workplaces. This is a must-read for those who are committed to positive change in criminal justice.

Wilmar Schaufeli, *Professor of Work and Organizational Psychology, Utrecht University, the Netherlands*

Improving Criminal Justice Workplaces

Whether public or private all organisations within the criminal justice system seek to improve, often from an evidence base, but often find it difficult to effectively translate research findings into policy or design best-practice interventions. This book provides a direct bridge between academic research in organisational behaviour and the management of workers within criminal justice agencies.

The public sector in particular is currently experiencing significant funding cuts and increasingly needs to create optimal workplace strategies to maintain frontline services and preserve the well-being of the workforce. The aim of this book is to equip managers with knowledge about key processes and appropriate research methods, thereby enabling them to more readily understand and apply academic research to their workplaces. The means to translate research findings into implementation strategies are also clearly explained. Furthermore, essential organisational issues that either impede or enhance productivity, employee effectiveness, and management responsiveness to change are discussed, following a common chapter template of problem definition, research and analysis, evidence translation, implementation, and evaluation.

Written by experts in the field, this book applies cutting-edge theoretical discussions and research findings to evidence-based policy. It examines new strategies and best practice in the context of widespread demoralization of staff in the criminal justice sector due to the impact of increased austerity. *Improving Criminal Justice Workplaces* is essential reading for leadership teams, managers and supervisors in the court, police, probation, and prison services, as well as allied professionals such as forensic psychologists and HR professionals.

Paula Brough is a Professor of Organisational Psychology at Griffith University, Brisbane, Australia. Her early research examining the psychological health and well-being of police officers was conducted in the UK and New Zealand. Paula has contributed over 90 scholarly outputs to the international academic literature in this field (books, book chapters, and journal articles).

Jennifer Brown is a visiting professor at the London School of Economics and Co-Director of the Mannheim Centre for the study of criminology and criminal justice. She has conducted research on occupational stress within the police service as well as making a special study of gender within policing. Most recently she was the deputy chair of an Independent Commission into the future of policing within England and Wales.

Amanda Biggs is a Lecturer at Griffith University, Australia. Her research focuses on psychological and physical health at work, intervention evaluation, positive occupational health psychology, and workplace bullying. Much of Amanda's research experience has been conducted in collaboration with criminal justice organisations, and has been presented at numerous national and international academic conferences.

Routledge frontiers of criminal justice

Improving Criminal Justice Workplaces

Translating theory and research into evidence-based practice

Paula Brough, Jennifer Brown and Amanda Biggs

Routledge
Taylor & Francis Group

LONDON AND NEW YORK

First published 2016
by Routledge
2 Park Square, Milton Park, Abingdon, Oxon OX14 4RN

and by Routledge
711 Third Avenue, New York, NY 10017

First issued in paperback 2017

Routledge is an imprint of the Taylor & Francis Group, an informa business

British Library Cataloguing in Publication Data
A catalogue record for this book is available from the British Library

Library of Congress Cataloging-in-Publication Data
Brough, Paula, author.
Improving criminal justice workplaces : translating theory and research into
evidence-based practice / Paula Brough, Jennifer Brown and Amanda Biggs.
    pages cm. – (Routledge frontiers of criminal justice ; 32)
    1. Criminal justice personnel. 2. Criminal justice, Administration of. 3.
Personnel management. 4. Organizational behavior. 5. Organizational
sociology. I. Title.
HV7419.B786 2016
364.068'3–dc23   2015020296

ISBN 13: 978-1-138-30478-9 (pbk)
ISBN 13: 978-1-138-01946-1 (hbk)

Typeset in Times New Roman
by Wearset Ltd, Boldon, Tyne and Wear

To Doug and Sylvester, for all the love, joy, and laughter.

To A.H.

To Ryan and Miki, Nana and Grandad, David and Samara, and Matt and Eleanor, thank you for your friendship and love.

To Maddison and Chelsea, being your aunty brings me immeasurable joy.

To my parents, Brian and Glennie, with all my love and gratitude for your kindness, generosity, and support.

Contents

PART III
Organisational problems and solutions 147

Figures

Tables

Acknowledgements

Paula Brough sincerely thanks the Australian Research Council, the Queensland Government (Smart State Senior Research Fellowships), and Griffith University for numerous years of funding which enabled this research to be conducted. She also thanks the members of Queensland Police Service and Queensland Corrective Services for supporting and collaborating with much of the research reported here.

Jennifer Brown thanks Lord Stevens for permission to quote from the Report of the Independent Police Commission which he chaired, Sue Woolfenden and Bill Williamson of Strategic Direction for their help in conducting the Delphi consultation, and Ben Bradford, University of Oxford, for his collaboration on the survey of police officers undertaken on behalf of the Independent Police Commission.

Amanda Biggs sincerely thanks the Australian Research Council, Griffith University, Queensland Police Service, and Queensland Corrective Service for their support and research collaboration. Amanda also thanks Dr Suzie Drummond for her assistance in sourcing materials cited in this book.

Abbreviations

ACPO	Association of Chief Police Officers
APA	Association of Police Authorities
BME	Black Minority Ethnic
CILP	Community Intelligence Led Policing
CIPD	Chartered Institute of Personnel Development
CJS	Criminal Justice System
CRC	Community Rehabilitation Companies
GIS	Geographic Information Software
LGB	Lesbian Gay Bi-sexual
MCSI	Magistrates Courts Service Inspectorate
MOJ	Ministry of Justice (UK)
NCPE	National Centre for Policing Excellence
NOMS	National Offender Management Service
NPIA	National Policing Improvement Agency
NPM	New Public Management
NPS	National Probation Service
OGRS	Offender Group Reconviction Scale
PA	Probation Association
PCC	Police and Crime Commissioners
PCMA	Police and Magistrates Courts Act
PSNI	Policing Service of Northern Ireland
SNOP	Statement of National Objectives and Priorities
TTA	Teacher Training Agency

Part I
Framing issues

1   Introduction

Introduction

Workplaces have over the last four decades changed dramatically (Sparks *et al.*, 2001). There has been the information technology (IT) revolution; introduction of techniques into the public sector from commercial businesses (New Public Management); and more recently the catastrophic failures of the global banking system resulting in reduction of staff numbers and pressure on service delivery. There can be little doubt that the criminal justice system (CJS) and its agencies are affected by the present turbulence. Many governments are engaging in reform programmes and responding to the stark realities of the economic downturn. Private companies are now running prisons (Andrew, 2006) and are involved in delivering policing services (Cheer, 2013; Rhodes, 2013).

King and Levy (2012) identified external politics as a key environmental stressor, and the uncertainty this creates increases psychological strain in employees. As part of the economic downturn they suggested that major organisational transformations have been accompanied by changes in how employees interact with each other on a daily basis, in addition to concerns about their continued employment. Under conditions of uncertainty and job insecurity people are more likely to withdraw both from their job and the organisation as a way of reducing the psychological impact of perceived or actual impacts of austerity. It is not surprising, then, that staff employed within the CJS are feeling anxious and confused by the magnitude and pace of new ways of working, while many managers are overwhelmed by having not only to deliver organisational changes, but also to respond to the operational demands of achieving more for less when delivering public services.

Researchers report job insecurity, lowered morale, and erosion of motivation and loyalty amongst the workforce generally (O'Driscoll and Brough, 2010). They also point out that managers in organisations may themselves, intentionally or unintentionally, cause stress in employees and adversely impact their well-being and productivity. When under strain, managers may react by exhibiting an inconsiderate or bullying management style, whilst members of the senior management team may, in conditions of crisis, become focused on self-preservation, limiting the flow of information to rank-and-file staff, and constraining their decision options

(Webster *et al.*, in press). Quick *et al.* (2004) ventured that executives have a tendency to adopt a depersonalised management style and reduce the variations in processes within organisational systems. In other words, they seek to control outcomes and results and limit the span of control exercised by their employees. Such an approach may place senior staff in a continuous state of struggle with employees, characterised by bullying behaviour, discrimination, and angry outbursts, that threatens subordinates' personal autonomy. Limiting control at work can, in turn, engender bad feeling and toxic emotions which, if ignored, can hamper productivity and learning. This is, of course, contrary to the working environments that most senior executives aim to build, i.e. a supportive and positive work environment constructed upon compassionate and humane employment conditions.

Organisational productivity is closely intertwined with the health of its members. There is a marked difference between over-controlling and potentially abusive behaviours which produce disengagement and distress and, in contrast, motivating and challenging employees for the release of human capital. There is a long history of evidence demonstrating that engaged and motivated employees are prepared to contribute discretionary effort (organisational citizenship behaviours) in achieving the organisation's goals (e.g. Brough *et al.*, 2009; Webster *et al.*, in press).

Increasingly, private and public sector organisations are seeking research evidence in order to improve their respective workplaces and the qualities of services they deliver. However, it is often difficult to effectively translate research findings into organisational policies or to design best-practice interventions. This is especially relevant in the current climate when public sectors are facing significant funding cuts. There is an urgent requirement to create optimal workplace strategies to maintain front-line services and preserve the well-being of the workforce currently in transition. As we describe in Chapter 13, professionals in the justice sector are experiencing a widespread demoralisation of staff through the impacts of austerity and correspondingly greater levels of both work disengagement, and occupational stress.

This book is divided into three parts. In Part I, current theoretical discussions of occupational culture, employee engagement, procedural justice, leadership, communication, and professionalisation are described as the conceptual bases underpinning organisational behaviours. Part II describes the essential research tools that form the basis of empirical evidence, including conducting organisational evaluations, focus groups, and surveys. Finally, in Part III we address five current key issues for CJS organisations (work–life balance, occupational stress, leadership, bullying, and discrimination) and clearly translate research findings into implementation strategies within each chapter.

Strategic foresight

Given the operational and organisational upheavals besetting the CJS, it seems timely not only to review the present situation faced by criminal justice organisations, but to also engage in forward-looking thinking optimising the welfare and well-being of those working in its agencies. In taking the criminal justice system as a whole, the strategic foresight framework (Hines and Bishop, 2006) provides a useful means to identify challenges and prepare for possible eventualities. We employ Hines and Bishop's six steps to outline the context and plan of the book: framing, scanning, forecasting, visioning, planning, and action.

Step 1 Framing

Framing the issue involves clear identification of the organisational problem requiring attention and is an antidote to the restricted attentional focus which may be adopted when under pressure or experiencing crises. A recurring theme of analyses of criminal justice reform and change (as well as resistance to change) has been the concept of the organisational culture. Mawby and Worrell (2013) declared that an analysis of organisational culture is important for the following five reasons:

1   To identify what really matters and how things are done (formally and informally) in an organisation;
2   To provide insight into how professionals perceive their occupation;
3   To reveal the influences on how work is done and how effective it will be;
4   To show how new members are introduced into ways of working (and how exiting members may resist new ways of working);
5   Finally, to locate the stable resources in periods of change and to identify the key obstacles to reform.

Thus in Chapter 2 we present an analysis of organisational culture and its supportive and problematic aspects. In Chapter 15 we provide a more detailed account of bullying and harassment that often occurs within criminal justice agencies, whilst in Chapter 16 we describe the problems associated with discrimination. Chapter 13 examines how toxic aspects of the working environment can lead to experiences of stress that may take place, especially in gendered workforces such as policing and prisons. In Chapter 3 we demonstrate the adverse effects of all these issues upon levels of employee engagement.

In recent years, much interest has been extended to employee engagement (Saks, 2006). As this has been a rather confused concept, Chapter 3 provides some clarification and discusses current research to show this has been linked to organisational success and performance as well as individuals' job satisfaction and their intention to stay or quit their job. Saks (2006) suggested that many of those in work are not fully engaged and estimates that in America alone the 'engagement gap' is costing $300 billion a year in lost productivity. Generally taken to mean the degree to which an individual is attentive and absorbed in and by their work, associations have been found between engagement and the fairness of the distribution of rewards and perceived levels of supervisor support. In addition, Richman *et al.* (2008) showed that supportive work–life balance policies are positively correlated with employee engagement. Chapter 12 provides the practice dimension giving consideration to the implementation of policies that promote full engagement.

As implied above, leadership style is another crucial concept that can directly influence a workplace in a positive or negative way. As Quick *et al.* (2004, p. 362) noted: 'organisational leaders, [and] executives have a responsibility to exercise power and influence in constructive ways to achieve positive organizational outcome and failure to do so is a failure of leadership.' In Chapter 4, therefore, we review the literature on effective leadership and the importance of instilling trust and confidence. Erosion of employee confidence undermines the legitimacy of the leader's authority and may result in active or passive resistance, especially under conditions of organisational change. Chapter 14 is the reciprocal practice discussion that takes the theoretical ideas and transforms them into ways of promoting effective leadership.

Another key framing issue is organisational communication. An unintended consequence of closed and controlled communications is a growth of the rumour mill and hidden agendas where people feel they cannot express their views or offer suggestions without recrimination or retribution (Quick *et al.*, 2004). Ways of cultivating open communication are through reflective listening and non-defensive consultation. This requires treating employees with dignity and respect. These ideas are discussed in Chapter 5 and the different modes of enacting consultation are described in Chapter 9. Finally, we look at the concept of professionalisation in Chapter 6. This has featured significantly in discussions about reforming aspects of the criminal justice system, particularly in relation to policing (Neyroud, 2013) and probation (Fitzgibbon and Lea, 2010).

Step 2 Scanning

Resources that provide the evidence base to reveal what is already known, is on the horizon or represents an area for which, as yet, little is known can be accessed through a scanning process. Part II of the book provides details of the key tools used for scanning (gathering evidence). In Chapter 9 we describe the method of rapid assessment evaluation whereby published sources are analysed to provide a clear summary of the already available information. Hearing directly from the affected constituencies is also an important part of scanning and we describe best-practice techniques in the areas of focus groups (Chapter 8), consultation (Chapter 9), and surveys (Chapter 10). Chapter 11 provides a detailed case study of the Delphi technique which is a way to achieve a consensual solution to an organisational question: e.g. how to achieve a procedurally just working environment. As part of the scanning process, it is important to be aware of the following five core external trends.

a Economic

The systemic failure of the global banking system and countries' balance of payment deficits have contributed to the current period of economic austerity. The police, courts, and prison system are facing present and future pressures on their funding (e.g. Horan and Maine, 2014; Independent Police Commission,

2013). Cuts are likely to be a continual feature of the criminal justice system for the foreseeable future and so efforts to improve organisational functioning are going to have to be cost-neutral at a minimum and cost-saving at best.

b Social

Patterns of migration and social mobility, increasing fragmentation of families and communities, and increasing levels of inequality have contributed to a transformation of the social conditions in which criminal justice agencies work. The internet and social media have created opportunities for new types of crime. The public generally are more sceptical and have a higher expectation about being consulted over changes in policy. The 24-hour news media coverage creates a spotlight in which managers and chief executives have to deal with ongoing operations and organisational failures within a public arena.

c Changing levels of crime

There has been a global trend of decreases in levels of crime. Tseloni *et al.* (2010) undertook a secondary analysis of European victimisation data, and found that between 1995 and 2004 the mean international crime reductions were 77 per cent for theft from cars; 60 per cent theft from a person; 26 per cent burglary; 21 per cent assaults; and 17 per cent theft of cars. Similar trends are observed in other Western countries. This general trend in decreasing crime levels reverses the upward trend which marked much of the twentieth century. The implications for criminal justice agencies in operating within climates of reduced changing patterns of crime are only just beginning to emerge.

d Scientific and technical trends

The considerable scientific developments, especially in the forensic science field, indicate that technological advances will lead to new forms of crime prevention and suspect identification. These technological advances place new demands on police investigations and pressure on prosecutors, expert witnesses, juries, and judicial functions (Horan and Maine, 2014). Emerging developments, for example, include the use of digital technologies to reconstruct three-dimensional crime scenes for juries, and the closer integrated networking of criminal justice agencies. These scientific developments will have a significant impact on current working practices. Neyroud and Weisburd (2014), for example, argued that policing must: value science and its potential contribution to policing; have knowledge about scientific methods; and be actively engaged in the advancement of science. Neyroud and Weisburd suggested there needs to be a greater valuing of scientific norms and procedures. We have taken this to mean an adoption of academic ethical practices and an awareness of the levels of rigour accompanying different scientific methods. We discuss these methods further in Part II of this book.

e Threats to legitimacy and trust

The catalogue of corruption scandals and operational failures (including the discrediting of victims and doctoring of police witness statements in the case of the Hillsborough football disaster, which has resulted in a new inquest being conducted in the UK) erode the contract between public and agencies of criminal justice. Bradford *et al.*, (2013) suggested that the perceived fairness of legal authorities is clearly linked to the public's propensities to both defer to and co-operate with those authorities. Moreover, just procedures generate a sense of legitimacy for those authorities to wield the power that they have been granted. Undermining people's belief in the trustworthiness of criminal justice agencies threatens the co-operative contact, without which people may be reluctant to come forward as witnesses, or be prepared to give evidence in court. Bradford and colleagues also noted that a sense of legitimacy is as important for senior staff to exert their authority and engage their respective workforces in a fair-minded way. Threats here may undermine the psychological contract between staff and senior managers.

Step 3 Forecasting alternatives

The forecasting step of this framework requires that attention be given to potential alternative scenarios in response to issues of identification and problem analysis. There are a number of ways in which CJS organisations could respond. The first is strengthening the personal resilience of the workforce, the second proposes the creation of a fair and just workplace, the third seeks greater professionalisation of the workforce (this last affects policing, probation, and prison, whilst ironically lawyers are facing a potential deprofessionalisation crisis). Finally, applying principles from rational choice models, such as stiffening of control, strengthening performance regimes, and introducing performance-related pay may offer another pathway.

a Increased resilience of workers

The idea of psychological resilience proposes that people have the capacity to move on in a positive way from negative or stressful experiences (Jackson *et al.*, 2007; Shochet *et al.*, 2011). Resilience differs from recovery in that the latter implies a period of suspended normal functioning, whereas resilience involves the maintenance of performance with no loss of functioning. Qualities associated with resilience include resourcefulness, self-confidence, and flexibility. Vulnerability, on the other hand, is likely to predict an adverse response to organisational stressors. Given the likelihood of people in the criminal justice system being exposed to human suffering and cruelty as well as turbulence in their working environments, recruiting employees with high levels of personal resilience and also enhancing personal resilience at work to reduce vulnerabilities, are important strategies to be considered.

b Introduction of organisational justice

Organisational justice consists of four key elements:

1   Distributive justice: perceived fairness of the distribution of inputs and rewards in the workplace (e.g. equality of access to promotion or job specialisms);
2   Procedural justice: perceived fairness of decision-making processes in the workplace (e.g. consistency in decision-making and having a voice in the process);
3   Informational justice: perceived fairness of information informing decision-making (e.g. clarity, completeness, and truthfulness);
4   Interpersonal justice: perceived fairness of interpersonal interactions (i.e. being treated respectfully and with dignity; Bradford *et al.*, 2014).

Bradford *et al.*, (2013) proposed that procedural justice is vitally important within policing organisations, while Tyler (2013) argued the same for prison staff. Bradford and colleagues proposed that perceptions of workplace procedural justice (particularly fairness of procedures, communications, and the quality of interactions with senior staff) are directly associated with compliance with organisational goals and demonstration of organisational citizenship behaviours (OCB), i.e. willingness to exert discretionary effort in dealings with the public. Perceived unfairness erodes internal legitimacy and discourages positive attitudes.

c Rational choice models

Government and private companies veer towards rational choice models. This is an instrumental approach to staff management based on the premise that employees make choices, and are motivated by their own self-interests. Thus people are said to respond to the risk of sanction because it may inflict pain (e.g. penalties for periods of sickness absence) or promote rewards (e.g. performance-related pay). In essence this logic proposes that on the one hand people comply with the rules of an organisation because they believe they may be punished in some way if they do not, while they will take on extra work because they are offered bonuses or other incentives. The introduction of the payment by results regime in the British Probation Service is an example of such an instrumental approach (Fox and Albertson, 2013).

Such approaches resonate with the discussion above about the exercise of controlling regimes in workplaces. In recent years, governments have sought to introduce performance indicators and targets as ways of directing activity and there is a danger that the cottage industry which develops to measure performance can be subverted. Munro (2011) suggested that managerial attention can thus become excessively focussed on the *process* rather than actual practice outcomes.

d (De)professionalisation and (de)regulation

Professionalisation and regulation represent two intertwined but somewhat contradictory trends. Recent contemporary discussions have occurred about methods to increase the accountability of police, probation, and prison officers that to some extent mimic the processes of the professional practice of the law. Thus lawyers are bound by professional and ethical codes of conduct. They are a regulated profession and can be struck off for misconduct. The newly established College of Policing in England and Wales, as a priority, issued a code of ethics for police officers, as part of a wider ambition to professionalise the police. This involves the development of a corpus of knowledge and the identification of evidence-based practices that contribute to police officers exercising their discretionary skills as autonomous, self-regulated professionals (Tilley and Laycock, 2013). Similar arguments have also been aired for prison and probation officers (Crewe *et al.*, 2008; Shepherd, 2013).

A related trend has been through the privatisation agenda. Thus Savage (2007) suggested that as governments sought to decentralise the provision of public services by inviting the private sector to deliver those services, they concomitantly introduced centralised oversight agencies. Thus, with the increase in the plurality of service provision, central control of public services is maintained through the regulatory machinery rather than through direct provision of those services.

Yet, to some degree there appears to be an opposite trend in the provision of legal services. Sherr and Thompson (2013) described how the Legal Services Act (2003) set about creating a new regulator in England and Wales, the *Legal Services Board*, taking away from the legal professions their ability to regulate themselves and open up new ways of delivering legal services. Some take this to be a 'dumbing down' of the profession and it has been colloquially referred to as 'Tesco Law', in the sense of cheaper legal services being comodified and literally supplied through a supermarket by lesser qualified legal executives. So, on the one hand, there has been an aspiration to improve the quality of services of CJS occupations such as policing, by attempts to enhance their professional status through the creation of chartered professionals (Independent Police Commission, 2013), while, on the other hand, through de-regulation of legal provision, there is a belief by some that this represents a deprofessionalisation of legal expertise.

Step 4 Visioning preferred futures

What evidence is available to assist in choosing between the various options identified above? Bradford *et al.* (2014) undertook an empirical test of the efficacy of the rational choice model compared to an organisational procedural justice model. Their study of officers in the Durham Constabulary in the North of England revealed that police officers' motivations across a whole range of positive behaviours were associated with their perceptions of fairness. This, in turn, was linked to the officer's sense of identification and loyalty to the force and predicted their greater likelihood of taking on discretionary actives (in other words showing greater organisational citizenship behaviours and contributing to the organisation's stock of social capital). Instrumental rewards and the threat of sanctions were not related to positive behaviours. Bradford *et al.* (2014, p. 110) concluded: 'the emphasis traditionally placed on instrumental incentives in performance management regimes seems misplaced. Positive orientation towards organisational goals in Durham was seemingly not fostered by threatening officers with sanctions for non-compliance.' Similarly, Lambert *et al.* (2007) demonstrated positive associations between distributive and procedural justice and stress outcomes, organisational commitment, and job satisfaction with US correctional employees.

Incentives such as performance-related pay has been a feature of New Public Management. Perry *et al.* (2009) reviewed the key publications between 1977 and 2008 assessing performance-related pay outcomes. They found:

- Where goals were clear, compensation adequate, and staff support for merit pay existed, there were positive outcomes. However, more often research reported little relationship between performance and compensation and a distaste amongst employees for the divisive side effects.
- Schemes in the public sector were frequently poorly implemented, a situation exacerbated by a lack of transparency and doubts about the fairness of the schemes.
- There is the potential for a public backlash when senior executives receive what the public perceives to be an excessive bonus relative to the average pay of the organisation.

Perry *et al.* (2009) concluded from the available research evidence that performance-related pay failed to produce significant performance improvements. Boosting employee resilience or only employing those having greater natural resilience might appear on its face value as a reasonable strategy, but this fails to address the structural and recurring problems that the workforce may encounter. 'Fixing' the individual employee to withstand inherently difficult working conditions or increasing their capacity to cope with problematic managers are only short-term strategies.

Professionalisation has been held to be an antidote to corruption and a way to improve delivery of service amongst the CJS's blue-collar workers (Fleming, 2013). Kakar (1998) found that police officers with a higher education perceive themselves as performing better in several performance categories including ethics and honesty. Paterson (2011, p. 294) concluded: 'Higher education adds value to the training and development of police in a number of areas and enhances the ability of officers to perform their role.' It is, therefore, apparent that the more promising candidate intervention to improve workplace performance and individual well-being is a combination of person-focused interventions (i.e. increased professionalisation) and organizational focused strategies to encourage a procedural justice style of management.

Step 5 Planning and action

The translation of conceptual ideas and drawing the lessons from empirical research is an essential part of this book. The five chapters in Part II of this book describing key tools adopted by CJS organisations provides the means to identify relevant issues and work towards developing solutions. The case studies in the chapters also act as demonstration projects of how to implement interventions.

Conclusions

We recognise that many of the problems identified in this book are currently affecting criminal justice agencies globally. By drawing on our own research experiences in Australia and the United Kingdom, as well as reviewing the literature from other jurisdictions, we have written this book with a strong international focus to appeal to criminal justice organisations around the world. We aim to provide a direct bridge between the available academic research of organisational behaviour and the management of workers' well-being within criminal justice workplaces (i.e. police, corrections/prison services, prosecution, and other justice services). Importantly, as well as describing research and explaining the underlying concepts, our coverage includes accessible accounts of tools that will provide managers with knowledge about key research methods, thereby enabling them more readily to understand and apply academic findings to their workplaces. We also provide some best-practice case study examples of these methods. Thus this book describes current thinking by drawing on the available research evidence, partnered with chapters translating this research evidence into practice.

We tackle the research–practice translation problem, by articulating theoretical ideas to inform criminal justice organisations about critical psychological and behavioural processes that may inhibit or facilitate the achievement of organisational goals. Each chapter identifies these processes which are most conducive to the good health and well-being of CJS employees, particularly in times of austerity and the challenges this brings.

References

Andrew, J. (2006) Prisons, the profit motive and other challenges to accountability. *Critical Perspectives on Accounting*, 18: 877–904.

Bradford, B., Jackson, J., and Hough, M. (2013) Police futures and legitimacy: redefining 'good policing'. In Brown, J. (ed.) *The future of policing*. Abingdon, UK: Routledge (pp. 79–99).

Bradford, B., Quinton, P., Myhill, A., and Porter, G. (2013) Why do 'the law' comply? Procedural justice group identification and officer motivation in police organisations. *European Journal of Criminology*, 11: 110–131.

Brough, P., O'Driscoll, M., Kalliath, T., Cooper, C.L., and Poelmans, S. (2009) *Workplace psychological health: current research and practice*. Cheltenham, UK: Edward Elgar.

Cheer, J. (2013) A wide-ranging partnership. In Neyroud, P. (ed.) *Policing UK 2013. Priorities and pressures: a year of transition*. London: Witan Media (pp. 38–39).

Crewe, B., Bennett, J., and Wahidin, A. (2008) Introduction. In Bennett, J., Crewe, B., and Wahidin, A. (eds) *Understanding prison staff*. Cullompton, UK: Willan (pp. 1–13).

Fitzgibbon, W., and Lea, J. (2010) Police, probation and the bifurcation of community. *The Howard Journal*, 49: 215–230.

Fleming, J. (2013) The pursuit of professionalism: lessons from Australia. In Brown, J. (ed.) *The future of policing*. Abingdon, UK: Routledge (pp. 355–368).

Fox, C., and Albertson, K. (2013) Payment by results and social impact bonds in the criminal justice sector: new challenges for the concept of evidence based policy. *Criminology and Criminal Justice*, 11: 395–413.

Hines, A., and Bishop, P. (eds) (2006) *Thinking about the future: guidelines for strategic foresight*. Washington, DC: Social Technologies.

Horan, J., and Maine, S. (2014) Criminal jury trials in 2030: a Law Odyssey. *Journal of Law and Society*, 41: 551–575.

Independent Police Commission (2013) *Policing for a better Britain*. London: The Commission.

Jackson, D., Firtko, A., and Edenborough, M. (2007) Personal resilience as a strategy for surviving and thriving in the face of workplace adversity: a literature review. *Journal of Advanced Nursing*, 40: 1–8.

Kakar, Suman (1998) Self-evaluations of police performance: an analysis of the relationship between police officers' education level and job performance. *Policing: An International Journal of Police Strategies and Management*, 21: 632–647.

King, A., and Levy, P. (2012) A theoretical framework for organisational politics during the economic downturn: the role of the economic crisis on occupational stress and well-being. *Research in Occupational Stress and Well Being*, 10: 87–130.

Lambert, E.G., Hogan, N., and Griffin, M.L. (2007) The impact of distributive and procedural justice on correctional staff job stress, job satisfaction and organisational commitment. *Journal of Criminal Justice*, 35: 644–656.

Mawby, R.C., and Worrell, A. (2013) *Doing probation work: identity in a criminal justice occupation*. London/New York: Routledge.

Munro, E. (2011) *The Munro review of child protection. Final report: a child centered system*. Cm 8062. London: Department of Education.

Neyroud, P. (2013) *Review of police leadership and training*. www.gov.uk/government/uploads/system/uploads/attachment_data/file/118227/report.pdf.

Neyroud, P., and Weisburd, D. (2014) Transforming the police through science: the challenge of ownership. *Policing*, 8(4): 287–293.

O'Driscoll, M., and Brough, P. (2010) Work organisation and health. In Leka, S. and Houdmont, J. (eds) *Occupational health psychology*. Chichester: Wiley-Blackwell (pp. 57–87).

Paterson, C. (2011) Adding value? A review of the international literature on the role of higher education in police training and education. *Police Practice and Research: An International Journal*, 12: 286–297.

Perry, J., Engbers, T., and Jun, So Yun (2009) Back to the future? Performance-related pay, empirical research, and the perils of persistence. *Public Administration Review*, 69: 39–51.

Quick, J.C., Mack, D., Gavin, J., Cooper, C., and Quick, J. (2004) Executives: engines for postive stress. In Perrewe, P.L. and Ganster, D. (eds) *Emotional and psychological processes and postive interventions strategies*. Research in occupational health and well-being, Volume 3. Bingley, UK: Emerald (pp. 359–405).

Rhodes, N. (2013) An outsourcing journey partnership. In Neyroud, P. (ed.) *Policing UK 2013. Priorities and pressures: a year of transition*. London: Witan Media (pp. 34–36).

Richman, A., Civian, J., Shannon, L., Hill, E., and Brennan, R. (2008) The relationship of perceived flexibility, supportive-life policies, and the use of formal flexible arrangements and occasional flexibility to employee engagement and expected retention. *Community, Work and Family*, 11: 183–197.

Saks, A.M. (2006) Antecedent and consequences of employee engagement. *Journal of Managerial Psychology*, 21: 600–619.

Savage, S. (2007) *Police reform: forces for change*. Oxford: Oxford University Press.

Shepherd, J. (2013) *Professionalising the probation service: why university institutes would transform rehabilitation*. London: Howard League for Penal Reform/London School of Economics Mannheim Centre for Criminology.

Sherr, A., and Thompson, S. (2013) Tesco law and Tesco lawyers: will our needs change if the market develops? *Oñati Socio-Legal Series*, 3: 595–610.

Shochet, I.M., Shakespeare-Finch, J., Craig, C., Roos, C., Wurfl, A., Hoge, R., Young, R., and Brough, P. (2011) The development and implementation of the Promoting Resilient Officers (PRO) Program. *Traumatology*, 17(4): 43–51.

Sparks, K., Faragher, B., and Cooper, C. (2001) Well-being and occupational health in the 21st century workplace. *Journal of Occupational and Organisational Psychology*, 74: 489–509.

Tilley, N., and Laycock, G. (2013) The police as professional problem solver. In Brown, J. (ed.) *The future of policing*. Abingdon, UK: Routledge (pp. 369–382).

Tseloni, A., Mailley, J., Farrell, S., and Tilley, N. (2010) Exploring the international decline in crime rates. *European Journal of Criminology*, 7: 375–394.

Tyler, T., and Jackson, J. (2013) *Future challenges in the study of legitimacy and criminal justice*. Yale Law School, Public Law Working Paper 264.

Webster, V., Brough, P., and Daly, K. (in press) Fight, flight or freeze: common responses for follower coping with toxic leadership. *Stress and Health*.

2 Occupational culture and organisational justice

Introduction

Most occupations share some common attributes by virtue of their knowledge base which are manifest through shared terminology, humour, sentiments, modes of dress, rituals, and norms of behaviour (Loftus, 2012). These attributes together with value sets, working practices, and rules guiding conduct (informally as well as formally) are often collectively referred to as the occupation's culture. Derived from and developed by anthropologists, the ideas conveyed by culture were adopted by psychologists to investigate work organisations and their responsivity to change (Millward, 2005). As applied to the world of work within criminal justice, the concept is not without its definitional problems but has nevertheless proved useful in explaining a number of processes such as job satisfaction, morale, ethical conduct, working styles, and attitudes towards reform (Kingshott *et al.*, 2004; Paoline, 2004; Stroshine *et al.*, 2008; Crawley and Crawley, 2008; Nalla *et al.*, 2010; Elliot and Daley, 2013; Dollard *et al.*, 2013). Culture has particularly been utilised to look at both causes of stress and coping adaptations (Chan,1997; Brown, 2004).

Whilst there are positive attributes of culture, it has more often been conceptualised in its negative aspects (Waddington, 1999). More recent research efforts have employed the concept of organisational procedure justice as an antidote to combat the adverse impacts of occupational culture (Bradford *et al.*, 2014). This chapter dissects various dimensions embedded within the notion of culture, shows how it has been used to explain both positive and negative workplace behaviours, and presents ideas from the literature on organisational justice to demonstrate how criminal justice agencies can build more supportive and productive working environments.

Twenty-first century workplaces

Work-related stress commonly arises from intrinsic factors, such as working conditions, levels of responsibility, and degrees of autonomy, role, relationships, and career factors. These stressors are found in criminal justice system (CJS) workplaces, such as prisons, police, and probation (Schaufeli and Peeters, 2000;

Baldwin *et al.*, 2002; Brown, 2004; Mawby and Worrall, 2013), as well as in the courts amongst lawyers (Kirby, 2014). There are, in addition, some stressors specific to CJS environments, including for example: confrontations and communication difficulties between prison officers and inmates (Launay and Fielding, 1989; Baldwin *et al.*, 2002; Nylander *et al.*, 2011); counsel being bullied by judges (Kirby, 2014); having to kill in the line of duty; or seeing a fellow officer killed (Lucas *et al.*, 2012).

There are also technological innovations and consequences of the economic cycle that have impacted work, including criminal justice organisations (Sparks *et al.*, 2001; King and Levy, 2012). During the 1980s and 1990s, the IT revolution, and increased competition created by privatisation, resulted in some major restructuring followed in the 2000s by austerity and recessionary reorganisation to cope with budget cuts. Workers experienced high levels of emotion as they ruminated about possible job loss and experienced a sense of helplessness (King and Levy 2012). King and Levy also note that when the economy deteriorates, overall stress levels increase as employees work in conditions of increasing uncertainty. The criminal justice system has not been immune to these political and socio-economic processes. Andrew (2006) discusses issues associated with privatisation in the Australian prison services, while Fox and Albertson (2011) describes the consequences of the introduction of payment-by-results regimes on the British Probation Service. More recently, the Independent Police Commission (2013) notes the impacts of staff reductions on the police services in England and Wales, and the amalgamation of the Scottish police into a new national police service.

As well as financial pressures, reform of informal practices of criminal justice professionals in the wake of various national scandals involving misconduct have also been drivers of change (Prenzler and Ransley 2002). The presence of corrupt and inefficient behaviour on the one hand, and the resistance to changing and streamlining working practices on the other, has been laid at the door of the organisation's culture (Audit Commission, 1989, 1990). Garland (2001) described the rapid and far-reaching impacts of politically imposed transformations that have literally turned the occupational cultures of probation officers, prison officials, prosecutors, judges, and police officers upside-down: 'hierarchies shifted precariously, settled routines were pulled apart, objectives and priorities were reformulated, standard working practices were altered, and professional expertise subject to challenge and viewed with increasing scepticism' (p. 4). These work changes and their (mis)management have been incredibly stressful (Brown 2004) and resulted in morale problems, job dissatisfaction, disengagement, and reductions in discretionary effort. Behavioural antecedents leading to the need for reform and reactions to change imposed by financial imperatives can be explained through understanding occupational and organisational culture.

Definitions and delineations

The construct of culture has caused much confusion (Furnham, 1997). Schein (1992, 2004) helpfully defined organisational culture as a template of the basic assumptions underpinning an organisation (in other words its raison d'être). These are developed as the organisation adapts and the surviving practices are taught to new members as the 'correct' way to perceive, think about, and respond to problems. Distinctions have been made between organisational and occupational culture. An organisational culture can be thought of as a general resource that shapes and provides the means of achieving goals and aspirations. These resources may be in the form of sanctions and rewards and communicated through mission statements and expression of core values. The culture dictates organising principles (e.g. hierarchical or flattened organisational structures), relationships (e.g. formalities of who has access to whom and styles of interaction), and the nature of the organisation's activities (prescriptive, reactive, or proactive). These tend to have been derived from historical precedents to which members feel loyal and are fiercely protected and, therefore, are difficult to change.

Organisational climate is a more fluid and affective concept. Furnham (1997) suggested that climate is less enduring than culture, and daily experienced by people in the form of morale. In the context of policing, Heady and Wearing (1989) conceptualised the police climate as stressors which arise as deviations from normal routine events. Thus police officers having to deliver a death message, or putting up with an oppressive senior officer, would be examples of negative 'hassles'. In contrast, examples of positive 'uplift' include obtaining a 'good' arrest, the public showing appreciation, or helpful supervision. Climate (or work hassles and uplifts) contributes to job satisfaction and is influential in performance. A healthy and motivating organisational climate is achieved through clarity of purpose, fair leadership behaviour, good communication networks, just reward systems, and versatile goal-setting techniques (Furnham, 1997).

Occupational culture often refers to the filtering down and frequently the holding of divergent views to that of the organisational culture as shaped by the experiences and roles of different subgroups within the organisation. As Paoline (2003) suggested, the difference is that organisational culture tends to be management-led and top-down, whereas occupational culture is more rank-and-file and bottom-up. Subgroups within an organisation may not always conform to the management rhetoric of the prescribed cultural values and internal fragmentation can occur when these are in conflict. Jermier *et al.* (1991) described the corporate mission of the police service as a morally informed, order-preserving service intended for public protection and contrasts this with the reality of divergent informal missions and practices of rank-and-file police officers having an occupational identity as 'crime fighters' where rules may be bent or broken to effect an arrest.

Manning (2007) proposes that there is a distinctive management culture within the police of more highly educated senior officers with the potential of alternative careers, which makes them less dependent on loyalty to rank-and-file officers. For Paoline (2003) management culture is more politically attuned and aware of competition for resources, and emphasises the need for efficient productivity and accountability. Management culture is learnt through courses in leadership, financial management, and training in governance arrangements. Street cop or 'canteen' occupational culture is acquired through on-the-job socialisation (Fielding, 1988). This has been characterised by Reiner (2010) as compromising: elements of mission (that policing is not just a job but a way of life); action (notably catching villains); and cynicism (that it's all a bit of a game with arrest providing a sense of personal satisfaction rather than necessarily public service). Reiner also emphasised the sense of social isolation felt by operational officers from wider society, partly because of feeling separated by virtue of actual or potential criminality, but also because of shift-working, erratic hours, difficulties of switching off from tensions created by having a discipline code, and possible hostility from those with whom they socially interact. This, in turn, creates a strong internal solidarity because of the need to rely on colleagues when in a tight spot, but also as a protection from possible infractions that might come to the attention of supervisory management officers.

Fielding (1988) describes how new recruits to the police in England and Wales learn to distance themselves from the emotion attached to distressing incidents as a way of protecting themselves from their adverse impacts. They do this through the use of gallows humour, irony, or cynicism, often deployed in the telling of stories about a fatal accident or violent encounter. These devices are modelled by older tutor constables or sergeants.

Similar analyses of the informal occupational culture have been described for prison officers (e.g. Martin and Jurik, 1996) and for probation officers (e.g. Mawby and Worrel, 2013). Crawley and Crawley (2008) catalogue a list of attributes that defines prison officers' occupational culture, in particular noting the use of humour as a defence mechanism serving to protect staff against emotional distress, as a 'wit sharpener', allowing officers to think on their feet, as a morale raiser which 'gees up' officers at the start of their shift or releases tension after work. These devices operate as either an incorporative joking with new recruits as a 'one-of-us' strategy, or alteratively reinforce belief that a 'deviant' officer is not one of us. These authors and students of police occupational culture suggest that not only are there varieties of competing cultures within these organisations, but also the sense of isolation, solidarity, and a loyalty to traditional working practices can make it difficult to respond to change.

Mawby and Worrell (2013, p. 103) recount the huge changes that have taken place within probation in the UK: 'It is beyond dispute that the job of the probation worker has changed dramatically in recent decades and that this has resulted in a considerable degree of pessimism, negativity and distress.' They note the pressures probation workers experienced when trying to balance the contact time spent with clients (described as emotionally taxing) and doing effective work with them and satisfying the demands of paperwork and keeping the computer updated. Officers often felt unsupported by management and were made to feel that inability to cope was due to their personal shortcomings. This, together with what officers experienced as constraints on their professional autonomy coupled with high levels of accountability, resulted in their sense of being bullied and subjected to 'emotional tyranny' (p. 109). This lack of 'voice' was a particular concern.

The culture–stress link

The relationship between police stress and police organisational culture has only recently received research attention (Chan, 1997, 2007). Earlier work suggested such a link: how 'cop' culture provides ways of coping with pressures and tensions of the job (e.g. Reiner, 2000); how female workers may be excluded by virtue of their gender (Brown, 2000). However, Chan (2007) undertook a more detailed and theoretically sophisticated analysis and argued that it is important to consider 'how police culture can both shape and be shaped by stressors' (p. 131). Chan draws on Bourdieu's theory of practice which she paraphrases as follows:

> [A] field is a social space of conflict and competition, where certain resources (capital) and constraints are at stake, whilst habitas is a system of dispositions that integrate past experiences and enable individuals to cope with a diversity of unforeseen situations.

> (p. 131)

As applied to policing, Chan proposes that officers acquire skills, attitudes, and values from the resources offered by the occupational culture, which are transmitted through induction, training, and informal socialisation, i.e. the habitas. Stressors are the operational and organisational demands of the field and are interpreted through the assumptions and shared values embedded in the occupational culture. Chan notes that organisational change has become an increasingly important stressor in policing (and Brown (2004) argued this is also true for other CJS agencies.) Chan points out that for policing, which guards its way of doing things, changes in policing philosophy such as community-based policing threatens previous practice, potentially devaluing work done and leading to loss of morale and engagement. Losing a sense of control has been established as a key stressor (Fletcher, 1988) and Brough and Biggs (2010) point out that job control is highly associated with work engagement.

Chan conducted research into Australia's New South Wales Police Service after a period of reforming change in the light of the Wood Commission. This Commission had found systematic and entrenched corruption. Chan's research results revealed rank-and-file officers were disenchanted and critical of management for not supporting the front line, and for what were believed to be ill-conceived organisational changes. Just over half (52 per cent) of her sample indicated they had thought about leaving the Service (a proxy measure of job morale). The UK Independent Police Commission (2013) found much the same percentage of officers had considered leaving the service because of a series of politically inspired reforms in changes in pay and conditions of service in England and Wales. In both cases, officers felt reward systems such as promotion were under pressure and unfair, and those accountabilities, in the Australian case, and performance measurement, in the British example, were impeding officers from doing their job properly. Interestingly, the police in both countries thought that the internal mutual support offered by the informal culture was still needed as they felt the job they loved had been eroded and was becoming unrecognisable from the one to which they had joined up.

Mawby and Worrel (2013) indicated similar concerns from probation staff who, as previously mentioned, have experienced a huge upheaval in their service. Their reactions as documented by these researchers constituted a form of psychological exit, i.e. thinking about leaving, and an increase in cynicism as a result of the breaking of the 'psychological contract' between them and their management. (This concept is described in Chapter 10.)

Identifying cultural attributes

There are a number of ways to identify cultural attributes of an organisation. These include surveys such as the organisational cultural inventory (Cooke and Szumal, 1993), which measures behavioural norms and expectations and categorises organisations into three types: *constructive*; *passive/defensive*; or *aggressive/defensive*. Other more qualitative methods are exemplified by the cultural web (Johnson and Scholes, 2007). This has been used diagnostically to map how members of the organisation perceive the rituals and routines, levers of power, formal and informal controlling mechanisms, and stories associated with the organisation. Once having established what these are, the exercise can be repeated to reveal people's views about how they would like the organisation to be. A gap analysis can then be conducted to identify the actual and ideal and provide an indication of how to achieve improvement. Another technique is using experts to review means of improving an organisation's processes and systems, called Delphi; a description of this technique is provided in Chapter 12.

Often, attempts to measure people's views about the occupational and organisational cultures reveal contrary views from those playing different roles or occupying different ranks within the organisation, and these different views can be helpful in identifying potential pinch-points impeding communication, locating sources of stress, or causes of toxic working conditions (see Chapter 13). Agencies of the CJS are under huge pressure to change their working practices and adapt to new ways of working, especially sharing responsibilities for delivering services to the public with the private sector and working in partnership with charitable trusts, as well as achieving better interconnectivity between agencies (Fox and Albertson 2011).

Organisational procedural justice

As demonstrated above, organisational change itself can be rather stressful and often is perceived by the rank-and-file members of the organisation to be mismanaged. Change through external reform, on the one hand, and failing to ameliorate sources of stressors such as poor communication, oppressive supervision, and lack of support from senior management, on the other, can be experienced by the rank and file as arbitrary and undermining. Vermunt and Steensma (2005) conceptualised this within a justice model. By justice they mean an evaluation of an event in which some authority allocates resources. An authority can be a person, a role, or an entity such as a promotion board. Allocation involves the distribution of the resource by means of a procedure (i.e. governed by procedural rules). Both the authority and the procedure can be evaluated in terms of the perceived (in)justice of the distributive or procedural fairness. A discrepancy between what is deemed to be a deserved outcome and what is experienced can result in a perception, or reality, that internal processes and procedures and the share of resources is unfair. This neatly maps onto the Person Environmental-fit model of stress in which there is an imbalance between demands and capability to fulfil them (Lazarus and Folkman, 1984). Imbalance of resources to manage a task can result in an adverse reaction such as anxiety or somatic symptoms. If an unfair allocation of resource blocks a person's attainment of a goal then an injustice (and stress) may be experienced. It is hard for a person to restore the balance when an injustice is experienced because often they lack the control or power to do so, hence the suffering of a stress reaction.

Resources can be material goods such as pay or immaterial such as status or regard. Vemunt and Steesma rather neatly equate stressors to resources as follows:

- job content (e.g. work under- or overload, conflicting or ambiguous demands) relates to goods;
- working conditions (e.g. equipment, environmental conditions) relate to goods;
- employment conditions (e.g. shift patterns, pay, career prospects) relate to money and status;
- social relationships (e.g. quality of leadership and social support) relate to services and regard.

A justice-based approach emphasises that the authority/organisation is crucial in the stress process because of the accountability of the authority for the occurrence of the stressor. The authority mediates the sources of stress, rather than stressors being merely a fact of working life. Employees attribute unfair distribution of resources and unfair procedures as potential stressors to the decision-making of their supervisor or manager. The magnitude of the injustice depends on outcomes received in the past. Moreover, communication about a potential unfairness can itself be seen as unjust. If the reasoning for an apparently unfair outcome is well communicated, the employee is more likely to see this as a challenge and respond positively. A notional or insincere communication often results in resistance (see Chapter 17 for a discussion of the impact of perceived inauthentic communication as an example of this).

Reactions to unfairness are summarised by Vermunt and Steensma (2005) as increasing or decreasing effort, leaving the situation, decreasing performance, retaliation, insubordination, protest, and/or absenteeism. It follows that a sense of injustice can leave the employee demoralised and prone to reduce their discretionary effort, for example, not going the extra mile by putting in unpaid overtime thereby reducing the social capital of the organisation.

A further element to this approach is the concept of legitimacy. Sunshine and Tyler (2003, p. 514) define this as 'a property of an authority or institution that leads people to feel that the authority is entitled to be deferred to and obeyed'. Bradford *et al.* (2013, p. 81) regard legitimate authority as being made up of three components:

1   legality – acting according to the authority's own rules and being seen to follow those rules;
2   shared values – the values of the authority are shared by those subject to that authority; and
3   consent – a moral obligation to obey the authority.

This idea of legitimacy has been applied to the relationship between the police and those they police. It seems people are less interested in the effectiveness of the authority, the police, or even the outcome, than in the process by which decisions are made and the motivations behind them. So when applied to the police, Hinds and Murphy (2007) demonstrated from a survey of 2,611 members of the Australian public that people who believed that the police use procedural justice in the exercise of their authority are more likely to view the police as legitimate and are more satisfied with their services. The components of procedural justice are described in the Independent Police Commission report as comprising:

•   *Quality of decision-making.* Are decisions made in a fair, neutral, and unbiased way? Key issues here are whether people believe officers are making decisions based on the facts, not personal opinion or prejudice; whether they treat people equally and without favour; and whether they make decisions based on the law (although this last is tempered by the fact that people tend to want police to enforce the law 'sensibly', giving proper attention to circumstance and exigency). Note that this presupposes that decisions can be justified; procedural justice is not about providing an emollient for poor decisions.
•   *Quality of treatment.* Here the questions are: Do police treat people with dignity and respect? Do they accord them their proper rights? Do officers explain the reasons for their actions? A lack of respect, conversely, can be communicated by discriminatory language, for example, but also by sarcasm, cynicism, superciliousness, and brusqueness.
•   *Voice.* The third element of procedural justice is 'voice'. Do police allow the public a chance to 'have their say' during encounters? Do police take account of their needs and concerns, and do they make an effort to find out what these are?

Bradford *et al.* (2013, p. 94) suggest that procedural justice is as important within policing organisations as it is in the relationship between the public and the police:

Police officers' perceptions of procedural justice in their relationships with managers and supervisors – particularly concerning the fairness of procedure and the quality of interaction and communication – are strongly linked to their compliance with organisational goals and to organisational citizenship behaviours.

Bradford *et al.* (2014) undertook an evaluation in the Durham Constabulary, a small non-metropolitan force in the North of England. Durham was going through a period of significant organisational change resulting from budget cuts, which involved a major structural reorganisation with impending reductions in staff numbers and a shift away from the traditional hierarchical management structure. Their results showed that police officers who strongly shared the values implicit in the changes were associated with a greater sense of leadership procedural justice. Threat of sanction for non-compliance with the required changes had no significant association with identification. Propensity to take on extra work, discretionary effort, was significantly and positively predicted by organisational identification and supervisory procedural justice. Police officers' motivations across a range of positive behaviours were associated with their perceptions of fair treatment by their immediate supervisors and the organisation as a whole. They related their results to the dynamics within the police occupational culture by suggesting they operate as a psychological defence mechanism to help officers deal with the realities of having to impose their authority, sometimes using force, by retelling often exaggerated versions in the canteen as a way to alleviate any stress experienced, but without necessarily dictating action in the field. Alternatively, the sharing of stories can help build the identity of officers and influence their decisions on the street resulting in problematic interactions with the public. Bradford and colleagues suggested it is possible that the experience of organisational justice within the police will foster positive identities based on a culture of co-operation and fair processes that, in turn, will influence their interactions with members of the public.

Lambert *et al.* (2007) note that a few studies have been conducted looking at procedural justice with correctional staff. The studies they cite demonstrated no relationship between distributive justice and organisational commitment; but both procedural and distributive justice had an impact on job satisfaction. The former but not the latter had a significant negative effect on correctional staff job stress. In their own study of a mid-western US state maximum security private prison housing young adults, they looked at job satisfaction, stress, and organisational commitment. They concluded from their results that organisational justice was a salient dimension of the prison working environment, shaping staff perceptions of stress and job satisfaction. It was distributive justice that had greatest impact on job stress, suggesting that prison staff felt increasing levels of stress when they felt outcomes were unfair. They seemed particularly irritated when they thought outcomes were similar, regardless of the amount of effort of work inputs. So if a prison officer viewed their workload as higher or more demanding than a colleague's, yet both received the same salary, their sense of injustice at the allocation of pay added to their levels of job-related anger and frustration. Lambert *et al.* also found that procedural justice, e.g. in terms of status and recognition, was not related to work stress levels. They put this down to differences between the experience of daily 'hassles' which was more immediate, compared to the more intermittent formal evaluation of a promotion board. Procedural justice was related to job satisfaction and reflected staff perceptions of legitimacy of what went on in the facility. In other words outcomes were of less concern that processes. Finally, they reported that both distributive and procedural justice significantly influenced organisational commitment.

Conclusion

In this chapter we looked at the concept of culture as a collective description of the values and practices of an organisation that help guide ways of doing things. It was noted that culture can apply to the organisation, which helps orient structures, communication patterns, and levers of power, and to the occupation itself, which has often been applied to the more informal rank-and-file membership and derives from socialisation and induction into the organisation. Professional cultures tend to be applied to more formal arrangements whereby there is a recognised learned body, knowledge requirements and ethical codes of practice, and a register of practitioners. The organisational and occupational cultures may clash and create sources of tension especially during periods of change. The informal culture also provides the means to alleviated stress through the support and camaraderie of fellow workers.

Ideas drawn from procedural justice sit comfortably with the person-environment fit models of stress and represent one way to create a healthy workplace and advance the well-being of members of the organisation (Dollard *et al.*, 2013). They extend the person-environment fit model to include external factors impinging on organisations which require them to adapt, especially under circumstances of 'tight' resourcing. They recommend that public agencies including the police should be more mindful of external environmental demands and that adaptation can be undertaken without necessarily reducing morale and creating undue distress.

A worked example of measuring organisational justice and assessing how to inculcate a more procedurally just working environment is provided in Chapter 11.

References

Andrew, J. (2006) Prisons, the profit motive and other challenges to accountability. *Critical Perspectives on Accounting*, 18: 977–904.

Audit Commission (1989) *The probation service: promoting value for money*. London: HMSO.

Audit Commission (1990) *Police paper 9: reviewing the organisation of provincial police forces*. London: HMSO.

Baldwin, P., Cooke, D., and Howison, J. (2002) *Psychology in prisons*. Abingdon, UK: Routledge.

Bradford, B., Jackson, J., and Hough, M. (2013) Police futures and legitimacy: re-defining 'good policing'. In Brown, J. (ed.) *The future of policing*. Abingdon, UK: Routledge (pp 79–99).

Bradford, B., Quinton, P., Myhill, A., and Porter, G. (2014) Why do 'the law' comply? Procedural justice, group identification and officer motivation in police organizations. *European Journal of Criminology*, 11: 110–131.

Brough, P., and Biggs, A. (2010) Occupational stress in police and prison staff. In Brown, J. and Campbell, E. (eds) *Cambridge handbook of forensic psychology*. Cambridge: Cambridge University Press (707–717).

Brown, J. (2000) Occupational culture as a factor in the stress experience of police officers. In Leishman, F., Loveday, B., and Savage, S. (eds) *Core issues in policing*, 2nd edn. Boston: Addison-Wesley (pp. 249–262).

Brown, J. (2004) Occupational stress and the criminal justice practitioner. In Needs, A., and Towl, G. (eds) *Applying psychology to forensic practice*. Oxford: BPS Blackwell (pp. 147–166).

Chan, J. (1997) *Changing police culture*. Melbourne: Cambridge University Press.

Chan, J. (2007) Police stress and occupational culture. In O'Neill, M., Marks, M., and Singh, A-M. (eds) *Police occupational culture: new debates and directions. Sociology of crime, law and deviance*, volume 8. Amsterdam: Elsevier (pp. 129–151).

Cooke, R.A., and Szumal, J.L. (1993) Measuring normative beliefs and shared behavioural expectations in organizations: validation of the organisational culture invemtory. *Psychological Reports*, 72: 1299–1330.

Crawley, E., and Crawley, P. (2008) Understanding prison officers: culture, cohesion and conflicts. In Bennett, J., Crewe, B., and Wahidin, A. (eds) *Understanding prison staff*. Cullompton, UK: Willan (pp. 134–167).

Dollard, M., Osborne, K., and Manning, I. (2013) Organizational-environment adaption: a macro level shift in modelling work distress and morale. *Journal of Organisational Behavior*, 34: 629–647.

Elliott, K., and Daley, D. (2013) Stress, coping and psychological well-being among forensic health care professionals. *Legal and Criminological Psychology*, 18: 187–204.

Fielding, N. (1988) *Joining forces: police training, socialisation and occupational competence*. London: Routledge.

Fletcher, B. (1988) The epidemiology of occupational stress. In Cooper, C.L., and Payne, R. (eds) *Cause, coping and consequences of stress at work*. Chichester: Wiley (pp. 3–50).

Fox, C., and Albertson, K. (2011) Payment by results and social impact bonds in the criminal justice sector: new challenges for the concept of evidence based policy. *Criminology and Criminal Justice*, 11: 395–413.

Furnham, A. (1997) *The psychology of behaviour at work: the individual in the organisation*. Hove, UK: Psychology Press.

Garland, D. (2001) *The culture of control: crime and social order in contemporary society*. Oxford: Oxford University Press.

Heady, B., and Wearing, A. (1989) Personality, life events and subjective well-being: towards a dynamic equilibrium model. *Journal of Personality and Social Psychology*, 57: 731–739.

Hinds, L., and Murphy, K. (2007) Public satisfaction with police using procedural justice to improve police legitimacy. *Australian and New Zealand Journal of Criminology*, 40: 27–42.

Independent Police Commission (2013) *Policing for a better Britain*. London: The Commission.

Jermier, J., Slocum, J., Fry, L., and Gaines, J. (1991) Organisational subcultures in a soft bureaucracy. *Criminology*, 35: 277–306.

Johnson, G., and Scholes, K. (2007) *Exploring corporate strategy*, 6th edn. London: Pearson Education.

King, A., and Levy, P. (2012) A theoretical framework for organisational politics during the economic downturn: the role of the economic crisis on occupational stress and well-being. *Research in Occupational Stress and Well-Being*, 10: 87–130.

Kingshott, B., Bailey, K., and Wolfe, S. (2004) Police culture, ethics and entitlement. *Criminal Justice Studies*, 17: 187–202.

Kirby, M. (2014) Judicial stress and judicial bullying. *QUR Law Review*, 14: 1–14.

Lambert, E.G., Hogan, N., and Griffin, M.L. (2007) The impact of distributive and procedural justice on correctional staff job stress, job satisfaction and organisational commitment. *Journal of Criminal Justice*, 35: 644–656.

Launay, G., and Fielding, P. (1989) Stress among prison officers: some empirical evidence based on self report. *Howard Journal*, 28: 138–148.

Lazarus, R., and Folkman, S. (1984) *Stress, appraisal and coping*. New York: Springer.

Loftus, B. (2012 [2009]) *Police culture in a changing world*. Oxford: Clarendon.

Lucas, T., Weidner, N., and Janisse, J. (2012) Where does work stress come from? A generalisability analysis of stress in police officers. *Psychology and Health*, 27: 1426–1447.

Manning, P. (2007) A dialectic of organisational and occupational culture. In O'Neill, M., Marks, M., and Singh, A.-M. (eds) *Police occupational culture: new debates and directions. Sociology of crime, law and deviance*, volume 8. Amsterdam: Elsevier (pp. 47–83).

Martin, S., and Jurik, N. (1996) *Doing justice, doing gender: women in law and criminal justice occupations*. Thousand Oaks, CA: SAGE.

Mawby, R.C., and Worrall, A. (2013) *Doing probation work: identity in a criminal justice occupation*. London/New York: Routledge.

Millward, L. (2005) *Understanding occupational and organisational psychology*. London: SAGE.

Nalla, M., Rydberg, J., and Meško, G. (2010) Organisational factors, environmental climate and job satisfaction among police in Slovenia. *European Journal of Criminology*, 8: 1–13.

Nylander, P.Å., Lindberg, O., and Bruhn, A. (2011) Emotional labour and emotional strain among Swedish prison officers. *European Journal of Criminology*, 8(6): 469–483.

Paoline, E. (2003) Taking stock: towards a richer understanding of police culture. *Journal of Criminal Justice*, 31: 199–214.

Paoline, E. (2004) Shedding light on police culture: an examination of officers' occupational attitude. *Police Quarterly*, 7: 305–236.

Prenzler, T., and Ransley, J. (2002) *Police reform: building integrity*. Sydney: Hawkins Press.

Reiner, R. (2000) *The politics of the police*, 3rd edn. Oxford: Oxford University Press.

Reiner, R. (2010) *The politics of the police*, 4th edn. Oxford: Oxford University Press.

Schaufeli, W., and Peeters, M. (2000) Job stress and burnout among correctional officers: a literature review. *International Journal of Stress Management*, 7: 19–47.

Schien, E. (1992) *Organisational culture and leadership*. San Francisco: Jossey-Bass.

Schein, E. (2004) *Organizational culture and leadership*, 3rd edn. New York: Wiley.

Sparks, K., Faragher, B., and Cooper, C. (2001) Well-being and occupational health in the 21st century workplace. *Journal of Occupational and Organizational Psychology*, 74: 489–509.

Stroshine, M., Alpert, G., and Dunham, R. (2008) The influence of 'working rules' on police suspicion and discretionary decision making. *Police Quarterly*, 11(3): 315–337.

Sunshine, J., and Tyler, T. (2003) The role of procedural justice and legitimacy on shaping public support for policing. *Law and Society Review*, 37: 513–548.

Vermunt, R., and Steensma, H. (2005) How can justice be used to manage stress in organisations? In Greenberg, J., and Colquitt, J. (eds) *Handbook of organisational justice*. New Jersey: Lawrence Elbaum (pp. 385–410).

Waddington, P.A.J. (1999) Police (canteen) subculture: an appreciation. *British Journal of Criminology*, 39: 287–309.

3 Employee engagement

Introduction

Research and practice concerning employee health management has disproportionately focused on identifying and eradicating physical and psychological hazards linked with ill-health and poor performance. This is especially evident within criminal justice occupations, where concerns such as bullying, stress, and burnout have been particularly dominant (Brough and Biggs, 2010). This negative focus is unsurprising, given the tangible threat posed to the well-being of employees within high-stress criminal justice environments (Botha and Pienaar, 2006; Lambert *et al.*, 2008; Neveu, 2007). Recently, this negative focus has shifted, as positive psychology concepts focusing on building human strengths and positive states have become more influential in criminal justice research. This has unquestionably provided a more balanced perspective of health, placing 'equal importance on the precursors and outcomes of both the negative and positive states present within the work environment' (Burney, 2011, p. 1).

One of the most influential constructs to emerge from the burgeoning interest in positive psychology is work engagement (also referred to as employee engagement), which has been linked with beneficial outcomes for individuals and organisations. This chapter will discuss the challenges of building engagement within high-stress, criminal justice work environments. This chapter first defines work engagement, followed by a discussion of the core individual and organisational outcomes. Key frameworks and research evidence are presented, integrating research conducted specifically within criminal justice settings. Finally, this chapter concludes with an overview of recommended intervention strategies to build work engagement.

What is work engagement?

Highly engaged employees 'find work meaningful, and consequently, they want to, and can, invest in their work to achieve personal and career benefits. The end product of being engaged is an energetic and passionate employee' (Brunetto *et al.*, 2012, p. 430). Engaged employees exhibit high levels of *vigour*, *dedication*, and *absorption*. Vigour entails a strong capacity to invest more energy into the completion of work tasks, and the ability to persevere in spite of challenges or difficulties (Schaufeli *et al.*, 2002). Dedication reflects a strong sense of involvement and commitment to the performance of work-related tasks, combined with a perception of those tasks as challenging and meaningful (Mauno *et al.*, 2007; Schaufeli *et al.*, 2002). Finally, absorption occurs when employees become engrossed in tasks associated with their work role, characterised by extensive periods of concentration and an inability to become detached from work (Schaufeli *et al.*, 2002). Absorption is especially likely to occur when work tasks are highly challenging and enable a high degree of skill utilisation (Mauno *et al.*, 2007).

What are the benefits of work engagement?

Work engagement is associated with positive outcomes that mutually benefit employees and organisations. It is connected to employee well-being (Halbesleben, 2010) and has a positive effect on employees' non-work lives (Bakker *et al.*, 2005; Timms *et al.*, in press). Engagement stimulates creativity and innovation (Sonnentag and Niessen, 2008), which enhances employees' capacity to devise novel solutions to work-related problems. Proactivity is another particularly desirable outcome, as it leads employees to take initiative at work to complete tasks aligned with the organisation's goals, even if those tasks are not formally specified in an employee's job description (Hakanen *et al.*, 2008; Sonnentag, 2003; Sonnentag and Niessen, 2008). Research has shown engagement directly affects an organisation's bottom-line, for example, by improving:

- employee retention (Halbesleben, 2010; Schaufeli and Bakker, 2004);
- service climate and customer loyalty (Salanova *et al.*, 2005);
- financial returns (Xanthopoulou *et al.*, 2009);
- job performance and organisational commitment (Halbesleben, 2010); and
- task performance (relating to the completion of tasks formally aligned with an employee's job description) and contextual performance, also known as organisational citizenship behaviours (relating to the completion of tasks that are beyond the scope of an employee's job description, but contribute to the achievement of organisational goals and facilitate a positive work environment; Christian *et al.*, 2011).

Research has also demonstrated the benefits of work engagement within criminal justice occupations. Engagement was significantly associated with: well-being, job satisfaction, and organisational commitment in an Australian sample of police (Brunetto *et al.*, 2012); work-related self-efficacy and organisational commitment in a Norwegian sample of police (Richardsen *et al.*, 2006); and job satisfaction, organisational commitment, and turnover intentions in a sample of New Zealand correctional officers (Burney, 2011). In a three-wave study conducted with Australian correctional officers (Biggs, 2011), high levels of engagement predicted lower levels of burnout and psychological strain over time, in addition to increased psychological resources (e.g. supervisor support, job control, and mentoring).

Similarly, longitudinal research with Australian police indicated that engagement was associated with higher levels of strategic alignment and job control (Biggs, Brough, and Barbour, 2014d) and greater supervisor, colleague, and work culture support (Biggs, Brough, and Barbour, 2014c). Maintaining high levels of work engagement, therefore, reduces future ill-health and generates resources required to perform tasks in criminal justice roles (Biggs, 2011).

Reduced turnover and ill-health, combined with increased organisational commitment, arising from high levels of engagement translates to significant costs savings for organisations. Criminal justice organisations dedicate substantial resources to recruitment, selection, and training of employees, and their premature loss as a result of disengagement and ill-health 'represents an economic as well as a human tragedy' (Winwood *et al.*, 2009, p. 1057). This is particularly pertinent for criminal justice occupations at greater risk of psychological injury, due to their increased exposure to critical and traumatic incidents (Winwood *et al.*, 2009). Criminal justice organisations are also obligated to maintain service standards with increasingly limited tangible resources, requiring greater initiative and output from employees, which can be attained in part by increasing levels of work engagement (Masson *et al.*, 2008).

Building work engagement: frameworks and antecedents

Individual, work, and non-work factors that contribute to work engagement have been identified, and several frameworks have been established to organise this research. For example, the job demands-resources model (JD-R; Demerouti *et al.*, 2001; Dollard and Bakker, 2010) explains how upstream organisational characteristics (e.g. leadership) shape job characteristics experienced by employees (i.e. job demands and job resources). These job characteristics in turn are linked with engagement and other outcomes according to two mechanisms (Bakker and Demerouti, 2007; Demerouti *et al.*, 2001; Dollard and Bakker, 2010):

1   The *energy* or *health impairment process* describes the progression from high demands to depleted energy, which, when prolonged, results in burnout and impaired health.
2   The *motivation process* explains the effect of psychological resources (e.g. autonomy and recognition) in the promotion of engagement, and subsequent positive outcomes.

This model simultaneously considers burnout and engagement, reflecting the origin of engagement in burnout research, and also adopts a holistic approach to the assessment of factors that stimulate optimal functioning *and* ill-health.

According to this model, engagement is primarily driven by job resources, which are aspects of the job that are both *intrinsically motivating* (because they stimulate employee's learning, development, and need satisfaction), and *extrinsically motivating* (because they are instrumental in assisting employees to achieve work-related goals and tasks; Bakker and Demerouti, 2007). Resources may be tangible (e.g. vehicles and computers) or psychological, the latter derived from tasks (e.g. autonomy), interpersonal relationships (e.g. social support), and the organisation's structure (e.g. participation in decision-making; Bakker and Demerouti, 2007). The beneficial effect of resources on engagement is amplified when job demands are also greater: that is, high levels of engagement are likely when an employee is challenged by their job, and also possesses the resources to meet challenges and cope with hindrances. In contrast, high levels of demands and insufficient tangible and psychological resources to meet demands may result in burnout and frustration. This framework has been validated and can assist in the development of research and initiatives to increase employee engagement. Studies testing this model, primarily within criminal justice organisations, are discussed below.

Individual and non-work antecedents

Demographic characteristics, such as age and gender, have a negligible effect on work engagement. For example, despite female correctional officers reporting higher levels of engagement, gender did not predict engagement when work characteristics were taken into account (Biggs, 2011). Stable personality traits and personal resources do predict engagement, however. Conscientiousness, emotional stability, and extraversion were positively associated with engagement in a sample of South African police officers (Mostert and Rothmann, 2006), consistent with results from non-criminal justice studies (e.g. Langelaan *et al.*, 2006). Similarly, in a sample of Norwegian police officers, the achievement striving component of Type A personality predicted higher levels of engagement, after accounting for job demands, job resources, and demographic characteristics (Richardsen *et al.*, 2006).

Non-work factors also influence levels of work engagement, demonstrating the nexus between work and non-work experiences. In a sample of police officers, for instance, job resources were associated with positive work–home interactions, which in turn were related to higher levels of engagement (Mostert *et al.*, 2006). The accumulation of recovery experiences during non-work hours, such as opportunities to relax, psychologically detach from work, or master non-work-related skills are also associated with subsequent levels of work engagement (Sonnentag and Niessen, 2008).

Job and organisational antecedents

Higher levels of work engagement are typically reported by officers of higher tenure and rank, and employees in managerial and professional roles (Biggs, 2011), reflecting the greater saturation of resources in high-status positions, such as greater control over work tasks (Mauno *et al.*, 2007; Schaufeli and Salanova, 2007). High levels of engagement are also reported by new recruits, and this is likely due to new recruits exhibiting a greater willingness to invest their personal energies and resources into performing work tasks (Richardsen *et al.*, 2006).

In line with the JD-R model, research has demonstrated the primacy of job and organisational resources in the development of engagement for criminal justice employees. Both organisational support and supervisor support predicted higher levels of self-determined motivation and engagement in multiple studies conducted with French police officers (Gillet *et al.*, 2013). Similarly, job resources (e.g. job autonomy and social support) and Type A personality were significantly related to engagement, organisational commitment, and self-efficacy in a sample of Norwegian police officers (Richardsen *et al.*, 2006). In our longitudinal research with Australian police officers, work culture, job control, and strategic alignment (referring to an employee's line of sight between their job tasks and the strategic priorities of the organisation) predicted work engagement over multiple time-lags (Biggs, Brough, and Barbour, 2014c, 2014d).

Research has also ascertained that different types of job demands are associated with work engagement. In our work with correctional officers we found that mentoring, job control, support, and job demands were positively associated with engagement, while corrections-specific stressors (such as dealing with offenders) were negatively associated with engagement (Biggs, 2011; Brough and Biggs, 2015). Our research highlights the differential impact of demands on engagement: cognitive demands that have the potential to produce growth and development tend to be positively associated with work engagement, whilst emotional demands and work pressure tend to be negatively related to work engagement (e.g. Crawford *et al.*, 2010). Overall, this evidence suggests that resources, particularly organisational-level resources, and, to a lesser extent, job demands, have an important influence on work engagement.

Work engagement interventions

Interventions discussed in published research usually target work problems, such as stress and ill-health, which is at odds with growing organisational interest in maintaining an engaged workforce. The lack of evidence-based work engagement strategies is especially problematic for criminal justice occupations, which possess unique work requirements and organisational cultures. A key challenge in conducting work engagement interventions for criminal justice employees is that work engagement is usually associated with resourceful work environments; however, the work tasks performed by many criminal justice employees typically:

- are high-stress in nature, with available resources being insufficient to meet high demands;
- are devalued or highly scrutinised by the public, often through the media, despite the important service provided to the community;
- require high levels of interaction with stigmatised populations; and
- lack intrinsic rewards, such as development opportunities and autonomy (Ashforth and Kreiner, 1999; Biggs, 2011).

As a result, training and interventions that are effective in other occupational contexts may not be suitable, or available, in criminal justice contexts, where access to certain resources is more difficult and the pathway to achieving a sense that work is meaningful and challenging may differ. Many of the demands and risks associated with criminal justice work, such as physical danger, are difficult to remove or minimise, given the nature of the roles. Furthermore, austerity measures adopted by criminal justice organisations worldwide have resulted in diminished tangible resources available to assist employees to meet their job demands, which is also a significant threat to developing an engaged workforce.

Despite the challenges of working within criminal justice environments, research has demonstrated that criminal justice employees do report levels of engagement comparable to, or even higher than, those reported in other occupations. For instance, a comparison of occupations demonstrated police officers reported the third highest rates of vigour and the highest rates of dedication and absorption (Schaufeli *et al.*, 2006). Gillet *et al.* (2013, p. 48) also noted 'in spite of many problems faced by police – a work environment characterized by violence, conflict, and threats – officers' willingness to engage and persist in their work is frequently observed.' Explanations for why this may be the case point to the increased salience of extrinsic rewards, such as camaraderie, in the absence of intrinsic rewards, and the capacity to focus on the positive contribution to offender rehabilitation and public service components of the role (i.e. meaningful work; Ashforth and Kreiner, 1999; Biggs, 2011; Biggs, Brough, and Barbour, 2014b; Brough and Biggs, 2010). Therefore, it is possible to maintain an engaged workforce in criminal justice occupations, although the lack of evidence-based interventions for criminal justice occupations is currently a significant barrier. Below, we suggest strategies for addressing engagement and avoiding over-engagement for criminal justice organisations.

Strategies for increasing work engagement

According to Schaufeli and Salanova (2010), a comprehensive approach to increasing work engagement and decreasing ill-health integrates *positive interventions* with *prevention* and *treatment interventions*. Both prevention and treatment are commonly included in stress management interventions, which aim to minimise or eliminate stressor exposure (primary intervention), increase individual's coping capacity (secondary intervention), and treat strain (tertiary intervention). In contrast, positive interventions 'promote, increase and improve employee health and well-being, including work engagement' (Schaufeli and Salanova, 2010, p. 399). Positive interventions broaden the scope of prevention and treatment, by integrating illness and well-being, and targeting the entire workforce, rather than only those who are at-risk or ill (Schaufeli and Salanova, 2010). Furthermore, both individual and organisational intervention strategies should be considered (Biggs, Noblet, and Allisey, 2014). Individual strategies focus on what an employee can do to 'flourish and thrive at work', while organisational strategies focus on what an organisation can do to 'promote a flourishing and thriving workforce' (Schaufeli and Salanova, 2010, p. 399).

The specific focus for interventions should be driven by an assessment of risks and strengths, for example by using the tools we discuss in Part II of this book (Chapters 7–11). Based on a review of empirical research, the following four organisational-level strategies are most pertinent for criminal justice agencies to consider.

Building resources

Work engagement is strongly related to resourceful working environments, and programmes that increase access to tangible and psychological job resources are recommended. Support from work colleagues and job control over when and how to perform tasks are two psychological resources most commonly linked with work engagement. In some criminal justice occupations, however, the level of control over when and how to perform tasks is difficult to vary, due to the strict requirement for adherence to procedure. There are other psychological resources, such as supportive organisational cultures and recognition, which are more malleable in these work contexts.

Building positive and supportive organisational cultures

Work engagement research within criminal justice occupations has identified the influence of positive and supportive organisational cultures (Biggs, Brough, and Barbour, 2014a, 2014c; Gillet *et al.*, 2013). Specific strategies include: establishing clear lines of communication between managers and front-line employees; investing in the development of effective and supportive leaders; providing opportunities for employees to voice concerns without fear of stigma or punishment; recognising good work; and establishing fair procedures (see Chapter 2 for an overview of organisational justice). Research has demonstrated that perceptions of organisational support are most strongly shaped by fair treatment, followed by supervisor support, and rewards (recognition, pay, and promotion opportunity) and job conditions (e.g. demands and resources; Brough *et al.*, 2009; Rhoades and Eisenberger, 2002).

Enhancing the meaningfulness of work

Enhancing the perceived importance or meaning of the job is another mechanism for developing work engagement. Meaningfulness can be fostered through job design (e.g. job enrichment), enhancing person-job fit, fostering positive co-worker relations, and increasing recognition for good work (May *et al.*, 2004). Increasing strategic alignment is an additional strategy for increasing engagement. Strategic alignment encompasses an employee's (a) awareness of the organization's strategic priorities, (b) perceived importance of those priorities, and (c) understanding of how their daily job tasks and roles directly contribute to the organization's capacity to achieve its priorities (Biggs, Brough, and Barbour, 2014d). Biggs, Brough, and Barbour (2014d) demonstrated that both strategic alignment and work engagement were enhanced as a result of a leadership development programme for police officers (described in more detail in Chapters 7 and 14).

Effective leadership

Leadership plays an integral role in shaping organisational cultures and allocating demands and resources (Dollard and Bakker, 2010). Specific leadership styles, such as empowering and transformational leadership, are also related to work engagement (Bakker *et al.*, 2011; Christian *et al.*, 2011). Investing in effective leaders is a recommended strategy for increasing work engagement. In Chapter 14 we discuss a leadership development programme that successfully increased work engagement within an Australian police organisation.

Psychological contract

Schaufeli and Salanova (2010) propose establishing and monitoring the psychological contract as an organisational strategy for increasing work engagement. A psychological contract (Rousseau, 1989) involves an employees' implicit understanding that an investment of effort on their part will result in organisational rewards and benefits. Research has linked fulfilment of psychological contract to work engagement, and additional positive outcomes, such as organisational commitment and reduced turnover intentions (Parzefall and Hakanen, 2008). Establishing and monitoring a fair psychological contract, clarifying mutual expectations, and providing adequate resources for employees to meet expectations is recommended for enhancing work engagement (Schaufeli and Salanova, 2010). See also the related discussion on organisational justice in Chapter 2.

Strategies for avoiding over-engagement

As discussed earlier in this chapter, work engagement is associated with positive outcomes that are mutually beneficial for individuals and organisations alike. The obvious implication is that intervention strategies aiming to increase work engagement amongst employees will optimise these favourable outcomes. It is important to consider, however, that high levels of engagement may not be sustainable over time, or may even produce negative outcomes:

1   Highly engaged employees tend to experience greater demands over time, as they proactively seek challenges, attract additional responsibilities from managers who recognise their high levels of engagement and commitment, and engage in organisational citizenship behaviours (Christian *et al.*, 2011; Sonnentag, 2011). While highly engaged employees tend to have access to

resources to cope with demands, there is a risk that increased demands will overwhelm their coping capacity, producing exhaustion and disengagement over time (Timms *et al.*, 2012).

2   Related to the previous point, increased challenges and responsibilities may result in employees being overly involved or 'over-engaged' in their work, resulting in work–life conflict and reducing recovery opportunities (Halbesleben, 2010).

3   Highly engaged employees willingly invest their effort in return for intrinsic, rather than extrinsic, rewards (Gillet *et al.*, 2013). In this way, engagement is particularly beneficial for organisations as it increases performance without requiring a subsequent increase in remuneration. However, it does not seem reasonable to expect employees to continually invest high levels of engagement purely for intrinsic rewards, and there is a risk that these employees may feel unappreciated or exploited over time.

Our research with Australian correctional employees demonstrated that workers with high levels of engagement reported declining resources and job satisfaction, and increased stressors and burnout, over a six-month period. The detrimental effects of over-engagement were most evident for high levels of absorption, suggesting that high levels of immersion in job tasks potentially has an energy draining effect on individuals over time (Biggs and Brough, 2014). This research highlights that while high levels of work engagement are certainly desirable for individuals and organisations, the goal for interventions should not purely be to increase engagement, but to assist employees with maintaining *sustainable levels* of work engagement over time. Therefore, we recommend the following considerations:

•   Reward engagement not workaholism: people who are highly engaged at work are equally engaged in their non-work roles.
•   Encourage recovery: this is counterintuitive to traditional notions of productivity, but there is increasingly a strong business case for encouraging employees to adequately recover from work.
•   Monitor levels of demands and challenges to ensure workload is manageable and employees possess resources to meet demands.
•   Recognise and express gratitude to highly engaged employees.
•   Avoid fostering unrealistic expectations about rewards, such as promotion opportunities, to prevent perceived inequity.

Conclusion

In recent years, research on work engagement in criminal justice occupations has increased, reflecting the wider influence of positive psychology. In this chapter we discuss how achieving an engaged workforce is possible, despite the high-stress nature of criminal justice work. This area of research is still rather limited, however, particularly in relation to the effectiveness of intervention strategies that both enhance *and* sustain high levels of work engagement over time. More research on positive relationships between job resources and work engagement in criminal justice contexts is required to better inform managers seeking to retain healthy and productive workers.

References

Ashforth, B.E., and Kreiner, G.E. (1999) 'How can you do it?': Dirty work and the challenge of constructing a positive identity. *Academy of Management Review*, 24(3): 413–434.

Bakker, A.B., and Demerouti, E. (2007) The job demands-resources model: state of the art. *Journal of Managerial Psychology*, 22(3): 309–328. doi:10.1108/02683940710733115.

Bakker, A.B., Albrecht, S.L., and Leiter, M.P. (2011) Key questions regarding work engagement. *European Journal of Work and Organizational Psychology*, 20(1): 4–28. doi:10.1080/1359432X.2010.485352.

Bakker, A.B., Demerouti, E., and Schaufeli, W.B. (2005) The crossover of burnout and work engagement among working couples. *Human Relations*, 58(5): 661–689.

Biggs, A. (2011) *A longitudinal evaluation of strain, work engagement, and intervention strategies to address the health of high-risk employees.* Doctoral Thesis, Griffith University, Brisbane.

Biggs, A., and Brough, P. (2014) *Sustainability of high levels of work engagement.* Paper presented at the 28th International Congress of Applied Psychology, July, Paris.

Biggs, A., Brough, P., and Barbour, J.P. (2014a) Enhancing work-related attitudes and work engagement: a quasi-experimental study of the impact of a leadership development intervention. *International Journal of Stress Management*, 21(1): 43–68. doi:10.1037/a0034508.

Biggs, A., Brough, P., and Barbour, J.P. (2014b) Exposure to extraorganizational stressors: impact on mental health and organizational perceptions for police officers. *International Journal of Stress Management*, 21(3): 255–282. doi:10.1037/a0037297.

Biggs, A., Brough, P., and Barbour, J.P. (2014c) Relationships of individual and organizational support with engagement: examining various types of causality in a three-wave study. *Work and Stress*, 28(3): 236–254. doi:10.1080/02678373.2014.934316.

Biggs, A., Brough, P., and Barbour, J.P. (2014d) Strategic alignment with organizational priorities and work engagement: a multi-wave analysis. *Journal of Organizational Behavior*, 35(3): 301–317. doi:10.1002/job.1866.

Biggs, A., Noblet, A., and Allisey, A. (2014) Organisational interventions. In Dollard, M.F., Shimazu, A., Bin Nordin, R., Brough, P., and Tuckey, M.R. (eds) *Psychosocial factors at work in the Asia Pacific* (pp. 355–376).

Botha, C., and Pienaar, J. (2006) South African correctional official occupational stress: the role of psychological strengths. *Journal of Criminal Justice*, 34: 73–84.

Brough, P., and Biggs, A. (2010) Occupational stress in police and prison staff. In Brown, J., and Campbell, E. (eds) *The Cambridge handbook of forensic psychology.* Cambridge: Cambridge University Press (pp. 707–718).

Brough, P., and Biggs, A. (2015) Job demands x job control interaction effects: do occupation-specific job demands increase their occurrence? *Stress and Health*, 31(2): 138–149. doi:10.1002/smi.2537.

Brough, P., O'Driscoll, M., Kalliath, T., Cooper, C.L., and Poelmans, S. (2009) *Workplace psychological health: current research and practice.* Cheltenham: Edward Elgar.

Brunetto, Y., Teo, S.T.T., Shacklock, K., and Farr-Wharton, R. (2012) Emotional intelligence, job satisfaction, well-being and engagement: explaining organisational commitment and turnover intentions in policing. *Human Resources Management Journal*, 22(4): 428–441. doi:10.1111/j.1748–8583.2012.00198.x.

Burney, M.R. (2011) *Testing the job demands-resources model of work engagement with a sample of corrections officers working within New Zealand.* Master's Thesis, Massey University, Wellington.

Christian, M.S., Garza, A.S., and Slaughter, J.E. (2011) Work engagement: a quantitative review and test of its relations with task and contextual performance. *Personnel Psychology*, 64: 89–136. doi:10.1111/j.1744–6570.2010.01203.x.

Crawford, E.R., LePine, J.A., and Rich, B.L. (2010) Linking job demands and resources to employee engagement and burnout: a theoretical extension and meta-analytic test. *Journal of Applied Psychology*, 95(5): 834–848. doi:10.1037/a0019364.

Demerouti, E., Bakker, A.B., Nachreiner, F., and Schaufeli, W.B. (2001) The job demands-resources model of burnout. *Journal of Applied Psychology*, 86(3): 499–512. doi:10.1037//0021–9010.86.3.499.

Dollard, M.F., and Bakker, A.B. (2010) Psychosocial safety climate as a precursor to conducive work environments, psychological health problems, and employee engagement. *Journal of Occupational and Organizational Psychology*, 83: 579–599. doi:10.1348/096317909X470690.

Gillet, N., Huart, I., Colombat, P., and Fouquereau, E. (2013) Perceived organizational support, motivation, and engagement among police officers. *Professional Psychology: Research and Practice*, 44(1): 46–55. doi:10.1037/a0030066.

Hakanen, J.J., Perhoniemi, R., and Toppinen-Tanner, S. (2008) Positive gain spirals at work: from job resources to work engagement, personal initiative and work-unit innovativeness. *Journal of Vocational Behavior*, 73: 78–91. doi:10.1016/j.jvb.2008.01.003.

Halbesleben, J.R.B. (2010) A meta-analysis of work engagement: relationships with burnout, demands, resources, and consequences. In Bakker, A.B., and Leiter M.P. (eds) *Work engagement: a handbook of essential theory and research.* New York: Psychology Press (pp. 102–117).

Lambert, E.G., Hogan, N.L., Barton, S.M., Jiang, S., and Baker, D.N. (2008) The impact of punishment and rehabilitation views on organizational commitment among correctional staff: a preliminary study. *American Journal of Criminal Justice*, 33: 85–98.

Langelaan, S., Bakker, A.B., Van Doornen, L.J.P., and Schaufeli, W.B. (2006) Burnout and work engagement: do individual differences make a difference? *Personality and Individual Differences*, 40(3): 521–532. doi:10.1016/j.paid.2005.07.009.

Masson, R.C., Royal, M.A., Agnew, T.G., and Fine, S. (2008) Leveraging employee engagement: the practical implications [Commentary]. *Industrial and Organizational Psychology*, 1: 56–59. doi:10.1111/j.1754–9434.2007.00009.x.

Mauno, S., Kinnunen, U., and Ruokolainen, M. (2007) Job demands and resources as antecedents of work engagement: a longitudinal study. *Journal of Vocational Behavior*, 70: 149–171. doi:10.1016/j.jvb.2006.09.002.

May, D.R., Gilson, R.L., and Harter, L.M. (2004) The psychological conditions of meaningfulness, safety and availability and the engagement of the human spirit at work. *Journal of Occupational and Organizational Psychology*, 77: 11–37. doi:10.1348/0963179 04322915892.

Mostert, K., and Rothmann, S. (2006) Work-related well-being in the South African police service. *Journal of Criminal Justice*, 34: 479–491. doi:10.1016/j.jcrimjus.2006.09.003.

Mostert, K., Cronje, S., and Pienaar, J. (2006) Job resources, work engagement and the mediating role of positive work-home interaction of police officers in the North West Province. *Acta Criminologica*, 19(3): 64–87.

Neveu, J. (2007) Jailed resources: conservation of resources theory as applied to burnout among prison guards. *Journal of Organizational Behaviour*, 28: 21–42.

Parzefall, M., and Hakanen, J.J. (2008) Psychological contract and its motivational and health-enhancing properties. *Journal of Managerial Psychology*, 25(1): 4–21. doi:10.1108/02683941011013849.

Rhoades, L., and Eisenberger, R. (2002) Perceived organizational support: a review of the literature. *Journal of Applied Psychology*, 87(4): 698–714. doi:10.1037/0021–9010.87.4.698.

Richardsen, A.M., Burke, R.J., and Martinussen, M. (2006) Work and health outcomes among police officers: the mediating role of police cynicism and engagement. *International Journal of Stress Management*, 13(4): 555–574.

Rousseau, D.M. (1989) Psychological and implied contracts in organizations. *Employee Responsibilities and Rights Journal*, 2(2): 121–139.

Salanova, M., Agut, S., and Peiro, J. (2005) Linking organizational resources and work engagement to employee performance and customer loyalty: the mediation of service climate. *Journal of Applied Psychology*, 90(6): 1217–1227.

Schaufeli, W.B., and Bakker, A.B. (2004) Job demands, job resources, and their relationship with burnout and engagement: a multi-sample study. *Journal of Organizational Behavior*, 25(3): 293–315. doi:10.1002/job.248.

Schaufeli, W.B., and Salanova, M. (2007) Work engagement: an emerging psychological concept and its implications for organizations. In Gilliland, S.W., Steiner, D.D., and Skarlicki, D.P. (eds) *Research in social issues in management: managing social and ethical issues in organizations*, volume 5. Greenwich, CT: Information Age Publishers (pp. 135–177).

Schaufeli, W.B., and Salanova, M. (2010) How to improve work engagement? In Albrecht, S.L. (ed.) *Handbook of employee engagement*. Cheltenham: Edward Elgar (pp. 399–415).

Schaufeli, W.B., Bakker, A.B., and Salanova, M. (2006) The measurement of work engagement with a short questionnaire: a cross-national study. *Educational and Psychological Measurement*, 66(4): 701–716. doi:10.1177/0013164405282471.

Schaufeli, W.B., Salanova, M., González-Romá, V., and Bakker, A.B. (2002) The measurement of engagement and burnout: a two sample confirmatory factor analytic approach. *Journal of Happiness Studies*, 3(1): 71–92. doi:10.1023/A:1015630930326.

Sonnentag, S. (2003) Recovery, work engagement, and proactive behavior: a new look at the interface between nonwork and work. *Journal of Applied Psychology*, 88(3): 518–528.

Sonnentag, S. (2011) Research on work engagement is well and alive. *European Journal of Work and Organizational Psychology*, 20(1): 29–38. doi:10.1080/1359432X.2010.510639.

Sonnentag, S., and Niessen, C. (2008) Staying vigorous until work is over: the role of trait vigour, day-specific work experiences and recovery. *Journal of Occupational and Organizational Psychology*, 81: 435–458.

Timms, C., Brough, P., and Graham, D. (2012) Burnt-out but engaged: the co-existence of psychological burnout and engagement. *Journal of Educational Administration*, 50(3): 327–345. doi:10.1108/09578231211223338.

Timms, C., Brough, P., O'Driscoll, M., Kalliath, T., Siu, O.L., Sit, C., and Lo, D. (in press) Positive pathways to engaging workers: work-family enrichment as a predictor of work engagement. *Asia Pacific Journal of Human Resources*. doi:10.1111/1744–7941.12066.

Winwood, P.C., Tuckey, M.R., Peters, R., and Dollard, M.F. (2009) Identification and measurement of work-related psychological injury: piloting the psychological injury risk indicator among frontline police. *Journal of Occupational and Environmental Medicine*, 51(9): 1057–1065. doi:10.1097/JOM.0b013e3181b2f3d8.

Xanthopoulou, D., Bakker, A.B., Demerouti, E., and Schaufeli, W.B. (2009) Work engagement and financial returns: a diary study on the role of job and personal resources. *Journal of Occupational and Organizational Psychology*, 82: 183–200.

4 Leadership and management

Introduction

Leadership influences numerous outcomes relating to the performance and well-being of employees and the organisation's capacity to strategically and successfully achieve its objectives. Leaders shape employees' actual and perceived work experience; allocate resources, punishment, and rewards; drive the pace and volume of work; and establish standards of acceptable behaviour (Christian *et al.*, 2011; Kelloway and Barling, 2010). Considering the position of criminal justice employees as leaders and managers within the community, this issue is particularly pertinent for these organisations. This chapter focuses on the conceptualisation of leadership, the distinction between management and leadership, and traditional versus emerging leadership perspectives. Finally, a discussion of the state of play of leadership in criminal justice organisations is presented. The issue of leadership development, which is highly relevant to the content of this chapter, will be discussed in greater depth later in this book in Chapter 14.

Leadership defined

Leadership refers to 'a process of social influence that is enacted by designated individuals who hold formal leadership roles in organizations' (Kelloway and Barling, 2010, p. 261). Although leadership qualities may be displayed by any employee within an organisation, this definition recognises that designated organisational leaders have a particularly influential role in shaping employee and organisational outcomes (Kelloway and Barling, 2010). Similarly, in this chapter we specifically focus on leadership in organisations as a social influence process enacted by formal organisational leaders.

Direct leadership, which occurs when leaders influence followers via direct interaction and communication, has also been contrasted with indirect leadership (Yukl, 2010). According to Yukl (2010), the latter occurs when a leader influences followers through non-direct means such as:

- the influence of senior leaders on their immediate subordinates, which has a 'cascading' effect as the influence is transferred down the organisation's hierarchy;

- the influence of the leader in shaping organisational programmes, policies, and procedures; and
- the influence of the leader in shaping the organisation's culture.

The distinction between direct and indirect leadership is especially pertinent for criminal justice organisations, with implications for leadership effectiveness and development. Due to the hierarchical organisational structures, the distance between senior leaders and frontline staff is substantial, as we discuss in Chapter 5. Effective direct and indirect leadership is essential for transmitting organisational priorities, achieving employee commitment at all levels, and maintaining positive relations throughout the organisation. Unfortunately, effective indirect leadership is complicated by the leader's lack of autonomy over policies and procedures, which are often driven by external factors beyond the leader's control, in addition to their limited capacity to effect cultural change, as many criminal justice organisations possess strong cultures that are resistant to change.

Leadership versus management

According to Stojkovic *et al.* (2008, p. 7), 'the criminal justice system has a well-established history of creating a cadre of managers whose experience and subsequent socialization has trained them to work heroically to protect their existing systems and culture from intrusion, outsiders, and environmental forces.' Strong management has served criminal justice organisations well during times of stability; however, a greater focus on developing *both* leadership and management capacity is required in order for organisations to strategically prepare for future challenges in a dynamic external environment, including the rapidly evolving nature of crime, increasing diversity of offender populations, and multi-agency collaboration (Stojkovic *et al.*, 2008). This brings us to consider the distinction between management and leadership.

Management refers to 'the process by which organizational members are directed toward organizational goals' (Stojkovic *et al.*, 2008, p. 6). The necessity for management was realised during the industrial revolution, in which optimal productivity required order and consistency of large numbers of people and processes (Kotter, 1990). Management is still relevant in modern organisations due to the complexity created by technology, geographic dispersion, and increased global competition. Modern management functions include setting goals, allocating resources, hiring employees, delegating tasks, developing rules and processes, creating structure, and performance monitoring (Kotter, 1990; Stojkovic *et al.*, 2008).

Although some overlap exists between management and leadership, the fundamental distinction is their ultimate goal: while effective management achieves consistency, order, and predictability, effective leadership achieves 'constructive or adaptive change' and 'produces movement' (Kotter, 1990, p. 4). According to Kotter (1990), leaders achieve this by:

1   identifying vision and providing direction for followers;
2   aligning people with the vision to ensure their commitment to achieving the vision; and
3   motivating and inspiring people, by appealing to their needs, values, or emotions, to continue to move towards change, overcoming any barriers they face.

In contrast, managers tend to be concerned with shorter time-frames, details, tasks, risk reduction, and compliance (Kalliath *et al.*, 2014; Kotter, 1990).

Leadership tends to be viewed with greater esteem than management; however, it is increasingly recognised that modern criminal justice organisations need proficient leaders *and* managers to achieve optimal outcomes. Criminal justice organisations require order and stability to provide consistently effective public services, but also require the capacity to adapt and transform in preparation for emerging challenges (e.g. evolving nature of crime), dynamic external conditions (e.g. political environment), and increased complexity within the criminal justice environment (e.g. inter-agency collaboration; Kotter, 1990; Stojkovic *et al.*, 2008).

Traditional and emerging perspectives on leadership

Trait, behavioural, and contingency perspectives

Earlier trait-based perspectives considered leadership to be innate, with specific traits associated with effective leadership (Kalliath *et al.*, 2014). Failure to reliably identify sets of traits associated with leadership effectiveness, in addition to research debunking the notion that leadership is innate and cannot be developed through training, led to rejection of this perspective (Kelloway and Barling, 2010). Behavioural perspectives of leadership emerged, focusing on behaviours exhibited by effective leaders, generally categorising them as autocratic versus democratic, or task-oriented versus people-oriented (Kalliath *et al.*, 2014). For instance, autocratic leaders make decisions without the input of followers, whilst democratic leaders and their followers 'jointly define the parameters of the decision process and outcomes, after which the group is empowered to make any decision within the specified parameters' (Kalliath *et al.*, 2014, p. 328). A major limitation of these approaches, however, was their presumption that certain behaviours were effective irrespective of the context, failing to account for situational or follower characteristics. Contingency (or situational) perspectives extended behavioural theories by recognising that leadership effectiveness was a function of the context, and different leadership behaviours were suited to different combinations of situational and follower characteristics (Kalliath *et al.*, 2014). This perspective also considered situations that constrain leadership, such as lack of autonomy (Stojkovic *et al.*, 2012). Nonetheless, contingency perspectives are considered to be limited as they 'practically ignored the transformational role of leaders and focused almost exclusively on the transactional aspect of leadership, treating "leadership" as a management tool for motivating subordinates to perform their routine jobs' (Kalliath *et al.*, 2014, p. 339).

Transformational and authentic leadership

Transformational leadership theory is currently one of the most influential leadership perspectives, acknowledging both the transaction between leaders and followers and the leaders' capacity to transform tasks, people, and organisations (Stojkovic *et al.*, 2012). The most current iteration of transformational leadership theory is the full-range leadership model, which integrates non-leadership, transactional leadership, and transformational leadership (Avolio, 2011). Transactional leadership focuses on the transaction between leaders and followers, in which leaders achieve outcomes by 'making, and fulfilling, promises of recognition, pay increases, and advancement for employees who perform well' (Bass, 1990, p. 20). Transactional leadership is aligned with the concept of management discussed earlier in this chapter and comprises three components (Avolio, 2011):

- **Contingent reward:** involves an exchange of reward for effort, in which leaders clarify expectations, reward good performance, and recognise accomplishments (Bass, 1990; Judge and Piccolo, 2004).
- **Active management-by-exception:** leaders actively monitor behaviour, anticipate problems, and provide corrective action before problems escalate (Judge and Piccolo, 2004).
- **Passive management-by-exception:** leaders do not actively manage performance or anticipate problems, and take action only in response to problems (Walumbwa and Wernsing, 2012).

In contrast, transformational leadership is apparent when

> leaders broaden and elevate the interests of their employees, when they generate awareness and acceptance of the purposes and mission of the group, and when they stir their employees to look beyond their own self-interest for the good of the group.
>
> (Bass, 1990, p. 21)

Transformational leadership comprises the following four facets (Avolio, 2011):

- **Idealised influence:** leaders display charisma and behave in a manner consistent with their underlying values and beliefs, resulting in followers identifying with them and striving to emulate them (Avolio, 2011; Judge and Piccolo, 2004; Walumbwa and Wernsing, 2012).
- **Inspirational motivation:** leaders inspire by articulating a vision that appeals to followers, motivating them to achieve the vision by cultivating optimism and meaning (Judge and Piccolo, 2004).

- **Intellectual stimulation:** leaders question the status quo, appeal to followers' intellect, stimulate innovative and creative problem solving, and encourage followers to question their assumptions (Walumbwa and Wernsing, 2012).
- **Individualised consideration:** leaders attend to individuals' concerns and needs, acting as a mentor or coach to their followers (Judge and Piccolo, 2004).

Transformational leadership has been linked with a wide range of positive outcomes. In a review of 49 studies (Skakon *et al.*, 2010), optimal health and well-being levels were reported by employees whose leaders demonstrated positive leadership behaviours, embodying consideration, support, feedback, integrity, and confidence; high-quality leader–employee relationships; and transformational leadership style. Nielsen *et al.* (2008) also demonstrated that transformational leadership increased perceptions of a meaningful work environment, role clarity, and development opportunities, which in turn predicted employee well-being over time. Research conducted with police officers, employing a variety of research techniques, identified 53 specific behaviours linked with effective police leadership, 50 of which resembled transformational leadership behaviours. These behaviours were linked with positive work attitudes, such as increased organisational commitment and job satisfaction (Dobby *et al.*, 2004).

While transformational leadership is often considered to be more effective, it 'is not a panacea. In many situations, it is inappropriate and transactional processes are indicated' (Bass, 1990, p. 30). In particular, the contingent reward component is important, as it clarifies goals and provides reward in exchange for effort (Walumbwa and Wernsing, 2012). For example, Judge and Piccolo (2004) demonstrated that *both* transformational leadership and contingent reward (transactional) leadership were associated with a range of positive outcomes, including (a) follower job satisfaction, (b) follower satisfaction with the leader, (c) follower motivation, (d) leader job performance, (e) group or organizational performance, and (f) leader effectiveness. Furthermore, evidence in criminal justice organisations suggests that leaders who blend transformational and contingent reward (transactional) leadership, role-model competent and ethical behaviours, and adapt styles to suit the context are likely to be more effective than leaders who rely too heavily on inspirational motivation aspects of transformational leadership (Campbell and Kodz, 2011; Fisher *et al.*, 2014; Neyroud, 2011).

The underlying authenticity and ethicality of transformational leadership has also recently been addressed, in order to distinguish between transformational leaders who use their influence and charisma to achieve shared goals, versus those who manipulate followers to serve their own personal interests (Hannah *et al.*, 2011). Authentic, ethical leaders generally possess the following characteristics:

- **Self-awareness** and accurate knowledge of their strengths and weaknesses, in addition to a clear understanding of the impact of their behaviour on others (Walumbwa *et al.*, 2008; Walumbwa and Wernsing, 2012).

- **Relational transparency**, in which the leader presents an authentic representation of their true self (Walumbwa and Wernsing, 2012).
- **Balanced processing**, demonstrating the capacity to objectively analyse all relevant information and solicit input from followers to make the most informed decision possible (Hannah *et al.*, 2011; Walumbwa and Wernsing, 2012).
- **Internalized moral perspective**, involving thinking and behaving 'in a more prosocial and ethical manner even when confronted with difficult ethical challenges' due to their tendency to 'act in line with their highly developed value structures' (Walumbwa and Wernsing, 2012, p. 5).

While research on authentic leadership is relatively new, studies have shown its positive impact on a range of outcomes relating to employee performance. A field-study conducted with US military squads undergoing training demonstrated that team leader authenticity was associated with teamwork behaviour and team productivity (Hannah *et al.*, 2011). Burgess and Hawkes (2013) also demonstrated that authentic leadership was associated with increased ethical climate, trust in leadership, and organisational commitment. Authentic leadership is, therefore, likely to have a positive influence on leader-follower relationships, which is often the source of much dissatisfaction in criminal justice organisations. Furthermore, the contribution of authentic leadership to trust and ethical climate is pertinent in light of the increased scrutiny surrounding eradicating corruption and misconduct. For example, recent reports concerning the advancement of leadership in policing have noted the importance of ethical behaviour at all levels throughout the organisation, and particularly noted the lack of value placed on role-modelling integrity and ethical behaviour in police leadership development programmes (Neyroud, 2011).

State of play of leadership and management in criminal justice organisations

Concern over the quality of leadership in public bureaucracies has been continually debated, resulting in intense scrutiny of the selection and development of senior officer appointments, and calls for the modernisation of leadership practices (Neyroud, 2011; Silvestri *et al.*, 2013). Autocratic, masculine leadership styles have traditionally prevailed, and remain influential due to the strong organisational cultures and the hierarchical, bureaucratic structure inherent in criminal justice organisations (Stojkovic *et al.*, 2012; Villiers, 2009). For example, the militaristic nature of the hierarchy, combined with cultural elements of solidarity, creates social norms that encourage compliance with direct orders, and discourage defiance of senior officers' commands (Villiers, 2009). The traditionally punitive culture experienced in criminal justice organisations is another factor perpetuating the acceptance of autocratic leadership (Paoline, 2003). Villiers (2009), for example, noted that the premise of police leadership historically emphasised strict and relentless supervision as a result of mistrust of junior officers, who could not be expected to do the right thing when unsupervised. From this perspective, the role of senior officers was to catch out and punish officers for failing to follow procedure. Furthermore, the common practice of appointing senior leaders based on seniority or technical expertise, rather than leadership and management capacity, reinforces the cultural acceptance of autocratic leadership, as internally promoted leaders are likely to emulate the style of leadership they themselves experienced as they ascended the organisational hierarchy (Stojkovic *et al.*, 2008; Villiers, 2009).

There are certainly instances in which autocratic leadership is functional in criminal justice organisations, for example, during critical incidents where decisions need to be made rapidly, procedures need to be adhered to, and adopting a consultative approach would be counterproductive. However, it is now recognised that traditionally accepted autocratic leadership styles are not optimal for the majority of criminal justice work (Stojkovic *et al.*, 2012). Unfortunately, the question of what constitutes effective leadership in criminal justice settings has not yet been conclusively answered, with much of the evidence base limited to evaluating the impact of leadership on subordinates, and subordinates' perceptions of effective leadership, primarily within the police (Campbell and Kodz, 2011; Dobby *et al.*, 2004; Neyroud, 2011). In particular, there is very little evidence assessing the impact of leadership on operational and organisational outcomes (Campbell and Kodz, 2011). Furthermore, it is not clear whether existing theory and research conducted in other contexts is transferable to criminal justice occupations, due to their unique operational requirements, external political contexts, and position of authority within the community (Stojkovic *et al.*, 2012).

Despite the limited evidence base, research in criminal justice settings has emphasised the value of blending authentic, transformational, and transactional leadership; the ability to apply different leadership styles to suit different organisational and operational contexts, including the capacity to provide 'directive, active leadership when required'; and role-modelling active, competent, and ethical practice (Campbell and Kodz, 2011, p. 21; Fisher *et al.*, 2014; Neyroud, 2011). Authentic, transformational leadership is particularly required to enable criminal justice organisations to successfully navigate the unprecedented cultural and procedural changes currently required to ensure their ongoing success. For instance, correctional services are no longer solely responsible for supervising incarcerated offenders, but are required to provide rehabilitation, supervise offenders serving probation and parole orders, and assist offenders to assimilate into society once their sentences are completed. Furthermore, increasing diversity and complexity of the offender population requires novel approaches to assist employees working with ageing populations of offenders, offenders with mental illnesses, and group affiliations. For police, technology has completely transformed crime prevention, with rising crimes involving identity theft, terrorism, and internet-based offences (e.g. internet sex predators; Stojkovic *et al.*, 2012). Transformational and supportive leadership styles are likely to facilitate the creativity and innovation required to formulate new practices for preventing crime and rehabilitating offenders (Stojkovic *et al.*, 2012).

Within criminal justice organisations, the adoption of contemporary leadership approaches is becoming increasingly commonplace. An example of this is the *Police Leadership Qualities Framework* (PLQF) introduced in the UK and discussed by Villiers (2009). According to Villiers, the PLQF advocates for transformational leadership within the police, characterised by self-awareness, integrity, and achievement. Although not explicitly acknowledged, these elements are also characteristics of authentic leadership. In addition, Stojkovic *et al.* (2012) noted that the influence of transformational leadership can be seen in the practice of modern criminal justice occupations in relation to three key areas: (a) establishing the organisation's mission and strategic direction; (b) setting strategic priorities; and (c) cultivating creativity and innovation. Although setting goals and strategic priorities are relatively straightforward, motivating followers to commit to a vision and effecting organisational culture change to support leadership development is more challenging.

Shifting focus to embrace contemporary leadership perspectives, however, should be tempered by consideration of the organisational constraints placed on criminal justice leaders, which may impede leadership development and change. For example, punitive cultures, focusing on attributing blame and fault-finding are inconsistent with transformational and authentic leadership styles that aim to build trust amongst leaders and followers (Villiers, 2009). Cynicism, particularly of outsiders and behaviours that defy norms, is also a strong feature of organisational culture (Loftus, 2010; Villiers, 2009). Charisma, a characteristic of transformational leadership, is often regarded with suspicion and is generally viewed as unnecessary and undesirable for criminal justice leaders (Villiers, 2009). Building leadership capability by appointing senior leaders from external sources, rather than relying on internal promotions, may also be compromised due to the cynicism and mistrust displayed towards outsiders (Biggs, 2011).

The level of autonomy leaders possess is an additional consideration when contemplating leadership development. Criminal justice leaders may have limited capacity to implement new leadership styles or to control the distribution of rewards and punishment, due to the strong reliance on routine, procedures, and policies (Stojkovic *et al.*, 2012). This is not only a barrier for transformational and supportive leadership, but also inhibits contingent reward (transactional) leadership (Bass, 1990). Furthermore, as many criminal justice organisations are public bureaucracies, the external context for criminal justice leaders is unique and inherently political, with multiple stakeholders to appease, multi-agency collaborations, and competition amongst agencies for resources (Stojkovic *et al.*, 2012). In these contexts, leadership needs to be 'understood as a process that reaches well beyond the formal boundaries of the organisation' to take into consideration the external factors inhibiting leadership development (Stojkovic *et al.*, 2012, p. 194).

A final point requiring consideration is the need to increase diversity amongst senior leaders within criminal justice organisations. Currently, there is a lack of representation of women and ethnic minorities at higher levels within criminal justice organisations (Silvestri *et al.*, 2013; Villiers, 2009). Interpersonal, structural, and cultural elements of work promote discrimination and impede the capacity for women and ethnic minorities to progress to positions of leadership in criminal justice organisations (Biggs, 2011). These include stereotypical attitudes, lack of fit within the organisational culture, exclusion from formal and informal social networks, difficulties acquiring developmental assignments, and lack of mentoring (Lyness and Thompson, 2000; Stokes *et al.*, 1995). Removing barriers to senior leadership positions for women and other minority groups is likely to enrich leadership capabilities within criminal justice organisations (Dobby *et al.*, 2004). For example, research has demonstrated that female leaders tend to display more transformational and contingent reward behaviours compared to men, which are associated with more positive outcomes (Eagly *et al.*, 2003). Attempts to address this lack of diversity by introducing multiple pathways to leadership, instead of relying solely on internal vertical promotions, have been recommended (Winsor, 2012). However, as noted by Silvestri *et al.* (2013), this may actually further undermine the position of women and ethnic minorities as organisational outsiders. We discuss these issues in more detail in Chapter 14 and Chapter 16.

Conclusion

It is widely accepted that organisations require effective leadership and management in order to function optimally. To date, existing evidence points to effective criminal justice leadership consisting of a blend between authentic transformational and transactional elements, flexibility to match leadership styles to the situation, and role-modelling of competent and ethical behaviours. A stronger evidence base is required to more precisely determine the nature of effective leadership in criminal justice organisations, however, as limited high-quality studies currently exist in these contexts, and recommendations for criminal justice leadership are often drawn from other research contexts (Neyroud, 2011). This is potentially problematic because work in criminal justice occupations is unique, due to employees at all levels being required to display effective leadership, operational requirements, and the strong influence of the external political context. As a result, existing theory and research may not be applicable to criminal justice organisations. Implications for leadership development are discussed in further detail in Chapter 14.

References

Avolio, B.J. (2011) *Full range leadership development*, 2nd edn. Thousand Oaks, CA: SAGE.

Bass, B.M. (1990) From transactional to transformational leadership: learning to share the vision. *Organizational Dynamics*, 18(3): 19–31. doi:10.1016/0090–2616(90)90061-S.

Biggs, A. (2011) *A longitudinal evaluation of strain, work engagement, and intervention strategies to address the health of high-risk employees.* Doctoral Thesis, Griffith University, Brisbane.

Burgess, M., and Hawkes, A. (2013) *Authentic leadership and affective, normative and continuance commitment: the mediating effects of trust in leadership and caring ethical climate.* Paper presented at the Proceedings of the 10th Industrial and Organisational Psychology Conference, Perth.

Campbell, I., and Kodz, J. (2011) *What makes great police leadership? What research can tell us about the effectiveness of different leadership styles, competencies and behaviours: a rapid evidence review.* London: National Policing Improvement Agency.

Christian, M.S., Garza, A.S., and Slaughter, J.E. (2011) Work engagement: a quantitative review and test of its relations with task and contextual performance. *Personnel Psychology*, 64: 89–136. doi:10.1111/j.1744–6570.2010.01203.x.

Dobby, J., Anscombe, J., and Tuffin, R. (2004) *Police leadership: expectations and impact.* London: Home Office Research, Development and Statistics Directorate.

Eagly, A.H., Johannesen-Schmidt, M.C., and van Engen, M.L. (2003) Transformational, transactional, and laissez-faire leadership styles: a meta-analysis comparing women and men. *Psychological Bulletin*, 129(4): 569–591. doi:http://dx.doi.org/10.1037/0033-2909.129.4.569.

Fisher, A., Weir, D., and Phillips, J.S. (2014) Beyond transactional and transformational leadership into the double helix: a case-study of blended leadership in police work. *Review of Enterprise and Management Studies*, 1(2): 16–28.

Hannah, S.T., Walumbwa, F.O., and Fry, L.W. (2011) Leadership in action teams: team leader and members' authenticity, authenticity strength, and team outcomes. *Personnel Psychology*, 64: 771–802. doi:10.1111/j.1744–6570.2011.01225.x.

Judge, T.A., and Piccolo, R.F. (2004) Transformational and transactional leadership: a meta-analytic test of their relative validity. *Journal of Applied Psychology*, 89(5): 755–768. doi:10.1037/0021–9010.89.5.755.

Kalliath, T., Brough, P., O'Driscoll, M., Manimala, M.J., Siu, O.L., and Parker, S.K. (2014) *Organisational behaviour: a psychological perspective for the Asia-Pacific.* North Ryde, Australia: McGraw-Hill Education (Australia).

Kelloway, E.K., and Barling, J. (2010) Leadership development as an intervention in occupational health psychology. *Work and Stress*, 24(3): 260–279. doi:10.1080/02678373.2010.518441.

Kotter, J.P. (1990) *A force for change: how leadership differs from management.* New York: The Free Press.

Loftus, B. (2010) Police occupational culture: classic themes, altered times. *Policing and Society*, 20(1): 1–20. doi:10.1080/10439460903281547.

Lyness, K.S., and Thompson, D.E. (2000) Climbing the corporate ladder: do female and male executives follow the same route? *Journal of Applied Psychology*, 85(1): 86–101.

Neyroud, P. (2011) *Review of police leadership and training.* London: Home Office.

Nielsen, K., Randall, R., Yarker, J., and Brenner, S. (2008) The effects of transformational leadership on followers' perceived work characteristics and psychological well-being: a longitudinal study. *Work and Stress*, 22(1): 16–32. doi:10.1080/02678370801979430.

Paoline, E.A., III (2003) Taking stock: toward a richer understanding of police culture. *Journal of Criminal Justice*, 31(3): 199–214. doi:10.1016/s0047–2352(03)00002–3.

Silvestri, M., Tong, S., and Brown, J. (2013) Gender and police leadership: time for a paradigm shift? *International Journal of Police Science and Management*, 15(1): 61–73. doi:10.1350/ijps.2013.15.1.303.

Skakon, J., Nielsen, K., Borg, V., and Guzman, J. (2010) Are leaders' well-being, behaviours, and style associated with the affective well-being of their employees? A systematic review of three decades of research. *Work and Stress*, 24(2): 107–139. doi:10.1080/02678373.2010.495262.

Stojkovic, S., Kalinich, D., and Klofas, J. (2008) *Criminal justice: administration and management*, 4th edn. Belmont, CA: Thompson Wadsworth.

Stojkovic, S., Kalinich, D., and Klofas, J. (2012) *Criminal justice organizations: administration and management*, 5th edn. Belmont, CA: Wadsworth.

Stokes, J., Riger, S., and Sullivan, M. (1995) Measuring perceptions of the working environment for women in corporate settings. *Psychology of Women Quarterly*, 19: 533–549.

Villiers, P. (2009) *Police and policing: an introduction*. Hook, UK: Waterside Press.

Walumbwa, F.O., and Wernsing, T. (2012) From transactional and transformational leadership to authentic leadership. In Rumsey, M.G. (ed.) *The Oxford handbook of leadership*. New York: Oxford University Press (pp. 392–400). doi:10.1093/oxfordhb/9780195398793.013.0023.

Walumbwa, F.O., Avolio, B.J., Gardner, W.L., Wernsing, T.S., and Peterson, S.J. (2008) Authentic leadership: development and validation of a theory-based measure. *Journal of Management*, 34(1): 89–126. doi:10.1177/0149206307308913.

Winsor, T.P. (2012) *Independent review of police officer and staff remuneration and conditions*. London: HMSO.

Yukl, G. (2010) *Leadership in organizations*. New Jersey: Pearson Education.

5 Organisational communication

Introduction

Effective systems of internal organisation communication have been described as akin to the nervous system in the human body; that is, an essential and wide reaching two-way feedback system that directly influences performance and learnings (Baskin, 2012). Effective internal communication systems are fundamental to the core functioning of an organisation and are directly associated with both organisational leadership practices and the organisational culture. Many organisations with a hierarchical structure experience communication problems, and these commonly consist of more one-way than dual two-way communication flows. Information is often equated with power, and thus the withholding of information and communications is built into most bureaucratic systems, including criminal justice workplaces. In this chapter we discuss how communication systems are commonly structured within criminal justice workplaces and the reasons why these communication systems are often a source of dissatisfaction amongst rank-and-file employees. The chapter also describes common communication problems within criminal justice workplaces including wilful blindness and whistleblowing, and discusses some of the key implications of these problems.

Hierarchical organisational structures and communication

Policing and corrections organisations obviously adopt a hierarchical formal rank organisational structure. Hierarchical organisations typically have well developed formal communication systems flowing downwards from the top to the bottom of the hierarchy. Downwards communication methods commonly include: directions, orders, and instructions; formal organisational policies and procedures; manuals and newsletters; and formal performance appraisals. Organisational departments and workgroups form specific intra-group communication channels which are usually associated with a greater speed of communication and more efficient job performance as compared to reliance upon a single central source of communication. However, the flow of information upwards from frontline operational workers is typically less developed and often primarily consists of employee suggestions and complaints. One of the common causes for employee whistleblowing activities, for example, is frustration at an organisational communications system which provides a perceived inability for communications to be effectively heard (or acted upon; Burke and Cooper, 2013).

Impact of communication technologies

Advances in technological communication systems, primarily with the development of email, internet, and intranet (internal) systems has typically resulted in an increased speed and ease of organisational communications, including a greater frequency of informal communications. It has been observed that these technological communication systems promote internal groups (networks) of personnel which weaken (to varying extents) formal management hierarchies (Langan-Fox, 2002). The widespread use of email has proven to be an effective method for the rapid dissemination (and storage) of organisational news and events. Some studies have associated email with organisational productivity increases, primarily due to being a far more efficient communication system as compared to the alternative of hard-copy memos and letters, multiple telephone calls, and meetings (Langan-Fox, 2002).

However, the increased speed and ease of email and other electronic communications is also associated with information overload, defined as a feeling of being overwhelmed by the quantity of incoming information and the need to respond to it. The term 'techno-stress' also describes this issue and refers specifically to the demands placed upon employees to constantly renew their technical skills and adapt to more complex technology/computer systems (O'Driscoll *et al.*, 2010). Reports of information overload have risen exponentially with the increased use of email as a primary mechanism for communication. For example, Bellotti *et al.* (2005) reported that managers in particular are likely to experience information overload from email and frustration over an inability to adequately monitor multiple concurrent tasks for which they have responsibility. The misuse of emails, including bullying and harassment experiences, are also of increasing concern for employee health and productivity (O'Driscoll *et al.*, 2010). Organisational policies which establish parameters for email usage and protocols for email communications are increasingly common, although in the twenty-four-hour operations of criminal justice workplaces, these formal communications policies are often not practical.

The importance of frontline supervisors in the organisational communications process is widely recognized within criminal justice workplaces. These supervisors have been referred to as an organisation's 'real opinion leaders' who have a strong influence on the adoption of organisation changes and initiatives (Langan-Fox, 2002, p. 193). It has been noted that due to the strength of direct personal communications compared to group electronic communications, senior managers are still recommended to communicate any organisation changes with frontline supervisors via face-to-face meetings. Supervisors are then, therefore, more likely to positively communicate these changes to their subordinates (Langan-Fox, 2002).

Problems with communications flow

Complaints about communication problems, typically of workers not having a 'voice' and/or an influence upwards within the organisational hierarchy, is commonly identified in many organisations, including criminal justice workplaces. In a 1956 discussion of (US) police service communications Kenney noted eight barriers which act to hinder communication flow between internal police departments and ranks. Two of these barriers concerning the upwards flow of communications are issues which numerous police services and other criminal justice organisations still grapple with today; namely *the receptiveness of executives to communications from subordinates* and *a lack of action by executives upon receipt of communications*. Kenney (1956, p. 550) observed: 'By refusing to act, subordinates may lose faith both in the sincerity of the executive and in the values of a communication system. In many instances, refusal to act serves to communicate disapproval in a manner as effectively as words.' It is pertinent that perceptions of upwards communications being dismissed and/or ignored are still key complaints among contemporary police and corrections officers. For example, in an investigation of internal communications within the then newly formed Police Service for Northern Ireland (PSNI), Quinn and Hargie (2004) observed that frontline officers desired more information about their duties and also perceived a distinct gap existed between themselves and senior management in terms of direct contact, openness, and communications flow. Quinn and Hargie also noted the vital role played by both inspectors and sergeants as 'communications gate-keepers' between frontline officers and senior managers, which reinforces the observations made above.

In our long-term research collaborations with the Queensland Police Service (QPS) we have also found that issues with the 'disconnect' between frontline employees and senior management is a repeatedly identified core item of job dissatisfaction, and this issue is fuelled by (perceived) inadequate communications. More specifically, we found that the job characteristics of *adequate recognition for good work* and *attention paid to suggestions offered* are consistently rated within the top five most dissatisfying aspects of police work (Biggs, Brough, and Barbour, 2014b; Brough and Biggs, 2010). Most recently, for example, in response to a 2014 self-report job attitudes survey administered to all QPS employees (approximately 15,000), the survey respondents commented again on communication problems within the hierarchy: 'a disparity of understanding between the work priorities of frontline policing and the understanding of what is required to be completed by senior management' (Brough et al., 2014, p. 52). Similarly we also found there to be a perceived lack of positive communications concerning work performance:

> An issue that was commonly reported was dissatisfaction with the levels of positive feedback in relation to the work performance. Many respondents reported that they did not receive encouragement in their workplace and expressed a desire to contribute by providing input to changes in workplace practices.
>
> (Brough et al., 2014, p. 52)

For example, one police officer stated it was the lack of positive recognition when performing unpaid overtime that had a greater (adverse) impact upon morale, rather than the financial component:

> What I found most shocking is that there is absolutely no recognition, zilch, none whatsoever … it's shocking … complete disregard for the effort and amount of work officers put in … I put in a lot of effort … I get a lot of criticism … there is no positive recognition … recognition is a basic human need. It's not about money.
>
> (Chataway, 2014, p. 91)

We have also reported similar findings concerning the perceived inadequate occurrence of (downwards) positive communications and an inadequate response to (upwards) communications reported by samples of Australian correctional workers (Brough and Biggs, 2015; Brough and Williams, 2007), New Zealand police officers (Brough and Frame, 2004), and UK police officers (Brough, 1998). For example, when invited to suggest potential organisational improvements, 15 per cent of responses from a sample of Australian correctional workers specifically focused on improving internal communications: 'More communication between staff and management, especially prior to implementing changes' (Brough and Biggs, 2007, p. 15). In follow-up discussions with this sample of correctional workers, seven key problems with internal communications were identified:

1   Communication between staff and managers could be greatly improved.
2   More consultation prior to workplace change would be beneficial.
3   Staff may have greater participation in work processes, by having forums between all levels of staff to discuss how work practices can be changed and improved without fear of repercussions.
4   There is a lack of consultation with ground staff prior to implementing new practices.
5   Communication skills training may help managers and staff to improve communication.
6   Staff at regional centres feel isolated from senior management based at Headquarters.
7   Staff feel frustrated when directives are approved that are inconsistent with the outcomes of staff consultation.

(Brough and Biggs, 2007, p. 18)

Similar observations have also been reported with samples of police and corrections employees in Europe, the USA, New Zealand, and South Africa (Gershon *et al.*, 2002, 2009; Kirkcaldy *et al.*, 1995; Lambert *et al.*, 2002; Stephens and Long, 2000). Clearly problems with the communications flow between the levels of criminal justice organisations all over the globe are a long-standing problem. Importantly, these communications problems also have a direct impact on numerous employee health, performance, retention, and well-being outcomes.

Impact of chronic communications problems

Job dissatisfaction

The key issue with any source of chronic job dissatisfaction is the adverse impact this can have upon levels of employee job commitment and work performance. Low levels of job satisfaction have strong associations with decreased commitment, performance, and work engagement, and increased experiences of strain and staff turnover. Research has consistently noted these associations with heterogeneous samples of workers, including criminal justice employees (e.g. Biggs *et al.*, 2014b; Brough and Biggs, 2010; Brough *et al.*, 2007; Brough and Frame, 2004; Lambert and Paoline, 2008). For example, in a sample of New Zealand police officers, Brough and Frame (2004) identified the impact that low levels of job satisfaction had upon patterns of leave taking and consequently upon long-term turnover intentions. Similarly, in a sample of Australian correctional workers, Brough and Biggs (2015) noted the long-term negative impact of experiencing high levels of job demands (including inadequate internal communications) upon four pertinent outcomes: job satisfaction, work engagement, psychological strain, and turnover intentions.

Work disengagement

A second key outcome of chronic job dissatisfaction is the impact this may have upon other workers, as well as for the individual employee themselves. Empirical evidence is increasingly collaborating the anecdotal observations that a supervisor who is 'disengaged' with their work has a distinct negative ('toxic') impact upon their colleagues and subordinates (e.g. Webster *et al.*, in press). For example, in our research with police services we have identified that up to 20 per cent of police officers rate themselves as 'actively disengaged' with their work (with the majority (approximately 70 per cent) rating themselves as 'engaged' with their work) (Biggs, Brough, and Barbour, 2014a). These work disengagement figures demonstrate higher levels for the officers who are middle managers: police sergeants and senior sergeants. The negative impact that these police sergeants and senior sergeants can have upon the officers they formally supervise, especially new police constables, is highly significant. In recognition of this point, work is currently being undertaken to target appropriate workplace interventions for these disengaged managers in attempts to 'move' them into the engaged sphere (Biggs *et al.*, 2014b).

Wilful blindness

As well as being a significant stressor for employees, inadequate organisational communications processes are also directly associated with grossly impaired organisation performance. Two of these concepts, *wilful blindness* and *whistle-blowing*, we briefly review here. Wilful blindness is a legal concept that refers to the active ignoring of wrongdoing – commonly referred to as turning a blind eye. Wilful blindness includes the direct knowledge of wrongdoing and more commonly the *indirect* knowledge; that is, an awareness that evidence *probably* exists of a wrongdoing (formally termed constructive knowledge). In this case an individual purposefully avoids acquiring knowledge and is referred to as having 'wilfully shut their eyes' to the wrongdoing (Heffernan, 2011). Numerous major organisational accidents and mistakes have been attributed to wilful blindness, where the seeking of knowledge and/or the effort to communication this knowledge to others in the organisation is, for various reasons, not seen to be in the individual employee's interests. Often, for example, an employee feeling chronically overworked avoids the reporting of a wrongdoing not necessarily due to a lack of personal integrity, but to avoid the additional work demands of the reporting (communication) process.

The occurrence of wilful blindness and associated communication errors have been identified as contributing factors to a number of significant organisational performance mistakes including, for example, corruption in police and prison services and the impaired performance of various professionals involved in child protection investigations (Munro, 1999; Punch, 2003). For example, in a review of UK child abuse inquiry reports from 1973 to 1994, Munro (1999) observed that in 40 per cent of the cases simple communications errors between social workers and other professionals directly contributed to the deaths of children. Recent reports of the mismanagement of child protection services including the 2014 Rotherham sexual exploitation scandal in the UK and the 2015 Royal Commission into Institutional Responses to Child Sexual Abuse in Australia, also demonstrate that wilful blindness remains a disturbingly common behaviour.

Whistleblowing

Whistleblowing can almost be described as the opposite of wilful blindness, and is formally defined as: 'the disclosure by organisation members of illegal, immoral or illegitimate practices under the control of their employers, to persons or organisations that may be able to effect action' (Miceli and Near, 1984, p. 689). Appropriate responses by managers to employee reporting of wrongdoing (i.e. whistleblowing) are vital to the health of every organisation, to effective business regulation and to the accountability of all institutions. Where employee reporting of wrongdoing was once perceived by many organisations as undesirable, research has now established that it is both common and important to organisational health, especially where it includes public interest whistleblowing (i.e. disclosures about suspected or alleged wrongdoing affecting more than the whistleblower's personal interests; Brown, 2008). Whistleblower protection reforms, including requirements for organisational policies or 'internal disclosure procedures', are predicated on these realisations: 'Because it can lead to the discovery and rectification of wrongdoing, whistleblowing is widely acknowledged as having potentially positive effects – for organisations and for society at large … Whistleblowing is valuable' (Brown, 2008, p. 1). The costs of not reporting wrongdoing can be extreme, amounting to billions of dollars in industrial fraud and corporate corruption. Reports indicate that up to 80 per cent of aircraft accidents, surgical errors, policing mistakes, and hospital patient care errors are attributable to inhibited employees unable to voice concerns to their supervisors (Burke and Cooper, 2013). Whistleblowing is typically triggered by, and may exacerbate, intra-organisational conflict, therefore, the inadequate management of whistleblowing can be expensive.

While whistleblowing can be perceived as a positive exercise to retain organisational integrity, the actual act of whistleblowing is, of course, universally disapproved upon by the highlighted organisation. There remains a strong overt negative stigma associated to the individual whistleblower. There are a myriad of whistleblowing instances reported within the criminal justice services and many of these cases are widely reported by the popular media, including the adverse consequences commonly experienced by the whistleblower. Most criminal justice agencies discourage whistleblowing and have a poor record in their management of whistleblowers. In fact, Johnson (2006, p. 83) in a discussion of police services and whistleblowing observed: 'The cost of retaliation against police whistleblowers is extraordinarily high.… The threat of retaliation prevents officers from coming forward to expose corrupt and abusive practices and it prevents serious wrongdoing from being addressed in-house.'

Both wilful blindness and whistleblowing arise due to inadequate internal organisational communications and reporting processes. The responsibility of employers to provide psychologically safe working environments for their employees is legislated in many European countries, Australia, New Zealand, and elsewhere; failure to do so is the basis of formal occupational health injury claims and litigation (Brough *et al.*, 2009). Importantly, in 2013, Australia followed the UK lead of incorporating remedies for whistleblower mistreatment into its national workplace relations system (Brown, 2013). This reinforces the centrality of managerial responsibility for whistleblowing in legal frameworks of whistleblower protection. The responsibility for employers to provide a safe and just working environment for employees, which includes effective communication processes is, therefore, of increasing emphasis.

Conclusions

This chapter has focused upon internal organisational communications systems within the criminal justice workplaces. Other relevant areas of interest exist but could not be a focus of this chapter; most notably the specialist communications workers who interact with calls for assistance from the public, media communications between organisations and media communication agencies (e.g. TV and radio networks), and communication practices between police services and the general public. We acknowledge that these three areas have recently received increased attention, particularly in relation to formal court and police media communications via social media (Brainard and Derrick-Mills, 2011; Johnston and McGovern, 2013; Reeves and Packer, 2013); the specific impact of work for police and other emergency service communications workers (Adams *et al.*, 2014; Forslund *et al.*, 2004; Garner and Johnson, 2006); and the use of new communication practices, such as online newsletters, to encourage community confidence and engagement with local police services and other criminal justice agencies (Mawby, 2010; Wunsch and Hohl, 2009). We acknowledge that these three areas of organisational communications for workers employed within criminal justice workplaces are of increasing interest and we encourage further research to assess the specific developments occurring in these areas. This chapter also discussed the issues of wilful blindness and whistleblowing both of which can be attributed to the inadequacy of existing organisational internal communication processes.

This chapter has succeeded in drawing attention to the long-standing problems associated with an inadequate upwards flow of communication which commonly occurs in many hierarchical organisations, including criminal justice workplaces. Whilst the use of technologies has generally enabled internal organisational communications to be quicker, easier, and more effective, the lack of 'voice' and recognition noted by many rank-and-file workers is an enduring problem. Certainly the presence of a committed and trustworthy supervisor significantly assists in mitigating some of these communication frustrations and this represents some of the newer research being conducted in this field.

References

Adams, K., Shakespeare-Finch, J., and Armstrong, D. (2014) An interpretative phenomenological analysis of stress and well-being in emergency medical dispatchers. *Journal of Loss and Trauma*, 20(5): 430–448.

Baskin, K. (2012) *Corporate DNA*. New York: Routledge.

Bellotti, V., Ducheneaut, N., Howard, M., Smith, I., and Grinter, R.E. (2005) Quality versus quantity: e-mail-centric task management and its relation with overload. *Human-Computer Interaction*, 20(1): 89–138.

Biggs, A., Brough, P., and Barbour, J.P. (2014a) Relationships of individual and organizational support with engagement: examining various types of causality in a three-wave study. *Work and Stress*, 28(3): 236–254. doi:10.1080/02678373.2014.934316.

Biggs, A., Brough, P., and Barbour, J.P. (2014b) Enhancing work-related attitudes and work engagement: a quasi-experimental study of the impact of an organizational intervention. *International Journal of Stress Management*, 21: 43–68. doi:10.1037/a0034508.

Brainard, L.A., and Derrick-Mills, T. (2011) Electronic commons, community policing, and communication. *Administrative Theory and Praxis*, 33(3): 383–410.

Brough, P. (1998) Police officers' work hassles and coping behaviours. *Police Research and Management*, 1: 63–72.

Brough, P., and Biggs, A. (2007) *Employee health and well-being: report phase III*. Brisbane: School of Psychology, Griffith University.

Brough, P., and Biggs, A. (2010) Occupational stress in police and prison staff. In Brown, J. and Campbell, E. (eds) *The Cambridge handbook of forensic psychology*. Cambridge: Cambridge University Press (pp. 707–718).

Brough, P., and Biggs, A. (2015) Job demands x job control interaction effects: do occupation-specific job demands increase their occurrence? *Stress and Health*, 31(2): 138–149. doi:10.1002/smi.2537.

Brough, P., and Frame, R. (2004) Predicting police job satisfaction, work well-being and turnover intentions: the role of social support and police organisational variables. *New Zealand Journal of Psychology*, 33: 8–16.

Brough, P., and Williams, J. (2007) Managing occupational stress in a high-risk industry: measuring the job demands of correctional officers. *Criminal Justice and Behavior*, 34: 555–567. doi:10.1177/0093854806294147.

Brough, P., Biggs, A., and Outerbridge, C. (2014) *Healthy Workplaces project 2014 report*. Brisbane: School of Applied Psychology, Griffith University.

Brough, P., Biggs, A., and Pickering, S. (2007) Predictors of occupational stress: work cover claims by correctional officers. *Journal of Occupational Health and Safety – Australia and New Zealand*, 23: 43–52.

Brough, P., O'Driscoll, M., Kalliath, T., Cooper, C.L., and Poelmans, S. (2009) *Workplace psychological health: current research and practice*. Cheltenham: Edward Elgar.

Brown, A.J. (2008) *Whistleblowing in the Australian public sector*. Canberra: ANU E-Press.

Brown, A.J. (2013) Towards 'ideal' whistleblowing legislation? Some lessons from recent Australian experience. *E-Journal of International and Comparative Labour Studies*, 2: 153–182.

Burke, R.J., and Cooper., C.L. (2013) *Voice and whistleblowing in organizations*. Cheltenham: Edward Elgar.

Chataway, S. (2014) *Change or continuity? A mixed-methods investigation of contemporary police culture*. Doctoral Thesis, Griffith University, Brisbane.

Forslund, K., Kihlgren, A., and Kihlgren, M. (2004) Operators' experiences of emergency calls. *Journal of Telemedicine and Telecare*, 10(5): 290–297.

Garner, M., and Johnson, E. (2006) Operational communication: a paradigm for applied research into police call-handling. *International Journal of Speech, Language and the Law*, 13(1): 55–75.

Gershon, R., Barocas, B., Canton, A.N., Li, X., and Vlahov, D. (2009) Mental, physical, and behavioral outcomes associated with perceived work stress in police officers. *Criminal Justice and Behavior*, 36(3): 275–289.

Gershon, R., Lin, S., and Li, X. (2002) Work stress in aging police officers. *Journal of Occupational and Environmental Medicine*, 44(2): 160–167.

Heffernan, M. (2011) *Wilful blindness: why we ignore the obvious*. New York: Simon and Schuster.

Johnson, R.A. (2006) Whistleblowing and the police. *Rutgers University Journal of Law and Urban Policy*, 1(3): 74–83.

Johnston, J., and McGovern, A. (2013) Communicating justice: a comparison of courts and police use of contemporary media. *International Journal of Communication*, 7: 1667–1687.

Kenney, J.P. (1956) Internal police communications. *Journal of Criminal Law and Criminology*, 46(4): 547–553.

Kirkcaldy, B., Cooper, G.L., and Ruffalo, P. (1995) Work stress and health in a sample of US police. *Psychological Reports*, 76(2): 700–702.

Lambert, E.G., and Paoline, E.A., III (2008) The influence of individual, job, and organizational characteristics on correctional staff job stress, job satisfaction, and organizational commitment. *Criminal Justice Review*, 33(4): 541–564.

Lambert, E.G., Hogan, N.L., Barton, S., and Clarke, A. (2002) The impact of instrumental communication and integration on correctional staff. *The Justice Professional*, 15(2): 181–193.

Langan-Fox, J. (2002) Communication in organizations: speed, diversity, networks, and influence on organizational effectiveness, human health, and relationships. In Anderson, N., Ones, D.S., Sinangil, H.K., and Viswesvaran, C. (eds) *Handbook of industrial, work and organizational psychology*, volume 2. London: SAGE (pp. 188–205).

Mawby, R.C. (2010) Police corporate communications, crime reporting and the shaping of policing news. *Policing and Society: An International Journal of Research and Policy*, 20(1): 124–139.

Miceli, M.P., and Near, J.P. (1984) Organizational position, and whistleblowing status. *Academy of Management Journal*, 27: 687–705.

Munro, E. (1999) Common errors of reasoning in child protection work. *Child Abuse and Neglect*, 23(8): 745–758.

O'Driscoll, M., Brough, P., Timms, C., and Sawang, S. (2010) Engagement with information and communication technology and psychological well-being. In Perrewé, P.L. and Ganster, D.C. (eds) *New developments in theoretical and conceptual approaches to job stress*, volume 8. New York: Emerald (pp. 269–316).

Punch, M. (2003) Rotten orchards: 'pestilence', police misconduct and system failure. *Policing and Society*, 13(2): 171–196.

Quinn, D., and Hargie, O. (2004) Internal communication audits: a case study. *Corporate Communications: An International Journal*, 9(2): 146–158.

Reeves, J., and Packer, J. (2013) Police media: the governance of territory, speed, and communication. *Communication and Critical/Cultural Studies*, 10(4): 359–384.

Stephens, C., and Long, N. (2000) Communication with police supervisors and peers as a buffer of work-related traumatic stress. *Journal of Organizational Behavior*, 21(4): 407–424.

Webster, V., Brough, P., and Daly, K. (in press) Fight, flight or freeze: common responses for follower coping with toxic leadership. *Stress and Health*.

Wunsch, D., and Hohl, K. (2009) Evidencing a 'good practice model' of police communication: the impact of local policing newsletters on public confidence. *Policing*, 3(4): 331–339.

6   Professionalisation

Introduction

In this chapter the concept of professionalisation is deconstructed. An examination is presented of how this relates to governments' imposition of professionalisation on policing, probation, the prison service, and the de-regulating tendencies applied to the Law. Chan (1999) noted that professionalism means different things to different people at different times and serves different purposes so we need to distinguish between the terms profession, professional, professionalism, and professionalisation.

- The Law is considered one of the traditional professions, by which is meant an acknowledged group enjoying a high level of social prestige whose claims rest on prolonged study of a recognised corpus of knowledge, whose practitioners are registered, and whose conduct is governed by a code of ethics regulated through a learned body. Fournier (2000, p. 76) suggests a key distinguishing factor is that services are rendered not sold, thus standing outside the market and concerned with the public good.
- Professional means having a high degree of skill, as in professional tennis player or actor. It is the opposite of amateur and provides recognition of being engaged, often full-time, as the means of earning a living.
- Professionalism, according to Mawby and Worrell (2013, p. 144), involves some form of recognised qualification, the holding of expertise in a recognised field of knowledge, and autonomy, i.e. recognition of the right to intervene in the world.
- Professionalisation is the project of developing a body of knowledge that supports practice through an evidence base and a licencing and credentialing of practitioners (MacDonald, 1995). Professionalisation may be an aspiration from within an occupation, often as a result of an external challenge or imposed on it from outside.

This chapter discusses these concepts and makes a link with some of issues mentioned in Chapter 2 on occupational culture and the creation of stress described in Chapter 14. We delineate some of the tensions between organisational and occupational professionalisation as applied to the police, probation, and the prison service. As explained above, we make a distinction between these groupings within criminal justice, and which may be thought of as 'semi professions', and the Law which enjoys a status accorded to a traditional profession. The Law has not been immune from these pressures, but paradoxically the direction of change is perceived by some to be in effect a process of de-professionalisation.

Unmaking of professions

Current economic trends, and technological and organisational change are challenging both the legitimacy and foundation of the professions and blurring the demarcations between managers and professionals, as the latter are under increasing pressure to take on managerial responsibilities or reconstitute themselves as entrepreneurs (Fournier, 2000). Fournier provides a number of characteristics that distinguishes professions from occupations. These include the erection of boundaries between their and other professions or occupational jurisdictions, and between themselves and the client or layperson, and a corresponding degree of passivity required of the latter. In part this is done through formalisation and a degree of mystification of knowledge. As implied above the professional is demarcated from the manager with the former not being accountable to the market but to rules defined by their professional body. What Fournier then explains is that the 'logic of the market' challenges these distinctions. A marketised view of the world declares:

* life is too complex and dynamic to be segregated into autonomous and fragment fields of knowledge;
* a reconceptualisation of problems falling under professional jurisdictions and an opening up to other solutions by laypeople or other occupations;
* laypeople or clients are no longer passive but are reconstituted into customers taking responsibility for and making informed choices.

Proposals by Government in the United Kingdom, and elsewhere, to reform the legal profession have attacked the exclusivity of practitioners in the delivery of services, on the one hand, and the self-regulation of the profession, on the other (Parker 2010). The argument supporting deregulation was to break the monopoly of lawyers whilst involving something of a deprofessionalisation of legal work. The global recession and the financial deficit led the Coalition Government in the UK to reform public funding of legal services, with an estimated saving of £270 million to be achieved by removing significant categories of law from the scope of Legal Aid (Sherr and Tompson, 2013). As a response, for the first time since 1466, criminal lawyers withheld their labour in towns and cities all over England and Wales.

The administration of justice and the management of the courts have also been incorporated into New Public Management initiatives In 1994 in the UK the Police and Magistrates Courts Act (PCMA) provided powers to impose mergers of magistrates' courts committees and established a new justices' chief executive. This resulted in an administrative officer working alongside justices' clerks thereby separating administrative and legal functions. The administrative officer is charged with meeting efficiency targets, such as listing cases and managing the magistrates' rotas (Fitzpatrick *et al.*, 2001). In addition the PMCA established the Magistrates' Courts Service Inspectorate (MCSI). Fitzpatrick *et al.* (2001) noted that MCSI introduced a management information system, performance targets, and mission statements. Accompanying these were concerns for judicial independence, and (rather as the potential clash between the exercising of clinical judgements by doctors and achieving value for money savings by managers within the NHS) critics have argued that cost saving has primacy over professional judgment.

Professionalisation of the semi professions

Evetts (2009) differentiates between:

1   organisational professionalism (i.e. having rational-legal forms of authority; hierarchical structures of responsibility and decision-making; standardised work procedures and practice, consistent with managerial controls; reliance on external regulation and accountabilities such as target setting and performance review); and
2   occupational professionalism (i.e. having collegial authority, based on practitioner autonomy and discretionary judgment dependent on lengthy education and vocational training; a trust relationships between the practitioner and client; regulation by the practitioners themselves guided by codes of professional ethics monitored by a professional body).

She suggests that governments increasingly uses organisational professionalism (at the expense of occupational professionalism) to control, rationalise, and motivate staff in the public sector. Witz (2005) described how nursing in the UK sought to increase its authority itself through registration and training standards but was still subjected to a modernisation programme through the Government's Agenda for Change programme (Law and Aranda, 2010). Previously, nurse training was a hospital-based apprentice-type training, steeped in immersive learning by practice. Agenda for Change introduced performance targets and changed training regimes. Francis and Humphreys (1999) observed that professionalisation of nursing has occurred in many Western countries. In Australia, the transfer of nurse training to the higher education sector took place in 1984. The achieving of greater professionalisation has been accompanied by some angst. On the one hand, the rewards of occupational professionalisation were grasped by many as a way to improve nursing's occupational standing and status especially when under threat. On the other hand, some thought the requiring of bachelor level degrees and practice certification would mean nurses losing touch with the vocational element (Evetts, 2011, p. 408). Thus initial efforts were often met with a certain amount of resistance from within.

The external pressures to professionalise occupations have largely been exerted by government, motivated by a combination of factors: a wish to combat militancy of unions, to increase accountability, to inculcate new ways of working, and to control expenditure (Beck, 2008). Fleming and Lafferty (2000) suggest that increasing accountability has been a particular concern of the Australian Government's reforms in policing, citing the Fitzgerald and Wood Commissions' investigations into malpractices as catalysts. The urgency with which reforms have been undertaken in Australia, and elsewhere, was exacerbated by the economic crisis of 2010 which resulted in severe cuts in public sector funding, although the process of professionalisation was well established before this. The reality of professionalisation is actually to reduce the control exerted by members of the occupation over entry qualifications and the content of the required knowledge (Evetts, 2011). Bach (2002) identified three ways in which government have sought to professionalise public sector occupations: *managerialism, modernisation* and *marketisation*.

- Managerialism is the introduction of market sector disciplines and has been termed New Public Management (NPM) as a way to improve service standards and increase government control over what is delivered. The stated objective of NPM is greater efficiency and effectiveness; Evetts (2009) describes two requirements to effect its implementation: the acceptance of the role of management to control work activities (as opposed to the discretion exercised by an autonomous practitioner); and the possibility to standardise working practices. It is when these requirements are actually or perceived to be absent, that tensions arise. A further element of NPM is the conversion of the relationship between professionals and clients to one between provider and consumer, evaluated through customer satisfaction surveys and quantitative measurement of performance. Evetts concludes that NPM works to promote organisational professionalism and undermine occupational professionalism.
- Modernisation, in this context, was a project of the Labour Government in the United Kingdom (1997–2010), whereby it sought to work in partnership with the relevant occupations. In this process there is a redefining of professionalism whereby professionals recreate themselves as managers with a degree of self-regulation and where the values of occupational professionalism are redeployed to promote more efficient organisations (Evetts, 2009). Gash (2008) noted that in respect of the police service the Government came to the view that despite increased funding, the returns were limited at best and decreasing at worst. What was needed was a radical modernisation which included creating a more skilled and specialised workforce and a new culture of supportive performance management.
- Marketisation is the introduction of direct competition through privatisation and outsourcing and includes performance-related pay and payment by results. The logic here is that through the creation of internal markets, competitive bidding for contacts, and incentivising the workforce, services could be provided more efficiently and cheaply as well as driving up the quality of service (Ludlow, 2014).

Government-inspired professionalisation

Beck (2008) in an instructive article describes the processes in the UK whereby the Government sought to reform teaching. The first phase took place during the Conservative administrations between 1979 and 1997 through a process of increased accountability to central government by way of managerialism. This was achieved in part by discrediting and delegitimating teachers: for example, by denigrating 'lefty' teachers and 'looney' experiments in learning and thereby forfeiting their entitlement to be trusted and exercise autonomy over their work. Through legislation, the Government aimed to make them 'fit for purpose' because it was argued that teachers ignored the demands of parents and students and instead were responding to their own agendas. Reform was accomplished by empowering management and increasing the power of central government through inspection and regulation. By means of managerialism – the issuing of performance indicators, creation of league tables, and increasing the remuneration responsibilities of head teachers – schools were to become more efficient and effective.

The succeeding Labour administration engaged in a modernisation project. This now invited teachers into partnership with Government driven by pragmatic economic pressures rather than the political ideology of their predecessors. A new professional body for teaching was established, the *General Teaching Council for England*, whose powers included the drawing up of a code of ethics and the regulation of misconduct. All teachers were obliged to be members as a condition of becoming and remaining qualified and registered. The formation of the *Teacher Training Agency* (TTA) in 2007 was intended to reshape the knowledge base, to provide a framework for teachers to pursue their professional development and career progression, and to publish professional standards. This represented a shift from the idea of a profession's autonomy to influence its knowledge base and practice standards to those being prescribed by Government.

The next Government, a coalition of Conservatives and Liberal Democrats, continued its reform programme with a mixture of marketisation and state regulation (Hatcher, 2011). In an attempt to create diversity of provision, the Labour Government had introduced *City Academies*, setting up opportunities for the voluntary sector, religions, or business to establish new schools. This was further extended by the incoming administration into free schools which are state-funded but privately run, free from the national curriculum and not bound by national union agreements. This is an overt market-oriented policy to raise professional standards in teaching and a means to tackle 'failing' schools (Painter, 2012). Thus over the last 40 years or so years Britain and other Western democracies have attempted to reform public sector organisations including those within the criminal justice system. Beck (2008) describes the logic for the imposition of managerialism, modernisation, and marketisation as government inspired ways to enhance 'professional accountability':

a   *to* some combination of government, managers, and consumers;

b   *for* achieving standards, targets, and other performance criteria imposed by government agencies (usually with minimal consultation); and

c   *within* [organisations] by empowered managerial teams [original italics].

Governments of various political hues identified policing, probation, and the prison sector as 'suitable cases for treatment' for much the same reasons as identified for education and nursing: concerns about cost; militancy of unions and staff associations; and irritation with misconduct and operational failures. During the 1990s crime rates were rising and seemed impervious to the additional resources being put into the CJS. In addition there was a sense in which the members of these agencies were thought resistant to change.

Policing

Savage (2007) illustrated how New Public Management was introduced into the UK police services in the early 1990s through the imposition of activity sampling, performance measurement, and targets. The setting of key performance indicators by Government and the monitoring of their achievement by the Audit Commission and Her Majesty's Inspectorate of Constabulary were designed not only to improve standards, but also to direct activity. In other words this exemplified the external professionalisation through greater accountability to Government and to the consumers of policing services. These requirements were met with dismay and antagonism by members of the service (Waters 1996), who saw this as an erosion of the quality of the services they should be delivering and a challenge to their professional autonomy, particularly the exercise of police discretion. As a reaction, the police engaged in a quality of service initiative issuing a declaration of common purpose and values. Waters (1996, p. 215) comments that this was 'firmly rooted in the traditional public service ethic with its emphasis on equity, probity and profesionalism' and represented the aspiration of professionalisation from within. James (2013) also noted other internal attempts to professionalise, such as the introduction of intelligence-led policing inspired by the chief constable of Kent, Sir David Philips. There was an uncomfortable tension between the police service and Government at this time, with the former resisting and the latter confirming its view that the police service was resistant to change. In addition, as Brown *et al.* (1999) showed, senior officers, who had previously been promoted on the basis of their professional operational knowledge, were exhibiting indications of stress as they were required to take on the demands of a more explicit managerial role for which they had not been trained. As mentioned above, reform was a means of increasing accountability within the Australian Police Service, which Fleming and Lafferty (2000) argued was attempted though new managerial techniques and were resisted by both officers and police unions.

Increasing accountability, through its modernising agenda, was the Labour Government's approach (Gash, 2008). The Government created a *National Centre for Policing Excellence* (NCPE) to promote evidence-based practice and develop a specification of theory and practice of investigation, and the *National Policing Improvement Agency* (NPIA) to support the delivery of more effective policing and foster a culture of self-improvement. The Government co-opted the pioneering work of the Kent Constabulary as the National Intelligence Model. Whilst the Association of Chief Police Officers (ACPO) endorsed these developments, James (2013, p. 127) noted that implementation was characterised by 'resistance and antipathy', in part due to knowledge gaps and a dislike of the model's academic structure and language. Tong (2009) argued there was still a strong 'old regime' perspective that saw detective work as a craft emerging from experience on the job, i.e. the apprentice-type immersion that had characterised nurses' hospital-based training. Fleming and Lafferty (2000) found a similar sentiment within Australian police unions vis-à-vis operational police officers who, it was suggested, gained more from the experience on the streets than could be achieved by hours in a lecture theatre.

Notwithstanding such misgivings, the chief executive of the NPIA was asked to provide a template for a new approach to police training and leadership (Neyroud, 2011) in which he argued for the development of a higher education model, the inculcation of scientific methods, and the creation of a chartered professional police officer. Fleming (2013) tracked Australian efforts to professionalise the police which were driven in part by a realisation, similar to that in the case of nurses, whereby on-the-job training, especially for those preparing for higher office, was insufficient to meet the complexity of present-day policing demands. The Australian aspiration was for an evidence-based body of knowledge, continuing professional development, a process for professional registration, and the establishment of a professional body. Fleming noted these aspirations have not yet been achieved in Australia in part due to jurisdictional disputes, continued antagonisms from the police unions, and ambivalence from police officers themselves.

In England and Wales, further progress towards government inspired professionalisation was achieved by the incoming Coalition Government who abolished the NPIA and established the *College of Policing*, which also hosts the *What Works Centre for Crime Reduction*. This undertakes systematic reviews and engages in translation from research to effective implementation (Brown *et al.*, 2015). Police officers are currently given membership of the College which, like the TTA, supports the education and professional development of staff and officers. The Government also introduced direct entry into senior ranks of the police service, again as a way to enhance professional knowledge and improve practice. In parallel to these developments increased marketisation in the provision of policing has occurred. Jones (2007) discussed the trend towards the plural provision of security exemplified by the increasing involvement of the private sector. In the face of the economic crisis, private companies in the UK were brought in as a means to access new technology, acquire specialist skills, as well as saving money in the face of restrictions in public expenditure on policing (Rhodes, 2014).

These and other changes to officers' pay and conditions had a profound effect on morale, demonstrated by an increase in the percentages of officers' declared turnover intentions (Independent Police Commission, 2013). As previously discussed, intention to leave is significantly associated with organisational disengagement (see Chapter 3). Thus an unintended consequence of these Government inspired efforts towards professionalisation has to some extent undermined the project, in that officers experience this process as one which devalues their expert judgment and frustrates the exercise of their discretion (Evetts, 2011).

Prisons

The prison system too has been subjected to external professionalisation interventions. Ten years after the election of the Thatcher conservative government, prisons in the UK were said to be in a state of crisis, staff out of control, declining regimes, and a lack of information about what anything cost, where money was spent or what was expected (King and McDermott, 1995). Bell (2013) described the rise of managerialist values and the adoption of measurable standards of performance, pre-set output measures and introduction of cost centres to control budgets. Liebling (2006, p. 427) argued that 'a new culture and service delivery ethos [was] demanded, via economic reasoning; that is instrumental means'.

The push towards privatisation of prisons in England and Wales and Australia was not only to save money but also 'to develop staff cultures that were more positive, respectful and rehabilitative, than those that existed in the public sector' (Crewe *et al.*, 2011, p. 94). They characterised a negative form of a tradition-resistant prison officer culture that is cynical, petty, disrespectful, and pre-occupied with control. There is also a tradition-professional officer who is confident, boundaried, having clear goals, is vigilant and knowledgeable. Outsourcing and privatisation are aspects of marketisation which Andrew (2006) suggested, in the case of Australia, was a way to resolve staffing difficulties in public sector prisons and circumvent a unionised workforce that was said to be 'difficult' and 'problematic'. Private provision was believed more likely to improve quality of service through innovation and increase flexibility. The common tensions created by managerialism and marketisation identified by Liebling (2006) included:

* how to adopt the new managerialist techniques without abandoning traditional core values of trustworthiness, integrity, and public service;
* how to align a sense of occupational identity with modernisation;
* how to reconcile new techniques of performance measurement with perceptions of fairness.

Liebling (2006, p. 428) asserted that 'Government-at-a-distance, or management by target, involving strong central direction and future-oriented improvement, was experienced as alienating by many staff'. There was a distinct lack of trust of senior managers. Inappropriate use of measurement can lead to staff concluding they are neither understood nor valued as professionals. In turn this may contribute to feelings of disaffection and non-compliance. Liebling found managers who wished to exert strong control and officers, particularly in times of change, preferring to trust 'what worked yesterday' with their confidence being grounded in experience.

Ludlow (2014) argued that government, certainly in the UK, presents market competition as a benign and neutral management tool to drive up service standards. She undertook a study of the privatisation of a prison in Birmingham and reported that the process was experienced by prison staff as 'deprofessionalising and laden with condemnation' (p. 75). The protracted nature of the process added to their sense of devaluation and demoralisation which Ludlow concluded, 'eroded some of Birmingham's organisational and cultural strengths, such as co-operation, trust and commitment ... [causing] staff to become distracted by their own "private troubles"; worries about job security and "forced" changes to their occupational identities' (p. 76). Managers who also cared about prisoners and their staff became overburdened to the point of 'burnout'.

The Probation and Prison Services

The Probation Service has probably seen the most dramatic version of top-down imposed professionalisation which (ironically) its members have experienced as a form of deprofessionalisation (Eadie, 2000; Mawby and Worrell, 2013; Fitz-gibbon and Lea, 2014; Ludlow, 2014). Probation's incorporation into the managerialist three Es (economy, efficiency, and effectiveness) began in the second Conservative administration with the publication in 1984 of the Statement of National Objectives and Priorities (SNOP). According to Mair and Burke (2012) the SNOP was a marker for the consolidation of probation's geographic areas, while the setting of national objectives eroded the power and autonomy of local chief probation officers. The introduction of computerisation and standardisation of record keeping and data entry was another trend towards a national approach and modernisation of the service. This, together with the Government's adoption of a computer-based assessment, the *Offender Group Reconviction Scale* (OGRS), substituted a formulaic calculation of risk rather than the clinical judgement approach used by many probation officers.

The move towards even more central control and national programmes coalesced in 2000 under the Labour Government's modernisation programme with the Criminal Justice and Courts Services Act which created a *National Probation Service* (NPS). Jack Straw, the Home Secretary, had previously announced a new probation officer training scheme which broke its traditional link with social work and its welfare-ist ethos, replacing it with a criminal justice orientation. Fitzgibbon and Lea (2014) argued that this aimed to bring about a fundamental change in the nature of probation from assisted rehabilitation within a welfare state, to one in which individuals were held to be entirely responsible for their own welfare, and probation's role was to attempt to teach offenders to make 'correct' choices and neutralise or warehouse them if they failed. As had police and prison officers, probation officers also resisted this agenda by attempting to retain their own sense of professional autonomy both in terms of working with offenders and their relationship to other criminal justice agencies. In part this was achieved by probation's continued links with academia, publishing research in its own journals, and convening workshops and conferences to disseminate knowledge (processes engaged in by traditional professions). Fitzgibbon and Lea (2014) suggested that professional autonomy was eroded by thematic inspection regimes, increasing workloads, and employment of an increasing number of semi-skilled practitioners. In an attempt to stem this the Probation Chiefs' Association (PCA), the Probation Association (PA), National Association of Probation Officers (Napo), and the trade union UNISON launched the Probation Institute. The avowed aim is to become a centre of excellence for probation by developing with researchers and academics evidence-based, rigorous, objective, and authoritative (Probation Institute, 2014).

The pace of marketisation was rapidly increased by the Coalition Government (Ludlow, 2014). In 2004 the Probation and Prison Services had been amalgamated into the *National Offender Management Service* (NOMS). Mawby and Worrell (2013, p. 76) asserted that the emergence of NOMS can be characterised by the desire of the Government 'to eradicate the concept of probation from the national psyche' and erode the professional identity of the probation officer. A probation service 'market' was created in order to stimulate innovation and improvement. Fitzgibbon and Lea (2014) explained that under present plans, Probation, managed by NOMS, was responsible for the 12 per cent of high-risk offenders (numbering approximately 31,000). The 35 local probation trusts were abolished and replaced by 21 *Community Rehabilitation Companies* (CRCs) with contracts being awarded to a combination of voluntary and private providers working to a payment-by-results regime. Fitzgibbon and Lea argued that the more skilled and labour intensive traditional forms of probation rehabilitation through community re-engagement were lost.

Therefore, in the space of 40 years, Probation in the UK has been transformed from an autonomous local service working with the consent of clients to support and rehabilitate, within a social services orientation, to an agency of criminal justice focusing on high-risk offenders. Bailey *et al.* (2007) characterised the probation officer of the 1980s as a semi-autonomous professional, but the rise of national standards and changes to supervision eroded this model. Their research on probation staff found poor morale, in particular feeling devalued, having less discretion than in the past, and thus feeling deskilled. All this was aggravated by a sense of powerlessness with the pace of change. Chief probation officers were also demoralised because they felt disheartened at their perceived loss of authority and status. For some it raised questions about whether they wished to remain working in a Probation Service that had changed so completely from the one they had originally joined. Whilst probation is feared by some to have lost its identity (Mair and Burke, 2012), Eadie (2000) states that the probation service has little option but to engage with the changes and been given the opportunity to revisit its theoretical base and practice shibboleths.

The judiciary

The lawyers and judges have also been incorporated into New Public Management initiatives. For example, Parker (2010, p. 175) noted that the 'legal professions around the world have been swept up in a broader movement of deregulation, in which professions are no longer seen as distinct from "business" and no longer immune from the demands of competition reform'. The argument supporting deregulation was to break the monopoly of lawyers and, whilst this involved something of a deprofessionalisation of legal work, Sherr and Thompson (2013) proposed this 'might engender more innovation … [and] encourage current legal practices to become more efficient'.

Conclusion

Professionalising occupations within the criminal justice service has been an avowed policy of governments in many Western countries. As budgets became tighter, and governments offer citizen greater choice, unionised workforces were increasingly seen as intransigent and resistant to change. Professionalisation was attempted through the processes of managerialism, modernisation, and marketisation. Evetts (2003) argued that these changes are often perceived by members of the occupation as more work and responsibilities but without the corresponding increase in status. If anything there is an increase in bureaucracy in the form of performance measurement and monitoring and a decline in the quality of service it is possible to deliver. Evetts concluded that one result of organisational professionalisation has been an occupational identity crisis often expressed as a form of discontent. As we illustrated above, this discontent has been manifest amongst both rank and file as well as senior staff in all the agencies examined. One particular expression of that discontent is in the form of disengagement which is discussed in more detail Chapter 3.

Hanlon (1999) proposed that governments have attempted to redefine professionalisation to encompass the 'semi-professions' of the CJS in order to create commercial awareness, and encourage focus on budgets and entrepreneurial initiatives. Thus professionalisation aims to convince, cajole, or persuade practitioners to perform and behave in ways that are deemed appropriate, effective, and efficient to promote organisational objectives as defined by government (Evetts, 2003). As demonstrated in this chapter, police, prison, and probation officers generally experience this as a deskilling and deprofessionalising process. The exertion of external control through top-down imposed, organisational professionalisation affects the autonomy of the individual and the exercise of discretion. As we suggest in this book, the less control a person has over their work the more likely this will result in adverse stress reactions (see Chapter 13). One antidote is for these occupations to lay claim to their own (occupational) professionalisation. One way for Probation to preserve its identity and its professional standing is to create, like the Police Service, a College to set and maintain professional standards (Shepherd, 2013). Shepherd's idea of a Royal College of

Probation and a strengthening of its historic link to university-based research institutes could return Probation to its rehabilitation ideals.

Tilley and Laycock (2013) endorsed the idea of the College of Policing as a way to ensure appropriate education and training drawn from an established body of knowledge which is scientifically and ethically defensible. They do however caution against the downside of professionalisation which they say is associated with 'pretentious status enhancement and self-aggrandisement' (p. 170).

The other theme in our discussion in this chapter is the erosion of trust between managers and rank-and-file membership of an occupation that is being subjected to externally imposed professionalisation, as well as between the CJS and the public. Evetts (2003) commented that those who master the requirements of this form of professionalisation and perform in the way that is deemed desirable will be rewarded with promotion and career advancement. Liebling (2006) draws attention to the cynicism of prison officers with governors who advance rapidly in the new regime, suggesting an increasing divide between 'the uniform and the suits'. These are ideas that we explored in Chapter 2 on organisational justice. In Chapters 14 (Leadership) and 16 (Discrimination) we discuss in more detail the processes that seek to encourage and increase levels of trust in the workplace.

References

Andrew, J. (2006) Prisons, the profit motive and other challenges to accountability. *Critical Perspectives on Accounting*, 18: 877–904.

Bach, S. (2002) Annual review article 2001. Public sector employment relations, reform under Labour: muddling through or modernisation? *British Journal of Industrial Relations*, 40: 319–339.

Bailey, R., Knight, C., and Williams B. (2007) The probation service as part of NOMS in England and Wales: fit for purpose? In Gelsthorpe, L. and Morgan, R. (eds) *Handbook of probation*. Cullompton, UK: Willan (pp. 114–130).

Beck, J. (2008) Governmental professionalism; re-professionalising or de-professionalising teachers in England? *British Journal of Educational Studies*, 56: 119–143.

Bell, E. (2013) Punishment as politics: the penal system in England and Wales. In Ruggiero, V. and Ryan, M. (eds) *Punishment in Europe; a critical anatomy of penal systems* (pp. 58–85).

Brown, J., Cole, T., and Shell, Y. (2015) *Forensic psychology; theory, research, policy and practice*. London: SAGE.

Brown, J., Cooper, C., and Kirkcaldy, B. (1999) Stressor exposure and methods of coping among senior police managers at time of organisational and managerial change. *International Journal of Police Science and Management*, 2: 217–228.

Chan, J. (1999) Police culture. In Dixon, D. (ed.) *A culture of corruption; changing an Australian police service*. Sydney: Harkins Press (pp. 98–137).

Crewe, B., Liebling, A., and Hulley, S. (2011) Staff culture, use of authority and prisoner quality of life in public and private sector prisons. *Australian and New Zealand Journal of Criminology*, 44: 94–115.

Eadie, T. (2000) From befriending to punishing; changing boundaries in the probation service. In Malin, N. (ed.) *Professionalism, boundaries and the workplace*. London/New York: Routledge (pp. 161–177).

Evetts, J. (2003) The construction of professionalism in new and existing occupational contexts; promoting and facilitating occupational change. *International Journal of Sociology and Social Policy*, 23: 22–34.

Evetts, J. (2009) New professionalism and new public management: changes, continuities and consequences. *Comparative Sociology*, 8: 247–266.

Evetts, J. (2011) A new professionalism? Challenges and opportunities. *Current Sociology*, 59: 406–422.

Fitzgibbon, W., and Lea, J. (2014) Defending probation; beyond privatisation and security. *European Journal of Probation*, 6: 24–41.

Fitzpatrick, B., Seago, P., Walker, C., and Wall, D. (2001) New courts management and the professionalisation of summary justice in England and Wales. *Criminal Law Forum*, 11: 1–22.

Fleming, J. (2013) The pursuit of professionalism; lessons from Australasia. In Brown, J. (ed.) *Future of policing*. Abingdon, UK: Routledge (pp. 355–368).

Fleming, J., and Lafferty, G. (2000) New management techniques and restructuring for accountability in Australian police organisations. *Policing: An International Journal of Police Strategies and Management*, 23: 154–168.

Fournier, V. (2000) Boundary work and the (un)making of the professions. In Malin, N. (ed.) *Professionalism, boundaries and the workplace*. London/New York: Routledge (pp. 67–86).

Francis, B., and Humphreys, J. (1999) Enrolled nurse and the professionalisation of nursing: a comparison of nurse education and skill-mix in Australia and the UK. *International Journal of Nursing Studies*, 36: 127–135.

Gash, T. (2008) *The new bill: modernising the police workforce*. London: Institute for Public Policy Research.

Hanlon, G. (1999) *Lawyers, the state and the market; professionalism revisited*. Basingstoke: Macmillan.

Hatcher, R. (2011) The Conservative-Liberal Democrat coalition government's 'free schools' in England. *Educational Review*, 63: 485–503.

Independent Police Commission (2013) *Policing for a better Britain*. London: The Commission.

James, A. (2013) *Examining intelligence-led policing; developments in research, policy and practice*. Basingstoke: Palgrave Macmillan.

Jones, T. (2007; 2012) Governing security: pluralization, privatization and polarization in crime control. In Maguire, M., Morgan, R., and Reiner, R. (eds) *The Oxford Handbook of Criminology*, 5th edn. Oxford: Oxford University Press (pp. 743–768).

King, E., and McDermott, K. (1995) *The state of our prisons*. Oxford: Clarendon.

Law, K., and Aranda, K. (2010) The shifting foundations of nursing. *Nurse Education Today*, 30: 544–547.

Liebling, A. (2006) Prisons in transition. *International Journal of Law and Psychiatry*, 29: 422–430.

Ludlow, A. (2014) Transforming rehabilitation: what lessons might be learned from prison privatisation? *European Journal of Probation*, 6: 67–81.

MacDonald, K. (1995) *The sociology of the professions*. London: SAGE.

Mair, G., and Burke, L. (2012) *Redemption, rehabilitation and risk management: a history of probation*. London: Routledge.

Mawby, R.C., and Worrell, A. (2013) *Doing probation work: identity in a criminal justice occupation*. London/New York: Routledge.

Neyroud, P. (2011) *Review of police training and leadership*. London: Home Office.

Painter, C. (2012) The UK coalition government: constructing public service reform narratives. *Public Policy and Administration*, 28: 3–20.

Parker, C. (2010) Lawyer deregulation via business deregulation: compliance professionalism and legal professionalism. *International Journal of the Legal Profession*, 6: 175–196.

Probation Institute (2014) Leaflet. http://probation-institute.org/wp-content/uploads/2014/04/Probation_Institute_brochure.pdf.

Rhodes, N. (2014) *12 golden rules of public sector outsourcing*. Lincoln: Lincolnshire Police.

Savage, S. (2007) *Police reform: forces for change*. Oxford: Oxford University Press.

Shepherd, J. (2013) *Professionalising the probation service: why university institutes would transform rehabilitation*. London: Howard League for Penal Reform/London School of Economics Mannheim Centre for Criminology.

Sherr, A., and Thompson, S. (2013) Tesco law and Tesco lawyers: will our needs change if the market develops? *Oñati Socio-Legal Series*, 3: 595–610.

Tilley, N., and Laycock, G. (2013) The police as professional problem solver. In Brown, J. (ed.) *The future of policing*. Abingdon, UK: Routledge (pp. 369–382).

Tong, S. (2009) Introduction: a brief history of crime investigation. In Tong, S., Bryant, R., and Horvath, M. *Understanding criminal investigation*. Chichester: Wiley-Blackwell.

Waters, I. (1996) Quality of service: politics or paradigm shift? In Leishman, F., Loveday, B. and Savage, S. (eds) *Core issues in policing*. Harlow: Longmans (pp. 205–217).

Witz, A. (2005) The challenge of nursing. In Gabe, J. and Kelleher, D. (eds) *Challenging medicine*. London: Routledge (pp. 23–45).

Part II
Tools

7 Evaluation

Introduction

'Knowing *why* a programme succeeds or fails is even more important than knowing that it does' (Feuerstein, 1986, p. 7). In order to establish whether any organisational intervention, change process, training programme or system is effective, it is required to be formally assessed. An accurate evaluation consists of several components, but at its most basic, it assesses whether the intervention has resulted in an *improvement* in performance. On the surface, evaluations are therefore quite simplistic: comparing performance pre- and post-intervention. Such before and after evaluations can be, therefore, easy to perform and the produced assessment will likewise be equally simplistic. Conducting an evaluation that is of more value requires the consideration of finer details of evidence, for example: Which specific performance indicators are being assessed? Whose opinions will be collected? How much change is required to demonstrate any significant improvement? What time period of change should be assessed? Increasingly criminal justice system organisations are adopting evidence-based practice approaches in which evaluation plays a critical role. This chapter discusses the complexities involved in performing organisational evaluations and highlights some successful examples of evaluations conducted within criminal justice workplaces.

The evaluation process

While numerous formal models of the process of evaluation exist, a basic model is illustrated in Figure 7.1.

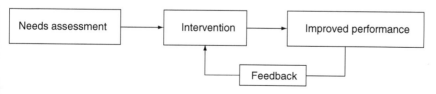

Figure 7.1 The evaluation process.

Identifying the **need for a change** in practice is the first step in the evaluation process. A thorough needs assessment will identify the specific issues (procedures/behaviours) to be changed and the specific employees requiring training. The needs assessment will often establish goals or indicators of the required change in performance, including measuring a baseline performance indicator. The assessment should also consider the costs–benefits ratio involved in the intervention, including, for example, consideration of the costs and practicalities of releasing employees from their daily work demands to complete the training.

The **intervention** requires an appropriate design process and should be based on clear evidence that the intervention will actually achieve the identified goals. Conducting successful organisational interventions and demonstrating their long-term success is difficult. Consideration of detailed organisational (macro) and individual (micro) processes is required, including the identification of the appropriate assessment of intervention success and the ethical requirement that the interventions will not cause harm (Biggs and Brough, 2015a; Biggs and Brough, 2015b).

The final stage consists of demonstrating with clear evidence that the intervention directly **improved performance** and achieved the goals stated in the needs assessment. One key consideration here is the period of time chosen to adequately demonstrate improvements. Cursory assessments of the content of training programmes with basic satisfaction questions or surveys are simple to conduct and typically produce positive results for a variety of meaningful and less meaningful reasons (including, for example, time away from 'real' work and socialising with colleagues over a free lunch). However, assessing the transfer of the training into actual work practices and the impact it has on performance levels is more complex and requires an adequate longer-term timeframe. It is also important to establish a **feedback process** so that performance levels inform future intervention programmes. This process of organisational learning and development is vital to ensure the validity and efficacy of the intervention programme delivered in the future.

In a review of the effectiveness of organisational interventions including evaluations, Biggs (2011, p. 270) noted that 'one of the greatest challenges in intervention research is to transform the aims of an intervention into measurable outcomes'. Biggs identified four key issues to be considered for the effective evaluation of an organisational intervention or training programme:

1   First, measures of assessment should be *evidence-based*. It is important to select measures which have been found to possess levels of validity and reliability and which are considered appropriate for the specific employees.
2   Second, programmes that are designed to target one domain (e.g. employee behaviours and/or performance) are best evaluated with outcomes from the same domain (e.g. employee-focused outcomes), rather than with group-level or organisational-level outcomes.
3   Third, assessing objective outcomes and conducting follow-up assessments rarely occur. Including follow-up assessments in an evaluation is essential,

as they provide evidence of the sustainability and cost-effectiveness of the training programme.

4 Finally, an evaluation should also include assessments of the cost-effectiveness of the programme. Again this assessment is rarely conducted in organisational evaluation processes.

Similarly, Farrington *et al.* (2002) described the *Maryland Scientific Measurement Scale* which contains five evaluation levels based on different depths of scientific rigour:

1 Level one addresses such research questions as: *comparing levels of crime in an area monitored by closed circuit television (CCTV) and an area not covered by CCTV.* The analysis conducted on the resulting data is simple (e.g. correlation analysis). This is the lowest quality evaluation as there are no means of establishing whether there are any other factors causing differences between the two crime areas.

2 Level two addresses the same problem by conducting a before-and-after study in the area in which the CCTV is situated. In other words, crime levels are measured before the installation of CCTV and then again afterwards. This at least can demonstrate some effect of CCTV but again does not rule out possible confounding factors such as less vigilance in the area after the CCTV was installed.

3 Level three compares the effect of the installation of CCTV in the experimental area and results are compared over the same period of time in a comparable area without CCTV. This is deemed the minimum quality for an evaluation.

4 Level four has multiple experimental and comparable control areas that can account for complex variations caused by, for example, differing vulnerabilities of premises or different patterns of use between people going to work and use of an area in the night-time economy.

5 Level five is a randomised control trial (RCT) in which there is a random assignment of victimised premises to having CCTV surveillance or being in the comparison condition of no intervention. This is considered to be the gold standard for conducting an objective and scientific evaluation study.

These five levels vary in sophistication, the skills required to conduct, length of time taken, and the costs incurred, with the RCTs being the most time consuming, expensive, and demanding a high level of skill to conduct successfully. In general, evaluations at levels three to five are likely to be conducted by professional researchers or external consultants. Proponents of RCTs argue that they are the most appropriate way to evaluate change based on the best evidence-based practice. On the other hand, critics of RCTs (e.g. Hollin, 2008; Hope, 2005) identify their difficulties, especially in terms of conducting RCTs within an organisational setting. Hollin suggested the method of quasi-experimental designs may be sufficient in many cases for organisational-based evaluations.

Evaluating the hits and the misses

Recent attention has been paid to understanding why some organisational programmes work whilst others fail (see, for example, a recent collection of expert views edited by Karanika-Murray and Biron, 2015). A better understanding of the 'process issues' behind both successful and unsuccessful programmes informs the planning of future (successful) programmes. Thus evaluations should focus not just on the direct outcomes of any programme, but also provide an assessment of the *process* of conducting the programme. So if the programme was to be administered again what specific details should be improved? Two types of 'process issues' have received the most recent attention:

1 **Macro-processes** are pragmatic factors that impact upon the design and implementation of an organisational programme. Macro-process factors predominately concern the perceptions and actions of individuals, managers, or other stakeholders that occur during the programme implementation and influence its effectiveness. These macro-processes are generally unanticipated and are usually only identified after they occur. Specific examples of macro-processes include: unsupportive attitudes towards the intervention; competing projects and organisational restructures that foster job uncertainty and poor morale; history of organisational intervention/ programme failures, particularly due to inadequate managerial follow-up and insufficient meaningful, long-term improvements; and conflicting perceptions regarding stress management roles and responsibilities (Biggs and Brough, in 2015b).

2 **Micro-process factors** are the mediators of change that link the intervention to its anticipated outcomes. Assessing these micro factors enables the mechanisms of change associated with particular outcomes to be specifically identified, and for subsequent programmes to be more targeted and effective. For example, engaging employees in an exercise to identify common problems existing in their work environments and then participating in a programme to specifically change these work environments problems is likely to result in a more successful and meaningful programme, compared to a programme without the initial employee involvement. Employee participation and engagement is an important micro process factor here.

Designing valid organisational evaluations

In consideration of the discussion above, it can be seen that producing an effective organisational evaluation is not necessarily a simple process. The plans for programme evaluations should be considered when the programme itself is being planned. Evaluations can be conducted in number of ways to gain meaningful data, including for example employee observations, focus groups, surveys, and 'rapid assessment and evaluations'. We discuss each of these four evaluation methods here.

1 Organisational evaluations by observations

Observational evaluation techniques can be informal and unstructured, such as the *observation by walking around* technique (Peters and Waterman, 1982), which purports to provide managers with direct interactions and opinions of a sample of their workforce. Similarly, the *goal-free evaluation* technique (Scriven, 1973) aims to consider both expected and unexpected information arising from the training programme/intervention. Both of these observational evaluation techniques are very flexible and importantly, are strongly dependent on the ability of employees to directly inform their managers in a face-to-face situation of any concerns or problems. This, of course, may not always be the easiest thing to do, especially within the hierarchical organisational structure of most criminal justice workplaces. A third evaluation technique is *participant observation* where the observer works alongside the employees/team to experience first-hand the issues arising (e.g. riding along on patrol with police officers). Again an issue of trust and participant interference may occur here, where 'normal' operational procedures and behaviours are adjusted due to the presence of the observer. Observational evaluation techniques can also be more structured and these include the use of *behavioural checklists* where the frequencies of specific (predetermined) behaviours are recorded.

The two main disadvantages of observational evaluation techniques are *observer bias* and *incorrect classifications/recordings of behaviours* (Guerra-López, 2008). Increasing the number of observers (raters) is a common method to improve the reliability of the collected data (as long as all the raters are assessing the same predetermined behaviours).

2 Organisational evaluations by focus groups or experts

A detailed account of both focus groups and the related Delphi technique are provided in subsequent chapters (see Chapters 8 and 11). It is pertinent to note here that focus groups are a commonly used method for providing evaluation information. The issues that are both discussed with relish and discussed with caution provide useful data to inform the evaluation process. Two important considerations for focus groups evaluations are: first, *who* conducts the focus groups (and indeed the broader evaluation process) – an internal organisational member or an independent external evaluator? The use of either internal or external personnel has both advantages and disadvantages, of course. Second, conducting focus groups across (police) ranks can be problematic (based on our own experiences); often officers are reluctant to speak out or be critical in the presence of senior officers. As is discussed in Chapter 8, the facilitation and composition of focus groups therefore requires careful consideration.

3 Organisational evaluations by surveys

A detailed discussion of conducting organisational surveys is provided in Chapter 10. For organisational evaluations based on surveys, two key components should be considered:

1   **comparison of performance assessments**, ideally of the same employees before and after the programme/intervention;
2   **comparison with controls**, comparing the performance of the employees receiving the programme with a similar group of employees who did not receive it (a 'control' group).

The research literature formally calls an evaluation process with these two components a *quasi-experiment* research design. A 'true' experimental research design involves the random allocation of employees to these two control and 'experimental' groups, but this rarely occurs in organisations due primarily to reasons of practicalities. Instead a group of employees based in a different work unit/branch/region often form the comparison (control) group and this, therefore, constitutes a quasi-experiment research design. The primary disadvantage of a quasi-experimental research design is that it cannot completely control for the influence of other factors that may impact the training outcomes, including for example participant characteristics (e.g. personality traits, experience) and organisational changes (e.g. staff transfers, staff leave).

4 Organisational evaluations by rapid assessment and evaluation

A final method is called *rapid assessment and evaluation* (McNall and Foster-Fishman, 2007). Rapid assessments are commonly undertaken when time is limited and the object of interest is very specific. Hallmarks of rapid evaluations are that they use multiple methods and are conducted by teams with some degree of local participation. The methods used may include direct behaviour observations, interviews with informed experts, and focus group discussions to derive a community perspective. The point of taking multiple perspectives is that if the same issues are revealed by each method used then greater credence may be placed on the genuineness of the identified problem. Rapid evaluations may also use a *social mapping technique* whereby participants draw a map of a particular place and indicate certain features such as anti-social behaviour. Aggregation of the maps then identifies specific 'hot spots' where there is a consensus about the location of such behaviour. (A useful resource which explains how rapid assessments may be undertaken is the UK civil-service website: www.civilservice.gov. uk/networks/gsr/resources-and-guidance/rapid-evidence-assessment.) Table 7.1 also explains in summary form the different requirements of reviews, including rapid assessments and evaluations.

Organisational evaluations: four examples of best practice

Example 1: LEAD leadership programme

In our long-term research collaborations with the Queensland Police Service (QPS), we have conducted a number of evaluations of training programmes for police officers, conducted by both internal and external trainers (see, for

Table 7.1 Summary of different types of reviews

Type	Method	Time-scale	Staffing	Comment
Review of reviews	Only review papers are selected and a summary of conclusions	Between one week and one month	One-person internet search	Does not need to be an expert, but limited to papers include in reviews and likely to be cursory
Literature review	Collates relevant studies	Between one week and two months	One-person internet search	Non-expert potential bias towards accessible and available studies and efficiency of search terms
Quick scoping review	Maps range of available studies	Between one week and two months	One-person internet search	Limited by potential search engine bias
Rapid Evaluation Assessment	Balanced assessment of what is known, promising, and unknown	Between two to six months	Team Expert in subject area Internet searching plus accessing 'grey' (unpublished) literature from networks of colleagues	More robust Systematic use of explicit search terms but still potential bias towards more accessible material
Systematic review	Explicit objective, uniform screening criteria for inclusion of papers	Between eight and twelve months	Team Expert in area Wide search	Most robust and comprehensive and also most time consuming and expensive

example, Biggs *et al.*, 2014). One example was a leadership programme for senior officers called 'LEAD'. An account of this programme is provided in Chapter 14 on leadership. Here we describe in more detail the evaluation component. In brief, the programme provided training and support to facilitate the participants' awareness of their own leadership styles and the impact of their leadership on the performance and well-being of the officers who reported to them (their subordinates). The police LEAD programme consisted of three components: (1) group action-learning workshops; (2) individual coaching; and (3) a 270-degree review process of the participants' leadership style. The LEAD programme was implemented in two of the QPS police regions and thoroughly evaluated using a quasi-experiment research design. Specifically:

- We statistically assessed each specific participant's scores on several criteria before and after they completed the LEAD programme, using two 'post-programme' assessments:

    - The first assessment occurred **immediately after the programme completion** to provide us with assessments of both immediate satisfaction and learnings of the LEAD programme.
    - The second assessment **occurred up to 12 months after the programme completion,** to provide us with assessments of long-term changes in leadership performance.

- We ensured the criteria measures we chose were valid, reliable, and meaningful to the participants (e.g. psychometrically sound measures of leadership, performance, and well-being drawn from the research literature).
- We statistically compared the performance of the LEAD programme participants with equivalent officers (same ranks) in other police regions who did not receive the LEAD programme (i.e. the 'control' groups). So both the LEAD programme participants and the officers in the control groups were assessed with the same leadership, performance, and well-being measures at the same time points.

The results we obtained from this detailed evaluation of the LEAD programme demonstrated that the programme was effective and significantly improved the participant's knowledge and confidence in their own leadership skills (see Figure 7.2). Importantly, the results also demonstrated significant improvements in their subordinate's assessments of their own levels of job performance and well-being.

Example 2: occupational stress intervention

We also conducted a similar quasi-experimental evaluation of an occupational stress intervention training programme for correctional workers (both prison officer and other employees; Biggs, 2011). Again, we adopted the same evaluations process as described above: namely, assessments of the same key criteria

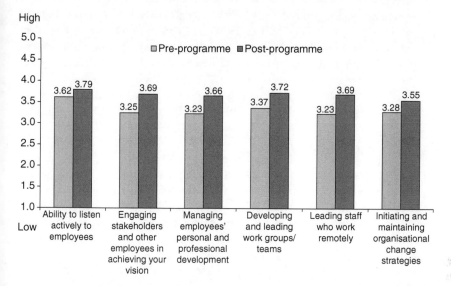

Figure 7.2 Evaluation of the police LEAD programme: pre and post-programme assessments (source: adapted from Brough *et al.* (2012)).

measures before and after the training programme (both six months and 12 months after programme completion) and statistical comparisons of the programme participants with correctional employees based in other prisons who did not complete the training programme (i.e. the control group). Whilst this evaluation produced some positive results, it also identified a number of 'process issues' which informed our learnings for subsequent organisational intervention and evaluation programmes. We have described these process issues and our learnings in detail elsewhere (Biggs and Brough, 2015a; Biggs and Brough, 2015b; Brough and Biggs, 2015) and these, for example, include:

- **the organisational context:** such as suspicion regarding the intent of the programme; inadequate resources to run the programme; adherence to rigid organisational practices; insufficient managerial support; and a highly bureaucratic, authoritarian organisational structure;
- **inadequate resources to run the programme:** particularly finances and time such as the impracticalities of removing staff from operational duties. Hence, training activities that are not linked to operational requirements may be viewed as unnecessary or too time-consuming when organisational resources are limited;
- **ineffective transfer of training:** As this training programme aimed to increase knowledge and skills pertaining to stress management, insufficient learning and transfer of skills and knowledge to the work context may have undermined its effectiveness. Although it is often assumed that stress management strategies

discussed during training sessions are absorbed and subsequently utilised in the workplace, in reality this does not apply to approximately one-third of training participants. Additionally if the organisational culture is 'transfer adverse' then uptake of the training into the actual workplace is also diminished. Characteristics of a transfer adverse organisational culture include: inadequate managerial and colleague support, and lack of job autonomy. As job autonomy is limited for correctional workers, the transfer of the taught stress management techniques was indeed limited (Biggs, 2011).

Example 3: Safe Street Team

An interesting evaluation study was conducted upon operational policing techniques by assessing the effectiveness of the Boston Police Department's *Safe Street Team* (SST). Braga *et al.* (2011) adopted a quasi-experimental method to assess the impact of this policing technique upon the frequency of violent crime between the years 2000 and 2009. Comparisons were conducted between the experimental group (locations where the SST was adopted) and a control group (locations which did not adopt the SST). This evaluation clearly identified the significant impact of the SST in reducing violent crime (robbery and assault). Braga *et al.* also discussed the value of this evidence-based policing approach and recommended the use of quasi-experimental evaluation methods to assist with meeting the demand for more evidence-based policing practices.

Example 4: rape investigations

Finally, a recent rapid evaluation assessment concerning the crime of rape was commissioned by the UK Stern Review (2010). In September 2009, Baroness Vivien Stern was invited by the British Government's Equalities Office to lead a review examining how public authorities including police, prosecutors, healthcare providers and local authorities responded to, and interacted with each other, in respect of rape complaints. A team of academic experts comprising Jennifer Brown, Miranda Horvath, Liz Kelly, and Nicole Westmarland undertook a rapid evaluation assessment of the available research evidence addressing the following questions. What do we know about:

- the prevalence and distribution of rape;
- reporting and disclosure;
- support and advocacy;
- the response of the criminal justice system;
- the response of the health system;
- attitudes and stereotypes relating to rape; and
- the impact of recent policy, practice, and legal changes?

The review took two months to complete. Nine on-line abstracting data bases were searched using 60 search terms and limited to 15 years (1995–2010). In addition, unpublished 'grey literature' was accessed by members of the review team contacting their network of researchers and through Google searches. Once all the materials were located they were coded as high relevance, not directly relevant, and not relevant for the present review. Criteria for inclusion was tiered with peer reviewed articles highly regarded, with the next tier being unpublished research reports by established researchers. This provided a yield of about 150 relevant and credible papers. Baroness Stern asked the research team to identify 'short wins and long hauls'. This involved an evaluation of the research evidence and included bridging the innovation and implementation gap. This was represented in the Stern review by noting that there was not a dearth of policies, but there was, critically, patchy implementation. The review also identified where there was little available research evidence. This included accuracy and completeness of reporting rates and impacts on victim survivors who do not report to the police but do access support services (Brown *et al.*, 2010).

These four examples of organisational evaluations demonstrate the value of forming formal research collaborations between criminal justice agencies and reputable university researchers. The university researchers bring an external, objective expertise to evaluation (and other research) processes and these skills are not always readily available within criminal justice organisations. The value of university–police agency research collaborations has a substantial history and has been discussed on numerous occasions. For example, a recent review of evaluation research actively undertaken by US police departments found this research occurred more frequently in larger police departments; a total of 70 US police departments each employing approximately 2,200 sworn (operational) police officers had conducted experimental and quasi-experimental evaluations between 1984 and 2011 (Cave *et al.*, 2014). Cave *et al.* suggested that in order for the findings of this police evaluation research to be more usefully applied, the participation of smaller police departments is also required. They also noted the difficulties for police departments that did not having a local university researcher interested in research collaboration.

Conclusions

This chapter has reviewed the practice of conducting evaluations of training programmes, interventions, and other initiatives within criminal justice organisations. We first described the basic evaluation process and stressed the value of planning evaluations simultaneously with the intended intervention programme. The most useful evaluations start *before* the planned intervention programme by gathering baseline (pre-test) performance data. We also discussed the recent interest in improving our understandings of the process issues which characterise successful and less successful organisational evaluations. We have recently described elsewhere the 17 key lessons we have learnt from conducting organisational evaluations within criminal justice organisations over the last ten years or so (Brough and Biggs, 2015). Our lessons learnt include both obvious issues (e.g. gaining the active commitment and participation of both *senior* and *local managers*) and more unexpected issues (e.g. the value of communicating to all employees exactly how the evaluation results impact the day-to-day work of the programme participants).

This chapter also described the four key methods of how to conduct organisational evaluations: via observation, focus groups, surveys, and rapid assessment evaluations. We particularly emphasised the value of designing careful data collections in order to empirically 'prove' the value of the programme. Thus, the ability to compare pre- and post-performance data of the training participants is important, as well as the ability to compare their performance data with a control group of employees who did not participate in the training programme (i.e. adopting quasi-experimental research designs). Finally, we described four examples of best-practice evaluation research conducted with police and corrections agencies. These examples also highlighted the value for criminal justice organisations of establishing enduring research collaborations with university-based experts.

References

Biggs, A. (2011) *A longitudinal evaluation of strain, work engagement, and intervention strategies to address the health of high risk employees.* Unpublished Doctoral Thesis, Griffith University, Brisbane.

Biggs, A., & Brough, P. (2015a). Challenges of intervention acceptance in complex, multi-faceted organisations: The importance of local champions. In: M. Karanika-Murray and C. Biron (Editors.). *Derailed organizational stress and well-being interventions: Confessions of failure and solutions for success.* (pp 151–158). Springer, UK.

Biggs, A., & Brough, P. (2015b). Explaining intervention success and failure: What works, when, and why?. In: M. Karanika-Murray and C. Biron (Editors.). *Derailed organizational stress and well-being interventions: Confessions of failure and solutions for success.* (pp 237–244). Springer, UK.

Biggs, A., Brough, P., and Barbour, J.P. (2014) Enhancing work-related attitudes and work engagement: a quasi-experimental study of the impact of an organizational intervention. *International Journal of Stress Management*, 21: 43–68. doi:10.1037/a0034508.

Braga, A.A., Hureau, D.M., and Papachristos, A.V. (2011) An ex post facto evaluation framework for place-based police interventions. *Evaluation Review*, 35(6): 592–626.

Brough, P., & Biggs, A. (2015). The highs and lows of occupational stress intervention research: Lessons learnt from collaborations with high-risk industries. In: M. Karanika-Murray and C. Biron (Editors.). *Derailed organizational stress and well-being interventions: Confessions of failure and solutions for success.* (pp 263–270). Springer, UK.

Brough, P., Biggs, A., and Barbour, J.P. (2012) *Healthy Workplaces project final report.* Brisbane: School of Applied Psychology, Griffith University.

Brown, J., Horvath, M., Kelly, L., and Westmarland, N. (2010) *Connections and disconnections; assessing evidence, knowledge and practice in response to rape.* London: Government Equalities Office.

Cave, B., Telep, C.W., and Grieco, J. (2014) Rigorous evaluation research among US police departments: special cases or a representative sample? *Police Practice and Research* (ahead-of-print), 1–15.

Farrington, D., Gottfredson, D., Sherman, L., and Welsh, B. (2002) The Maryland Scient-ific Methods Scale. In Sherman, L., Farrington, D., Welsh, B., and McKenzie, D. (eds) *Evidence-based crime prevention*. London: Routledge (pp. 13–21).

Feuerstein, M.T. (1986) *Partners in evaluation: evaluating development and community programmes with participants*. London: Macmillan.

Guerra-López, I.J. (2008) *Performance evaluation: proven approaches for improving program and organizational performance*. San Francisco: John Wiley and Sons.

Hollin, C. (2008) Evaluating offending behaviour programmes: does only randomisation glister? *Criminology and Criminal Justice*, 8: 89–106.

Hope, T. (2005) Pretend it doesn't work? The anti-social bias in the Maryland Scientific Methods Scale. *European Journal of Criminal Policy and Research*, 11: 275–296.

Karanika-Murray, M., and Biron, C. (2015) *Derailed organizational stress and well-being interventions: confessions of failure and solutions for success*. London: Springer.

McNall, M., and Foster-Fishman, P.G. (2007) Methods of rapid evaluation, assessment, and appraisal. *American Journal of Evaluation*, 28(2): 151–168.

Peters, T.J., and Waterman, R.H. (1982) *In search of excellence: lessons from America's best-run companies*. New York: HarperBusiness.

Scriven, M. (1973) Goal-free evaluation. In House, E.R. (ed.) *School evaluation: the politics and process*. San Pablo, CA: McCutchan (pp. 319–328).

Further resources

For a tool kit to conduct rapid evaluations, see:

www.civilservice.gov.uk/networks/gsr/resources-and-guidance/rapid-evidence-assessment.

For examples of randomised control trials, see:

Braga, A., Weisburd, D., Waring, E., Green Mazerolle, L., Spelman, W., and Gajewski, F. (1999) Problem-oriented policing in violent crime places: a randomised control experiment. *Criminology*, 37: 541–580.

Sherman, L., and Weisburd, D. (1995) General deterrent effects of police patrols in crime 'hot spots': a randomised control trial. *Justice Quarterly*, 12: 625–648.

Telep, C., Mitchell, R.J., and Weisburd, D. (2014) How much time should the police spend at crime hot spots? Answers from a Police Agency directed randomized field trial in Sacramento, California. *Justice Quarterly*, 31(5): 905–933.

For an example of a systematic review, see:

Braga, A.A., Papachristos, A.V., and Hureau, D.M. (2014) The effects of hot spots polic-ing on crime: an updated systematic review and meta-analysis. *Justice Quarterly*, 31(4): 633–663.

Memon, A., Meissner, C., and Fraser, J. (2010) The cognitive interview; a meta analytic review and study space analysis of the past 25 years. *Psychology, Public Policy and Law*, 16: 340–372.

Weisburd, D., Telep, C., Hinkle, J., and Eck, J. (2010) Is problem-oriented policing effective in reducing crime and disorder? Findings from a Campbell systematic review. *Criminology and Public Policy*, 9: 139–172.

For an example of a quasi-experimental design, see:

Piza, E.L., and O'Hara, B.A. (2014) Saturation foot-patrol in a high-violence area: a quasi-experimental evaluation. *Justice Quarterly*, 31(4): 693–718.

For secondary sources, see:

www.ipsos-mori.com (opinion polling data and reports).
www.justice.gov.uk (victimisation surveys, portal to Inspectorate websites, criminal statistics).

8　Focus groups

Introduction

Several methods of data collection are available to criminal justice researchers, with the most suitable method depending on a number of issues, including whether the research questions will most effectively be answered with qualitative or quantitative research. Qualitative research methods have been applied in criminal justice research to provide in-depth, context-specific information about issues, such as:

- reasons why people seek employment in corrective services (Biggs, 2011);
- the nature of the contemporary police culture in a specific national context (Chataway, 2014);
- the experience of occupational stress experienced by police (Toch, 2002); and
- barriers to achieving positive health outcomes among correctional employees (Morse *et al.*, 2011).

This chapter first discusses the distinction between quantitative and qualitative research, accompanied by suggestions for when one or the other may be required. The remainder of the chapter provides an overview of how to conduct focus groups, which is one of the most commonly applied methods for collecting qualitative data in criminal justice occupations.

Quantitative versus qualitative research

A basic distinction between quantitative and qualitative research methods is that the former generate data in the form of numbers, while the latter generate data in the form of text (Merriam, 2009). Quantitative methods allow for data collection in large, representative employee samples and enable associations between different work and non-work characteristics to be tested, as a large variety of statistical analyses are available to assess simple and complex relationships within the data (Eatough and Spector, 2013; Merriam, 2009). As many research projects are concerned with examining relationships amongst individual and work characteristics, quantitative data collection methods are most often used in organisational research (e.g. Eatough and Spector, 2013). For example, quantitative methods have been used to explore the effect of involvement in a major disaster relief effort on work-related attitudes and well-being experienced by Australian police officers (Biggs *et al.*, 2014a). Surveys represent the most popular quantitative data collection tool, and are discussed in detail in Chapter 10.

In contrast, qualitative data is appropriate when the purpose of research is to uncover 'the meaning of a phenomenon' or understand 'how people interpret their experiences, how they construct their worlds, and what meaning they attribute to their experiences' (Merriam, 2009, p. 5). For instance, focus groups conducted by Toch (2002) were primarily interested in achieving social consensus of the meaning of stress experienced by police officers. Qualitative approaches are generally applied in much smaller samples than quantitative methods. Bachiochi and Weiner (2004) suggest several key questions that can assist criminal justice researchers to determine whether qualitative approaches are most appropriate:

1   Are the issues of interest specific to an occupational or organisational context?
2   Are employees' interpretations of an event or issue integral to the research?
3   Is in-depth data about an issue or event required?
4   Is the investigation primarily exploratory, that is, are the issues being investigated well established organisational issues, or are they novel, complex issues that have seldom been investigated in the past?
5   Are there sufficient resources to support labour intensive qualitative research?
6   Are there sufficient levels of trust and support within the culture of the organisation to support qualitative research?

According to Bachiochi and Weiner (2004), affirmative responses to some or all of these questions indicate that qualitative approaches are appropriate. Some example research aims that would be appropriately addressed by qualitative data include:

•   Determining reasons for why people seek employment with corrective services (Biggs, 2011). Qualitative research is appropriate in this case, as investigating factors that attract employees to working in a correctional facility may be beneficial for recruitment and selection within that specific occupation, and the in-depth information provided for the specific context outweighs the lack of ability to transfer findings to other occupational groups.
•   Documenting current police organisational culture within a specific national context (i.e. Australian police officers; Chataway, 2014). Again, the occupational context is central to this research question, and in-depth information expressed by the participants themselves is required. Furthermore, the

research is exploratory as it focused on modern police culture, rather than attempting to replicate previous investigations of police culture.

• Investigating sources of police stress (Toch, 2002). This study combined several methods, including interviews, focus groups, personal observations, and surveys, to investigate the experience of police stress and reform in two New York police departments, one that had undergone diversification and one that had not. The occupational context was central to the research question, and in-depth data and individuals' interpretations of stress were required. Furthermore, although stress is well established, the relationship between stress and police reform was novel.

• Identifying obstacles to achieving health among correctional services employees (Morse *et al.*, 2011). The study combined focus groups, interviews, surveys, and physical assessments to explore the nature of risk factors associated with indicators of ill health. Qualitative methods were utilised as it was determined that health promotion interventions need to take into account context-specific constraints and risk factors.

As indicated in the examples provide above, in some cases, mixed-methods approaches that collect both quantitative and qualitative data are needed to address complex organisational issues. For example, the research conducted by Toch (2002) initially utilised qualitative methods (i.e. interviews, focus groups, and personal observation) to understand the experience of police stress and to facilitate the development and analysis of a survey instrument. When used together, mixed-methods complement one another and strengthen research conclusions (Bachiochi and Weiner, 2004). The remainder of this chapter will focus on the collection of qualitative data via focus groups.

Focus groups: what are they and when should they be used?

While there are several methods for collecting qualitative data, including one-on-one interviews, observation, and case studies, organisational research is often conducted with focus groups. Focus groups involve a facilitated discussion with a pre-selected group of participants to answer specific research questions (e.g. Bachiochi and Weiner, 2004; Parker and Tritter, 2006). They may be conducted alone to develop new theories and provide insight into novel organisational issues, or may be used in conjunction with surveys to identify key topics, generate items for new measures, and provide clarification of unexpected research findings (Bachiochi and Weiner, 2004). Focus groups are generally preferred over other qualitative methods (such as individual interviews) as they provide rich data from a large number of people in a short amount of time (Grumbein and Lowe, 2010).

Focus groups are particularly valuable when the purpose of the research is to gain an in-depth, focused understanding of *issues of shared importance* amongst employees (Bachiochi and Weiner, 2004). Work-related attitudes tend to be socially formed, and focus groups provide a rich social environment for experiences and attitudes to be explored, clarified, and shared (Breen, 2006; Freeman, 2006). The communication that occurs between focus group members additionally assists in clarifying similarities and differences in opinions amongst employees (Freeman, 2006).

Despite commonly being referred to as a *type of group interview*, focus groups are distinct from interviews due to their emphasis on both the content of the discussion *and* the interaction amongst participants, with data collected reflecting both sources of information (Parker and Tritter, 2006). The role of a focus group facilitator is different from that of a group interviewer: while interviewers ask questions to elicit responses, focus group facilitators stimulate discussion *amongst* participants to uncover the meaning and norms underlying their opinions, achieving a greater level of self-disclosure than would occur in a traditional interview (Grumbein and Lowe, 2010; Parker and Tritter, 2006). As a result, data obtained from focus groups is likely to be more in-depth than that achieved by individual interviews, as the group interactions encourage participants to elaborate and respond to comments made by others, and allows for participants' experiences and interpretation of events to be challenged and explored by others (Tewkesbury, 2009). This is in contrast to the more intimate and singular views expressed in one-on-one interviews (Toch, 2002).

Conducting focus group research

As with any organisational initiative, substantial preparation is required to increase research acceptance and participation, prior to commencing any actual research activities. The process for preparing for research in criminal justice occupations is outlined in Chapter 10, and is also applicable to focus group research. Once research preparation is complete, the actual process of conducting focus group research involves planning the sessions, recruiting a sample, conducting the focus groups, and analysing the data generated (e.g. Bachiochi and Weiner, 2004; Breen, 2006; Grumbein and Lowe, 2010; Parker and Tritter, 2006). Here, we provide a summary of some of the key tasks associated with conducting focus groups.

Planning and recruiting a sample

1   It is essential to articulate clear research goals to determine if focus groups will provide the information required: this will also assist in developing focus group questions (Breen, 2006; Grumbein and Lowe, 2010).

2   Select a skilled focus group facilitator, who can effectively summarise and seek clarification; keep the discussion on track; control verbose participants and encourage reserved participants; avoid engaging in discussions, which should primarily occur between participants; and probe for similarities and differences in opinion (Bachiochi and Weiner, 2004; Breen, 2006; Grumbein and Lowe, 2010). Furthermore, focus group facilitation requires an understanding of the need for methodological rigour in research in addition

to facilitation skills (Milward, 2000). Skilled facilitation of focus groups is one of the key factors determining the quality of data obtained (Milward, 2000).

3   Plan the total number of focus groups required, as well as the quantity and balance of participants within each group:

a   The number of groups required should be enough to achieve *theoretical saturation*, which occurs when conducting new sessions no longer generates new knowledge (Bachiochi and Weiner, 2004). At least ten to 12 groups may be required, although it depends on the complexity of the research question, the time available, and the size and composition of the organisation (Bachiochi and Weiner, 2004; Breen, 2006).

b   Each focus group should be small enough to ensure participation of all members, but large enough to achieve diverse opinions (Freeman, 2006; Milward, 2000). Suggested group sizes include four to six employees (Breen, 2006), eight to ten employees (Bachiochi and Weiner, 2004), and six to 12 employees (Freeman, 2006). So aim for approximately 6–10 members in each focus group. It is also recommended that focus groups be over-recruited, in the event that some group members do not attend on the day (Milward, 2000).

c   Carefully consider the composition of each focus group, aiming for homogeneity within groups and heterogeneity across groups (Bachiochi and Weiner, 2004; Breen, 2006). According to Milward (2000) group members should exhibit some common characteristics in order to facilitate the sharing of experiences. For example, if the research is concerned with gender differences in perceptions of correctional job characteristics, it may be beneficial to conduct separate sessions for male and female correctional officers. Similarly, if the research is concerned with management quality issues in a police occupation, it may be beneficial to stratify focus groups according to rank, so officers of only the same rank are included in the same group.

4   Select an appropriate location for the focus groups. Conducting focus groups within police stations or correctional centres is cost-effective and convenient for participants, although they are likely to be concerned about their anonymity and confidentiality, especially if the questions are of a sensitive nature (Breen, 2006). On-site locations can also result in greater disruptions, which adversely impacts focus group dynamics. This is especially likely to occur for criminal justice occupations, where participants are likely to be called to attend to operational matters, which are (understandably) prioritised over research activities (Biggs, 2011). Furthermore, conducting focus groups on-site in secure facilities introduces additional logistic challenges, as security checks may be required, limitations placed on the equipment brought into facilities, and recording sessions is likely to be prohibited. If conducting focus groups on-site, ensure facilitators are aware of policies and procedures at each location, liaise with a local contact to schedule venues

and assist with entry to the facility, and be prepared for delays (Wakai *et al.*, 2009). Conducting focus groups off-site addresses some of these issues but tends to be more expensive and less convenient for participants.

5   Develop a focus group protocol outlining the structure of the focus group, in order to keep the discussion on topic, facilitate coding of responses, and enhance standardisation across focus groups (Bachiochi and Weiner, 2004).

6   Select participants. Focus group participants are usually selected strategically and non-randomly, targeting participants who will provide the most meaningful information related to the objectives of the research (Milward, 2000; Parker and Tritter, 2006). Milward (2000) recommended making personal contact with the research population at the outset of the project in order to select appropriate participants and to facilitate rapport in the actual sessions. Common methods of recruitment include purposive sampling of participants from a specific population to meet a specific research need, convenience sampling of participants who are easy to recruit and readily available, and snowball sampling in which participants recommend additional participants (Kelley *et al.*, 2003; Parker and Tritter, 2006). It is important to take into account rostering systems when selecting participants. Several criminal justice occupations rely on strict roster systems, and it may be necessary to involve rostering staff and supervisors in the selection process to minimise disruptions to the service. Furthermore, consider staff who usually perform shift-work; it may be necessary to conduct focus groups at night or on weekends to accommodate all participants.

7   Distribute invitations to participants prior to the focus group, containing information about the location, date, and time; research purpose; participant expectations; and ethical issues (e.g. confidentiality and use of recordings). It may be useful to include a list of discussion questions for participants to consider, and a letter of support from a relevant stakeholder, such as a senior manager or union representative (Bachiochi and Weiner, 2004).

8   Consider pilot testing to obtain feedback on questions, focus group structure, and effectiveness of the facilitator and note-taker (Breen, 2006).

Conducting focus group sessions

Session structure

The actual structure of the session is informed by the focus group protocol, and several authors have provided guidelines for developing the protocol (e.g. Bachiochi and Weiner, 2004; Breen, 2006). Generally, a recommended focus group structure includes the following elements:

1   Welcome and introduction, providing an overview of the research, what is expected from participants, how data will be collected and stored, and actions that are expected to be taken in response to focus group results.

2   Establishing ground rules, for example, requesting confidentiality, encouraging honesty and involvement, and discouraging individuals from dominating the conversation.

3   Questioning, starting with more general introductory questions, and leading to more specific questions pertinent to the goals of the research (Breen, 2006). A reasonable duration for a focus group is between 60 and 90 minutes (Bachiochi and Weiner, 2004). Therefore, to ensure the discussion remains on track and to avoid running out of time for the substantive research questions, it is useful to include pre-established time-limits for each question (Breen, 2006).

4   Summary and closing, in which the facilitator provides a tentative overview of issues raised, to seek confirmation or clarification, as it is often impractical to reconvene the focus groups at a later date (Kidd and Parshall, 2000).

The purpose of a focus group protocol is mainly to ensure that the key issues are addressed and there is some level of methodological rigour maintained. However, the facilitator should maintain flexibility over the session in order to follower unanticipated and relevant lines of inquiry (Milward, 2000).

Focus groups in criminal justice occupations

As already noted, careful consideration of focus group composition is important, especially when distinct subcultures exist within an organisation, which is extremely likely in large, multifaceted criminal justice organisations. Unfortunately, conflict between employees and the existence of subcultures is seldom overt, and facilitators may need to spend time talking to employees and managers to better grasp employee dynamics in the planning stage (i.e. before the focus groups take place). It is difficult to manage these dynamics during the focus groups, but if they do arise emphasise mutual goals of the research, research benefits, and clarify ground rules (Apa et al., 2012). Milward (2000) also suggested that if a focus group participant is extremely hostile in the session, the best course of action may be to discretely ask the participant to leave (e.g. during a coffee break).

An additional challenge is the solidarity amongst employees within criminal justice occupational cultures (e.g. Biggs et al., 2014b). This solidarity is advantageous in many circumstances, for example, during critical incidents when officers need to rely on one another. However, solidarity can adversely affect the quality of focus group dynamics, if individuals are reluctant to share personal opinions that conflict with the opinions of others, or are concerned about being viewed as critical of their colleagues, superiors, or the service (Sollund, 2005). Solidarity can also produce an 'us-versus-them' mentality, which can foster mistrust and cynicism towards the intent of the research and interfere with facilitators' attempts to build rapport (Sollund, 2005). In this instance, it is extremely important to maintain rigorous and ethical research methods, particularly relating to confidentiality and security of data collected, to build trust between participants and researchers (Apa et al., 2012).

The prevailing culture within many criminal justice occupations is one that values stereotypical masculine traits, such as 'toughness' (Biggs *et al.*, 2014b). Participants may be unwilling to honestly discuss sensitive issues such as stress, harassment, and ill health, due to the stigma attached to being viewed as 'weak' and concern about punitive outcomes, such as losing promotional opportunities. If addressing sensitive topics, education to reduce stigma associated with these topics may be required prior to conducting the focus groups (Biggs, 2011; Biggs *et al.*, 2014b; Brough and Biggs, 2010).

Finally, Toch (2002, p. 73) noted 'focus groups happen to lend themselves to the surfacing of dissatisfactions. On their own – given the right subject – they verge on ebullient gripe sessions in which discontents can be shared and explored and sometimes even socially reinforced.' Milward (2000) provided the following recommendations to prevent focus groups from veering off topic and becoming overly negative:

- Apply gentle questioning techniques to ensure that overly negative issues are provided adequate context and perspective.
- Use assertive skills to get the conversation back on track if problems raised are off-topic. Even if they are on-topic, it is still important to maintain a positive conversation and avoid the session from becoming a venting session.
- Remind the group of the role of the facilitator and the aims of the focus group at the beginning and end of the session to avoid unrealistic expectations.
- Try to end the focus groups in a positive manner so the participants leave in a positive frame of mind.

For example, researchers investigating police stress attempted to avoid the focus groups becoming overly negative venting sessions by asking police officers to reflect on both positive and negative aspects of their work (Toch, 2002).

Recording or note-taking in focus groups

Focus group discussions can be recorded and transcribed, or notes can be taken during the session. Recording sessions allows the facilitator to focus on the flow of discussion, prevents reliance on notes, and, in the case of visual recording, can keep track of speakers and record non-verbal actions (Bachiochi and Weiner, 2004). Using recording devices, however, is not always possible or appropriate, especially when (a) sensitive topics are discussed; (b) identification of participants may cause harm; (c) unanimous permission is not provided by participants; and (d) local privacy laws or organisational policies prohibit the use of recording devices in criminal justice facilities (Bachiochi and Weiner, 2004). Furthermore, recording and transcribing can be an expensive and laborious process.

Note-taking is recommended, even when sessions are recorded, to provide a back-up in case of recording device failure and to assist the facilitator in summarising and checking accuracy of key issues during the focus group closing (Breen, 2006). It is preferable that the facilitator is not the note-taker, so they can concentrate on the flow of conversation and provide an independent view of the discussion (Breen, 2006; Kidd and Parshall, 2000). Bachiochi and Weiner (2004) provided the following advice for note-taking:

1   Devise a map of the seating arrangement and assign a number to each parti-
    cipant, so comments can be associated with individual participants. This
    helps avoid weighting comments of verbose individuals too heavily during
    analysis.
2   Record as much verbatim as possible, avoiding summarising or forming
    conclusions during the focus groups.
3   Record non-verbal actions as well as discussion content.

Regardless of which approach is taken, it is important that focus group particip-ants are (a) informed that the sessions will be recorded or notated, (b) given the opportunity to provide or withdraw permission for the recording, and (c) advised of how the data will be stored and whether any third-parties will have access to the data (e.g. use of transcribing service; Bachiochi and Weiner, 2004). Consider also the potential impact of recording or note-taking on group dynamics. The use of recording devices or the presence of a note-taker can make people feel uncom-fortable, leading them to change the way they respond to questions and interact with other participants, ultimately influencing the quality of the data (Bachiochi and Weiner, 2004; Breen, 2006).

Analysing focus group data

Focus groups generate an unwieldy amount of text, which is not amenable to systematic analysis unless it is summarised and categorised (Bachiochi and Weiner, 2004; Berg, 2012). Content analysis and thematic analysis are the most frequently employed methods for analysing focus group data, and both adopt a similar process of condensing and categorising data into meaningful themes, with the assistance of a coding scheme (Marks and Yardley, 2004). Coding is central to focus group data analysis, and involves an iterative process of recog-nising patterns in the data, dividing the data into small portions of text, and assigning meaningful codes to those portions (Marks and Yardley, 2004). Codes are words or short phrases that summarise or capture the essence of a portion of text, and are useful for retrieving and analysing data (Marks and Yardley, 2004; Saldaña, 2009). The overall coding scheme may be based on an existing theoret-ical framework and developed prior to analysis, or may be data-driven, in which the codes are developed as a result of an iterative coding process of the raw data (Marks and Yardley, 2004). Coding schemes are often hierarchical, with codes arranged into sub-categories and categories, which are grouped into overarching themes (Saldaña, 2009). When coding is complete, codes can be analysed by examining their frequency of occurrence in the data (content analysis) or patterns of themes (thematic analysis; Marks and Yardley, 2004). The coding process can be conducted manually or with the assistance of a computer program, such as NVivo. It is recommended that experienced researchers be involved in the complex process of analysing focus group data.

Finally, there are additional considerations to take into account when analysing focus group data, these include:

- Assess whether a theme represents the opinions of the majority or a vocal minority, and make adjustments for this in the analysis (Bachiochi and Weiner, 2004; Kidd and Parshall, 2000).
- Avoid attributing too much importance to catchy or interesting quotes, unless they are representative of the group's opinions. Summarise findings initially, and then use quotes representative of the majority of participants' opinions as examples of a particular theme (Bachiochi and Weiner, 2004).
- Pay attention to consensus and controversy, to understand how different perspectives arise and are modified within the group (Kidd and Parshall, 2000).
- Reflect on the reliability and validity of focus group data. For instance, consider assigning more than one researcher to independently develop the coding scheme and code the data, and examine the level of consensus between the independent researchers (Bachiochi and Weiner, 2004).

Focus group ethical issues and limitations

Focus groups are less resource intensive to prepare and conduct than other qualitative methods, although the complexity of data generated can negate this benefit (Kidd and Parshall, 2000). Furthermore, data quality may be diminished by poor group dynamics and ineffective facilitation. Finally, ethical issues may complicate the use of focus groups, and are important to consider throughout the planning and implementation stages.

Over-disclosure by participants, particularly when discussing sensitive topics, is one of the most important ethical issues to consider (Halcomb *et al.*, 2007; Smith, 1995). In focus group settings, maintaining confidentiality of participant's involvement is difficult, as the identity of participants and the source of comments are known to researchers, other focus group participants, and transcribers (Parker and Tritter, 2006). As researchers cannot control the actions of other group participants after the focus group, it is not possible to guarantee confidentiality of participants' identity or comments outside of the focus group (Smith, 1995). The risk to participants can be minimised during the informed consent process prior to the focus group by: (a) acknowledging in the informed consent materials that confidentiality cannot be guaranteed; (b) asking participants to sign an undertaking that they will not disclose experiences shared by others in the group; and (c) advising participants to avoid disclosing information they would not want to be shared with others outside the focus group context (Halcomb *et al.*, 2007; Smith, 1995).

Another related ethical issue is the disclosure of legally reportable incidents or behaviours that potentially cause harm to others (Smith, 1995), for example, police officers revealing instances of criminal misconduct. In these cases, professional ethical codes or legislation may dictate a particular course of action, and the facilitator may need to consider whether to address the issue immediately in the session or discretely at the end of the session (Smith, 1995). Again, it is optimal to discuss upfront the consequences of disclosing legally reportable incidents at the beginning of the session, so that participants are clear of the obligations of researchers in the event of such disclosures. When conducting research on sensitive issues or vulnerable populations, where there is a greater chance of such issues being uncovered, it may be necessary to ensure appropriate support and infrastructure is available to deal with these situations (Halcomb *et al.*, 2007).

Additional ethical issues include the importance of clearly informing participants about the confidentiality of their data, such as how responses will be treated in reports (e.g. feedback based on de-identified data), how data will be stored, and whether any third-parties will have access to the data (e.g. use of transcription service; Bachiochi and Weiner, 2004). Finally, debriefing at the end of the session is an important consideration, to ensure that the session is concluded in a positive manner (Smith, 1995).

Conclusion

Focus groups are useful for collecting in-depth data about organisational issues of shared importance amongst employees. They allow employees to express their personal opinions in a social context, so both the content of the discussion and the interpersonal dynamics amongst participants can be observed. This chapter outlined practical steps to take to plan and conduct focus groups within criminal justice occupations, and discussed important analytic and ethical issues.

References

Apa, Z.L., Bai, R., Dhritiman, V.M., Herzig, C.T.A., Koenigsmann, C., Lowy, F.D., and Larson, E.L. (2012) Challenges and strategies for research in prisons. *Public Health Nursing*, 29(5): 467–472. doi:10.1111/j.1525–1446.2012.01027.x.

Bachiochi, P.D., and Weiner, S.P. (2004) Qualitative data collection and analysis. In Rogelberg, S.G. (ed.) *Handbook of research methods in industrial and organizational psychology*. Malden, MA: Blackwell Publishing (pp. 161–183).

Berg, B.L. (2012) *Qualitative research methods for the social sciences*, 8th edn. Boston, MA: Pearson.

Biggs, A. (2011) *A longitudinal evaluation of strain, work engagement, and intervention strategies to address the health of high-risk employees*. Doctoral Thesis, Griffith University, Brisbane.

Biggs, A., Brough, P., and Barbour, J.P. (2014a) Exposure to extraorganizational stressors: impact on mental health and organizational perceptions for police officers. *International Journal of Stress Management*, 21(3): 255–282. doi:10.1037/a0037297.

Biggs, A., Brough, P., and Barbour, J.P. (2014b) Relationships of individual and organizational support with engagement: examining various types of causality in a three-wave study. *Work and Stress*, 28(3): 236–254. doi:10.1080/02678373.2014.934316.

Breen, R.L. (2006) A practical guide to focus-group research. *Journal of Geography in Higher Education*, 30(3): 463–475. doi:10.1080/03098260600927575.

Brough, P., and Biggs, A. (2010) Occupational stress in police and prison staff. In Brown, J. and Campbell, E. (eds) *The Cambridge handbook of forensic psychology*. Cambridge: Cambridge University Press (pp. 707–718).

Chataway, S. (2014) *Change or continuity? A mixed methods investigation of contemporary police culture*. Doctoral Thesis, Griffith University, Brisbane.

Eatough, E.M., and Spector, P.E. (2013) Quantitative self-report methods in occupational health psychology research. In Sinclair, R.R., Wang, M., and Tetrick, L.E. (eds) *Research methods in occupational health psychology: measurement, design, and analysis*. New York: Routledge (pp. 248–267).

Freeman, T. (2006) 'Best practice' in focus group research: making sense of different views. *Journal of Advanced Nursing*, 56(5): 491–497. doi:10.1111/j.1365–2648.2006.04043.x.

Grumbein, M.J., and Lowe, P.A. (2010) Focus group. In Salkind, N.J. (ed.) *Encyclopedia of research design*. Thousand Oaks, CA: SAGE. doi:http://dx.doi.org.libraryproxy.griffith.edu.au/10.4135/9781412961288.n156.

Halcomb, E.J., Gholizadeh, L., DiGiacomo, M., Phillips, J., and Davidson, P.M. (2007) Literature review: Considerations in undertaking focus group research with culturally and linguistically diverse groups. *Journal of Clinical Nursing*, 16: 1000–1011. doi:10.1111/j.1365–2702.2006.01760.x.

Kelley, K., Clark, B., Brown, V., and Sitzia, J. (2003) Good practice in the conduct and reporting of survey research. *International Journal for Quality in Health Care*, 15(3): 261–266. doi:http://dx.doi.org/10.1093/intqhc/mzg031.

Kidd, P.S., and Parshall, M.B. (2000) Getting the focus and the group: enhancing analytical rigor in focus group research. *Qualitative Health Research*, 10(3): 293–308. doi:10.1177/104973200129118453.

Marks, D.F., and Yardley, L. (2004) Content and thematic analysis. In Marks, D.F. and Yardley, L. (eds), *Research methods for clinical and health psychology*. London: SAGE (pp. 56–69).

Merriam, S.B. (2009) *Qualitative research: a guide to design and implementation*, 2nd edn. San Francisco, CA: Jossey-Bass.

Milward, L.J. (2000) Focus Groups. In Breakwell, G.M., Hammond, S., and Fife-Shaw, C. (eds) *Research methods in psychology*, 2nd edn. London: SAGE (pp. 303–324).

Morse, T., Dussetschleger, J., Warren, N., and Cherniack, M. (2011) Talking about health: correction employees' assessments of obstacles to healthy living. *Journal of Occupational and Environmental Medicine*, 53(9): 1037–1045. doi:10.1097/JOM.0b013e3182260e2c.

Parker, A., and Tritter, J. (2006) Focus group method and methodology: current practice and recent debate. *International Journal of Research and Method in Education*, 29(1): 23–37. doi:10.1080/01406720500537304.

Saldaña, J. (2009) *The coding manual for qualitative researchers*. London: SAGE.

Smith, M.W. (1995) Ethics in focus groups: a few concerns. *Qualitative Health Research*, 5(4): 478–486. doi:10.1177/104973239500500408.

Sollund, R. (2005) Obstacles and possibilities in police research. *Outlines. Critical Practice Studies*, 7(2): 43–64. http://ojs.statsbiblioteket.dk/index.php/outlines/article/view/2103.

Tewkesbury, R. (2009) Qualitative versus quantitative methods: understanding why qualitative methods are superior for criminology and criminal justice. *Journal of Theoretical and Philosophical Criminology*, 1(1): 38–58.

Toch, H. (2002) *Stress in policing.* Washington, D.C.: American Psychological Association.

Wakai, S., Shelton, D., Trestman, R.L., and Kesten, K. (2009) Conducting research in corrections: challenges and solutions. *Behavioral Sciences and the Law*, 27: 743–752. doi:10.1002/bsl.894.

9   Consultation and consultancy

Introduction

One of our key aims with this book is to prompt criminal justice organisations to enhance the well-being of staff under the particularly difficult conditions of cut-backs and organisational change. As part of that agenda we are promoting an organisational justice approach which emphasises treating both members of an organisation and the public with dignity and fairness as a way to increase co-operative engagement. A critical aspect in creating a procedurally just organisa-tion as well as enhancing organisational legitimacy is an appreciation of how the affected constituencies feel about the management of processes and procedures as well as the quality of interactions. Monitoring and communication are essen-tial ingredients in achieving such understanding and we discussed organisational communication issues in detail in Chapter 5. This chapter focuses on consulta-tion: asking who is consulted and how this may be done. Evaluation is another means of gaining feedback about processes and procedures particularly during periods of organisational change (see Chapter 7).

Consultation and evaluation may be relatively 'quick and dirty' or more soph-isticated in scope and can be conducted with readily adaptable tools for the organisation itself to employ. At other times, the complexity and skill require-ment is not within the organisation's competency and the expertise of external consultants is required. This chapter provides some examples to illustrate this process of consultation.

The chapter includes a discussion of the ethical dimensions implicated in using these tools and draws attention to the importance of making the rules of engagement explicit when canvassing views of staff or service users. A funda-mental principle of social science is that no harm is experienced by people who are participants in research projects (Ward and Willis, 2011). This is a moral responsibility that addresses two questions: how research is conducted and how the researcher conducts themselves towards the participants. This may involve assessing the risk of participation, especially if the issues are sensitive and potentially distressing. Adequate consideration must be given to the vulnerabili-ties of all potential participants. We are advocating that good practice from aca-demic research be extended to organisations when conducting internal staff consultations and evaluations as well as when engaging with the public. Finally, these are big topics and there is insufficient space to provide a detailed account of methods. The chapter will point to resources that provide richer descriptions of the various tools discussed.

Consultation

Over the last decade or so, the process of consultation has become an increasingly important part of engaging the public in policy and local implementation (Cook, 2002) but the means of achieving this are often tokenistic and unrepresentative. A recurring feature of employee surveys of stress in whichever environment measured is a complaint about poor communication, especially during times of organisational change (Millward, 2005). Millward explains that in part this is due to a disruption in people's ability to make sense of what is happening and why. This can create both anxiety and result in a decrement of performance, as well as causing confusion and creating resistance to change. A procedural justice approach (Chapter 2) argued that process is more important than outcome and that people who experience fair and open communication are more likely to comply even if the outcomes are difficult or uncomfortable (Bradford *et al.*, 2013). In essence consultation is about conveying, receiving, interpreting and acting upon information. When considering a consultation it is useful to establish a strategy with four component elements: the intended audience; source of the message; content of the message; and the channel of communication (Brown and Campbell, 1991).

Audience

This may be the staff within the organisation, members of the general public, target communities (especially those who are hard to reach, such as excluded young people or non-English speaking immigrants) or professional stakeholders. These differ in terms of numbers, knowledge, interest, and heterogeneity. Thus consulting with the general public may involve a large-scale survey of a random representative sample in which broad trends of opinion may be solicited, perhaps seeking an indication of preferences of one policy option over another. For example, the establishment of Police and Crime Commissioners in England and Wales has been a particularly controversial idea. A YouGov poll asked a sample of UK adults whether they thought this was a good or bad idea (people were actually split almost equally between those thinking it was a good idea, a bad idea, or they did not know). Such a consultation can only hope to elicit some general indicative trends from a broad swathe of the population.

A more targeted consultation might be directed at specific groups in a particular location. The Home Office Research, Development and Statistics Directorate commissioned a research group (Pain *et al.*, 2002) to look more particularly at the crime and disorder experiences of a 'hard to reach' group of excluded young people living in Tyneside. This involved careful consideration in defining and locating the participants and in the methods employed to engage with the young participants.

Clearly the intended audience will determine the appropriate methods to identify those to be included and indicate how they may be located and approached. Where the audience is the general public, a 'hard to reach' group or staff within the organisation it is important to be clear about the terms of engagement. In other words, be open and honest about the purpose of the consultation, the use the information will be put to, and if the results will be fed back in some form to the participants. Minimally the consultation may be in the form of an instructional leaflet informing people about a change of opening times of a police station or the relocation of offices, or introducing a new neighbourhood officer to the community. Often it will involve some interaction, for example permitting people to voice their concerns or complaints about the running of a service. Potential participants will wish to know whether and how this information may influence development of new policies.

Source of the message

The identity of the initiator of the consultation is also significant. It could be a government Department, a national organisation such as the Crown Prosecution Service or the Association of Chief Probation Officers. It might be a specific organisation such as a particular police force or prison. The initiator is not always the organisation carrying out the consultation. A critical feature of a successful consultation is the credibility of the source. Clearly if the organisation has a poor public image or has been discredited this may influence people's responsiveness and willingness to participate. Sometimes it may be helpful for a source that is considered independent, such as a university or a commercial company, to run the consultation on behalf of an organisation. If this is the case, ethically it is important to indicate to potential participants who the sponsor is and explain that the exercise is being run independently.

Content of the consultation

The primary purposes of consultation are:

- educational – informing people about policy options or organisational change;
- generating ideas – garnering innovations and novel solutions from the workforce or a user group;
- motivational – facilitating new ways of working;
- feedback – reaction to innovative policies or procedures;
- monitoring – checking on process and outcomes.

Some of these aims can be achieved through secondary sources. These may be publically available (often on-line) and include for example:

- national public opinion polling, such as those carried out by IPSOS-MORI and other polling organisations whose reports and raw data can be accessed through their websites;
- government statistics and victimisation surveys which include details of demographics of staff employed in justice agencies (for example, a police force can look at the number of its ethnic minority or women officers and compare against the national average);
- regulatory bodies such as Her Majesty's Inspectorates undertake reviews and thematic inspections which may also include consultations with the public. For example, Her Majesty's Inspectorate of Constabulary (2011), as part of its investigation into police corruption, commissioned a consultative process involving 3,571 respondents and qualitative interviews with 42 respondents across England and Wales. This process aimed to ascertain public perceptions of what represents integrity and corruption, their respective prevalence, and whether attitudes are affected by recent events (e.g. the Leveson enquiry, 2013, concerning relationships between the police and the media).

Other secondary sources of information may be available within the organisation itself, including for example, rates of sickness absence broken down by location or unit can be a proxy indicator of morale or discipline problems. Exceptionally high performance may actually bear investigation as well as poor performance. The Independent Police Commission (2013) report showed that forces in England and Wales with the highest detection rates also showed the greatest number of complaints from the public about incivility. The report speculated that a force with a driving performance culture might achieve its results at the cost of the quality of officer's interactions with members of the public.

Mode of consultation

Two particular aspects of communication are discussed here: structure and power. Furnham (1997) provided a description of basic communication structures, which vary in terms of the speed and accuracy of the information conveyed and the satisfaction of the participants. Structures in which communication is controlled centrally or hierarchically (i.e. a hub at the centre of a wheel or at the branch of a Y shape) convey information quickly and accurately but are low on participants' satisfaction (see Figure 9.1). A circle arrangement where participants are adjacent gains greater satisfaction but is poor on speed and accuracy of the information conveyed. The optimal arrangement is complete connectivity although this configuration may have no designated leadership and whilst more satisfying to participants, may impede decision-making.

Centralised structures of communication are preferable for relatively straight-forward and simple tasks, such as conveying information, whereas connected networks are better for more complex interactions and are experienced as more democratic.

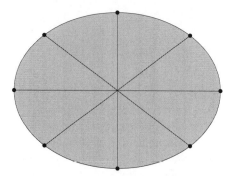

Figure 9.1 Optimal communication structure for speed and accuracy of information transmission.

Power is also related to the levels of interaction permitted and the degree to which participants can actually influence outcomes. As just explained, decentralised networks permit greater levels of participation, but where people feel that the consultation is purely notional (for example, simply informing the workforce about a major reorganisation), this is likely to have a negative effect on morale and will increase resistance.

Use of social media is another way to promote connected networks and criminal justice agencies are increasingy making use of this means of communication (Independent Police Commission, 2013). We illustrate this approach in example two of the case studies at the end of the chapter. Ballentyne and Fraser (1998) discussed the benefits of participatory consultation as follows:

- Often communities or workgroups understand their problems better than service professionals and actively engaging communities about their own experiences can yield novel as well as meaningful solutions.
- Communities are often more flexible and creative than large service conglomerates or bureaucracies in problem-solving, solution focusing, and implementation.
- It can be a cost effective way to identify problems as well as proffering solutions.
- There is potential added value as a result of the development of sustainable empowerment and involvement within local communities, there is often a greater acceptance of solutions and more enthusiastic implementation.

Further benefits associated with participatory consultation include improved legitimacy and accountability. Participatory consultation is also useful in re-establishing the social capital which may have been damaged by a particular scandal or bruising period of change. A detailed worked example of a participatory method (the Delphi technique) is provided in Chapter 11. Focus groups are also an excellent means of working participatively and these were described in Chapter 8.

Consultancy

Two models of consultancy arrangements are considered in this chapter: private public partnerships and academic collaborations.

Private public partnerships

Cheer (2013) and Rhodes (2013), both chief constables of police forces in England and Wales, described the process whereby their respective forces entered into partnership arrangements with private companies to deliver 'back office' administrative services. In both cases the commercial enterprise brought in new IT expertise and transferred employees from the public to the private sector. Significant amounts of money were involved in these contracts. Lessons learnt from these experiences included:

- greater appreciation of the need for a psychological contract between individuals and the force and staff moved from a public sector emergency service to a commercial private company;
- greater understanding of the complexity and diversity of policing tasks;
- need to fully engage with collaborating partner at all levels in the organisation and consult with staff and stakeholders at each stage of the process;
- importance of risk assessments to ensure commercial imperatives did not distort the police mission;
- establishment of key objectives with a clear separation of tasks and responsibilities;
- added value of transferred learning from the private sector.

Academic collaborations

Academic interest in criminal justice agencies began in the early 1900s (Engel and Henderson, 2013) and we have described our own collaborative research experiences with criminal justice agencies throughout this book. Some of the main advantages of collaborations with academic researchers include:

- increased effectiveness in basing innovation on empirical findings;
- provision of externally validated sources of accountability when operational/ organisational change is scrutinised;
- provision of formative and on-going feedback through the duration of the research collaboration;
- mutual appreciation of the importance of theory and practice;
- enhancement of the participating agency's knowledge;
- greater confidence in academic research.

There are different types of academic collaborative arrangements. They may be long-term and enduring (Bradley and Nixon, 2009) or involve a single specific project aim (Fleming, 2012). A more elaborate arrangement is exemplified by the Scottish Institute for Policing Research (SIPR) and the Scottish Police Service (Fyfe and Wilson, 2012). Here three research networks have been created: police–community relations; evidence and investigation; organisational issues. There is a co-ordinating hub and appropriate researchers are paired with practitioners to work on specific projects. Often external funding is obtained to support the project. Weisburd and Neyroud (2011) argued for a logical extension of such collaborations by suggesting that police–academic collaboration ultimately leads to greater professionalisation of policing. Shepherd (2013) made a similar point in reference to the probation service.

Three case studies

Example 1: Community Intelligence Led Policing (CILP)

A procedural justice approach, in which the community has a direct input, was undertaken in the South Wales Police in the form of a consultancy led by an academic (Innes, 2014). Under the rubric of a neighbourhood policing model, Innes and colleagues developed an evidence-based approach towards the relative distribution of harm caused by crime and disorder incidents in the city of Cardiff. The objective was to devise a way to allocate the most resources to where harm was the greatest. The aim was to focus local policing resources on where they are most needed, while ensuring that all communities continue to receive a guaranteed minimum standard of service. The value of this approach is threefold:

- It integrates a method for democratic influence in terms of deciding how the public's problems are defined as police priorities. By using community intelligence to spot emerging trends and the precursors of more serious crimes, police can operate more effectively through influencing effects and reducing reliance upon coercive social control.
- Community intelligence identifies the most vulnerable people, places, and events to ensure that they are supported.
- Community engagement provides the basis for more effective partnership working by providing a common picture of what are the key problems to be tackled.

The method comprises of five stages:

1   Instead of holding community meetings and waiting to see who turns up, or conducting a survey and see who responds, local police officers go and actively seek out the views of residents in a neighbourhood via face-to-face interviews. They use a structured interview (designed by the consultants) to elicit the prevalence and distribution of different kinds of crime, physical disorder, and social disorder in the local area, along with a measure of the relative harm these are causing.

2   The data from the interviews are processed by the consultants and mapped onto Geographic Information Software (GIS).
3   The consultants analyse the data to identify those places and issues where there is a collective view that a problem exists. The analysis seeks to identify both those problems affecting a lot of people, as well as those that affect a relatively small number of individuals. Data are represented graphically showing the spatial distribution of the harm impacts of crime and disorder in Cardiff. The hot spots are where crime and disorder is impacting negatively upon neighbourhood security, calculated not on the basis of the amount of crime or anti-social behaviour, but on their aggregated impact.
4   The analysis is taken back to the community through meetings to prioritise interventions.
5   Finally, targeted interventions are designed to provide solutions to enact these public priorities.

The utility of this approach is brought home if this is compared to a standard crime hot-spot analysis. In Cardiff the recorded crime hot spot gravitates very clearly and distinctly upon the city centre area, reflecting issues to do with the night-time economy and property offences. In contrast, the mapping of impacts provides a more nuanced and variegated picture, about where neighbourhood security is being harmed. This approach allows attention to be drawn to crime and disorder 'cold spots' – in other words, where crime and disorder is happening but where there is a greater degree of resilience. These areas do not require the same level of police resourcing.

Example 2: public counter service review consultation evaluation

Police Scotland was formed in 2013 by amalgamating the six pre-existing regional forces. This involved considerable administrative, operational, and organisational change. The new national service proposed changes to the provision of counter services, whereby the public entered police stations with queries and questions or to report a crime. The proposals included a rationalisation of opening times and having 61 of 214 police stations without a staffed counter service. A programme of consultation was designed and is summarised in Table 9.1.

The results of concerns arising from this consultation process were collated and Police Scotland responded in two ways:

a   formulated a response, e.g. general concern over reduction or removal of counter provision (Police Scotland, n.d.) highlighted the downward trend in public attendance at counters and alternative methods to contact police;
b   supplied a set of criteria to assess the viability of public, staff, and stakeholder suggestions and as a result nine specific proposals were modified.

Table 9.1 Consultation methods

Method	Comment	Criticism
The proposals were announced to the media and posted on Police Scotland website and simultaneously on the internal intranet	This achieved speed and accuracy of information dissemination but resulted in low levels of staff satisfaction	Staff would have preferred to have been told in person rather than indirectly through the inter/intranet
Affected staff were invited to attend a briefing on the proposed changes	258/466 staff attended and DVD of the presentation was made available to staff who could not attend	55% attendance rate credible but more might have been done to increase presence at briefings
A four-week public consultation was planned	Contact by internet	Time-scale considered too short Concentration on internet contact potentially exclusory
Stakeholder contacts	Correspondence and petitions	Problems identified in wording of the petitions

Example 3: an outsourcing consultation – Lincolnshire police

Lincolnshire Police were obliged to achieve considerable levels of savings, needed to replace outdated computer systems and an estate infrastructure badly in need of refurbishment. The steps they took in engaging a private sector partner included the following:

1 scoped the services that Lincolnshire Police had to offer;
2 made explicit organisational values;
3 soft market testing – meetings with a number of potential partners for a provisional exploration of what might be achieved and what organisational development and investment as well as organisational transformations could be achieved;
4 published a notice in the Official Journal of the European Union which set out the invitation to tender;
5 organised a bidders' day in which 105 organisations attended;
6 issued an invitation to submit an Outline Solution, 12 consortia subsequently responded;
7 assessment against criteria resulting in five bidders;
8 interaction between force and bidders for the latter to refine their bids;
9 submission of a Detailed Solution;
10 evaluation of the bids resulting in two contenders;
11 construction in parallel of two potentially binding contacts;
12 issued an Invitation to Submit a Final Tender when one bidder chosen.

Neil Rhodes, Chief Constable of Lincolnshire Police, provides greater detail of these 12 'golden rules' of public sector outsourcing in a pamphlet published by the force in 2014. In a review of this consultancy partnership arrangements it was noted in a report by Lincolnshire Police, the Police and Crime Commissioner (PCC) for Lincolnshire and G4S (Rhodes, 2014) that after two years:

*   999 emergency call response rates had improved from 93 to 95 per cent of calls answered within ten seconds;
*   95 per cent of arrest summons were processed to the Police National Computer within 24 hours compared to the national target of 90 per cent;
*   the force's Crime Management Bureau completed action fraud reports on behalf of officers thereby saving the equivalent of 16 weeks of officers' time; and
*   over £5 million worth of savings achieved.

All three parties, the chief constable, PCC, and G4S, expressed satisfaction with the arrangements and were fully expecting year three to yield further improvements. (The first annual report of this arrangement is available at: www.g4s.com/~/media/Files/United%20Kingdom/Sector%20content/G4SLincs%20Annual%20Report%202013FINALSINGLE.ashx and the second year report at: www.au.g4s.com/media/1592/g4s_lincs_police_year_2_annual_report.pdf.)

Conclusions

Consultation and consultancy are tools available to agencies within the CJS and are particularly important during times of change. Many agencies are facing reform, streamlining of staff and introduction of new working practices, both operational and organisational. Innovation and change often are accompanied by uncertainty and anxiety from within the workforce. Consultation is key to explaining what is happening and why, and there are distinct advantages in gaining the trust and confidence of staff by engaging them in the early stages of the change process. Not only is this perceived as more democratic, research evidence suggests that explaining both the why and how of change is more likely to encourage acceptance of the process.

It may well be within the capability of CJS organisations to undertake their own evaluations. However, when either a more complex evaluation is required or it is important to establish the independence of such an exercise, some collaboration may be required, either with an academic or other research institution or with the private sector. In this chapter we have outlined the importance of conducting both consultation and consultancy within an ethical framework. Insincere consultation or ill-prepared collaborative arrangements probably lead to worse outcomes than if neither had taken place.

References

Ballentyne, S. and Fraser, P. (1998) It's good to talk, but it's not good enough: Active Consultation as a key to safer communities. In Ballentyne, S., Pease, K., and McLaren, V. (eds) *Secure foundations: key issues in crime prevention, crime reduction and community safety.* London: IPPR (pp. 164–188).

Bradford, B., Jackson, J., and Hough, M. (2013) Police futures and legitimacy: redefining 'good policing'. In Brown, J. (ed.) *The future of policing.* Abingdon, UK: Routledge (pp. 79–99).

Bradley, D., and Nixon, C. (2009) Ending the 'dialogue of the deaf': evidence and policing policies and practice. An Australian case study. *Police Practice and Research: An International Journal*, 10: 423–435.

Brown, J., and Campbell, E. (1991) Risk communication: some underlying principles. *International Journal of Environmental Studies*, 38: 297–303.

Cheer, J. (2013) A wide-ranging partnership. In Neyroud, P. (ed.) *Policing UK 2013. Priorities and pressures: a year of transition.* London: Witan Media (pp. 38–39).

Cook, D. (2002) Consultation for a change? Engaging users and communities in the policy process. *Social Policy and Administration*, 36: 516–531.

Engel, E., and Henderson, S. (2013) Beyond rhetoric: establishing police-academic partnerships at work. In Brown, J. (ed.) *The future of policing.* Abingdon, UK: Routledge (pp. 227–236).

Fleming, J. (2012) Changing the way we do business: reflecting on collaborative practice. *Police Practice and Research. An International Journal*, 13: 375–388.

Furnham, A. (1997) *The psychology of behaviour at work: the individual in the organisation.* Hove, UK: Psychology Press.

Fyfe, N., and Wilson, P. (2012) Knowledge exchange and police practice: broadening and deepening the debate around research-practitioner collaborations. *Police Practice and Research: An International Journal*, 13: 306–314.

Her Majesty's Inspectorate of Constabulary (2011) *Without fear or favour: a review of police relationships*. London: HMSO.

Independent Police Commission (2013) *Policing for a better Britain*. London: The Commission.

Innes, M. (2014) Reinventing the office of constable: progressive policing in the age of austerity. In Brown, J. (ed.) *The future of policing*. Abingdon, UK: Routledge (pp. 64–78).

Millward, L. (2005) *Understanding occupational and organisational psychology*. London: SAGE.

Pain, R., Francis, P., Fuller, I., O'Brian, K., and Williams, S. (2002) Hard to reach young people and community safety: a model for participatory research and consultation. Briefing note. www.dur.ac.uk/resources/cscr/outputs/PRS_152.pdf.

Police Scotland (n.d.) Public counter service review: consultation evaluation. www.scotland. police.uk/assets/pdf/138327/229858/public-counter-consultation-evaluation? view=Standard.

Rhodes, N. (2013) An outsourcing journey partnership. In Neyroud, P. (ed.) *Policing UK 2013. Priorities and pressures: a year of transition*. London: Witan Media (pp. 34–36).

Rhodes, N. (2014) *Twelve golden rules of public sector outsourcing*. Pamphlet. Lincolnshire Police.

Shepherd, J. (2013) *Professionalising the probation service: why university institutes would transform rehabilitation*. London: The Howard League for Penal Reform/ London School of Economics Mannheim Centre for Criminology.

Ward, T., and Willis, G. (2011) Ethical problems arising in forensic and correctional research. In Sheldon, K., Davies, J., and Howells, K. (eds) *Research in practice for forensic professionals*. Abingdon, UK: Routledge (pp. 16–33).

Weisburd, D., and Neyroud, P. (2011) *Police science: toward a new paradigm.* New Perspectives in Policing. Harvard Kennedy School/National Institute of Justice.

10 Surveys

Introduction

Research conducted within criminal justice organisations often utilises surveys to measure employees' perceptions of their work environments. Surveys provide a relatively time-efficient and cost-effective means for collecting data from large samples representative of the overall workforce (Kelley *et al.*, 2003). They are extremely versatile: several facets of work can be assessed in a single survey and numerous statistical analyses are available to interpret the data (Eatough and Spector, 2013). Surveys have been employed to answer numerous research questions, for example:

- The relative importance of generic versus occupation-specific predictors of work engagement and psychological strain experienced by Australian correctional employees (Brough and Biggs, 2015).
- The effect of involvement in a major disaster relief effort on work-related attitudes and well-being experienced by Australian police officers (Biggs *et al.*, 2014b).
- Gender differences in the relationship between sex discrimination and sexual harassment on psychological strain experiences by UK police employees (Brown *et al.*, 1995).
- Attitudes to punishment within England and Wales assessed via the British Crime Survey, conducted with a nationally representative sample of respondents (Hough and Roberts, 1998).

Despite their utility and versatility, surveys are frequently misused and overused, limiting their capacity to provide high-quality data to support organisational initiatives. In this chapter we initially outline the basic process to follow when conducting survey research in criminal justice occupations, followed by a brief discussion of common pitfalls associated with this research method.

Survey process

A systematic approach is required to conduct surveys that produce high-quality data to inform organisational issues and initiatives. Too often, survey efforts are haphazard, producing questionable data, and diminishing the relevance of findings. Here, we outline the key steps for conducting systematic survey research within criminal justice occupations (see also Church and Waclawski, 2001; Rogelberg *et al.*, 2004). These steps are not necessarily sequential; rather, several steps may be revisited throughout the process, especially those relating to stakeholder support.

Step 1: establishing a survey action plan

Within criminal justice occupations, the need to conduct a survey may be identified by internal stakeholders, such as managers and human resource management (HRM), or external stakeholders, such as union representatives, government officials, and university researchers. Steps are then taken to commence the survey process. Additional internal and/or external stakeholders are often engaged to provide the required expertise, resources, or authority to conduct the survey.

An important initial task is to develop a survey action plan, articulating the survey's purpose, outlining the process, and clarifying roles and expectations, ultimately ensuring progress remains on track and research objectives are achieved (Church and Waclawski, 2001). According to Church and Waclawski (2001), developing a survey action plan involves:

- Articulating the survey's purpose, which should be 'grounded in the broader strategic fabric of the organization' (Church and Waclawski, 2001, p. 28).
- Identifying broad content areas, drawing on identified organisational issues, theoretical frameworks, and empirical research.
- Establishing the availability of human and financial resources to support the survey process.
- Clarifying roles of people involved in the survey process, including who will:
    - i take responsibility for managing the survey process (e.g. a steering committee, university researchers, or a pre-existing organisational group, such as HRM);
    - ii contribute to the survey design;
    - iii assist with survey logistics (e.g. internet and computer security staff, senior managers, local managers); and
    - iv provide expert support (e.g. research design experts and statisticians).
- Identifying who the survey participants will be, and how many participants will be required (ensuring sufficient numbers of respondents while also allowing for non-response).
- Determining whether organisational or local authorities need to be informed about the research (e.g. human research ethics committee).
- Establishing the timeframe and method for data collection, and the analytic strategies employed to interpret the data.

- Identifying the structure that the resulting reports will take and who will be authorised to access the survey results.
- Establishing the nature and timing of actions in response to survey results.

While the action plan provides a solid foundation for the research, decisions made are not final, allowing flexibility to tailor the research to the organisation's needs.

Step 2: building and maintaining stakeholder involvement and support

Initiating and maintaining stakeholder involvement and support is perhaps the most challenging aspect of conducting research. Criminal justice organisations are traditionally hierarchically structured, rely on routine and security, and possess strong cultures that are resistant to change (Sollund, 2005; Wakai et al., 2009). Although these characteristics can facilitate operational functions, they are not always conducive to research activities (Wakai et al., 2009). Criminal justice organisations also tend to be heavily scrutinised by external parties, such as the media, community leaders, and the general public. As a result, surveys may be regarded with suspicion and negatively appraised if there is a perceived risk they will attract additional scrutiny.

Furthermore, whilst some criminal justice occupations, such as police, are 'over-researched,' others, such as correctional officers and judges, generally have less experience working collaboratively with researchers. Gaining involvement and support may be a lengthier and more complex process in under-researched occupations and in over-researched occupations with previous experiences of ineffective research. Additionally, criminal justice organisations often have mandatory reporting requirements in the event of disclosure of illegal or unethical behaviours. This presents a dilemma for researchers if there are open-ended questions, or close-ended questions relating to topics such as crime, misconduct, or harassment in the survey. It may be necessary to ensure that data collected is completely anonymous so that individual responses cannot be traced. Finally, criminal justice occupations traditionally possess 'tough cultures,' characterised by elevated cynicism, mistrust, and stigma associated with admissions of weakness (Dollard and Winefield, 1998; Neveu, 2007). Survey accuracy may be diminished if employees view the intention of the survey with suspicion or cynicism, and may be unwilling to answer questions honestly for fear of punishment or stigma.

Overcoming resistance to research is challenging but necessary, as research fails to have a significant impact unless it is 'endorsed by organizational members' and integrated within existing organisational frameworks (Church and Waclawski, 2001, p. 27). For survey research, stakeholder involvement and support facilitates the development of an accurate and relevant survey instrument, a smooth data collection process, an acceptable response rate, and increases the adoption of research-based recommendations. At the outset of any research project, consideration must be given to initiating and maintaining involvement and support (Biggs and Brough, 2015a).

The endorsement of *senior managers* is essential as they have the capacity to allocate resources and facilitate organisational change, and their expressed support infuses the survey with credibility and significance (Church and Waclawski, 2001; Wakai *et al.*, 2009). As criminal justice occupations are hier-archically structured, a top-down approach to gaining support and involvement is particularly important. Identifying senior managers with autonomy over organisational decisions and resources, obtaining their approval to conduct the research, and ensuring that the proposed research will benefit staff and support the mission of the organisation are effective strategies for increasing their support (Apa *et al.*, 2012; Wakai *et al.*, 2009).

The process of attaining managerial support for surveys within hierarchical, multifaceted organisations is additionally complicated when separate organisa-tional entities, such as police regions or correctional facilities, are managed autonomously by *local managers*. While it is important to first obtain senior management's support, it does not guarantee the support and engagement of local managers. It may even exacerbate resistance to the research if poor com-munication or conflict exists amongst the various levels of management and organisational entities (Biggs, 2011; Biggs and Brough, 2015a).

Resistance expressed by senior and local managers is often due to concerns that (a) resources required to conduct a survey are better invested elsewhere; (b) nega-tivity expressed by employees will be unduly directed at them; and (c) they will be pressured to action recommendations, despite them being expensive, implausible, or beyond their control (Church and Waclawski, 2001). As mentioned above, resistance may be exacerbated when conflict or poor communication exists between organisational entities. Strategies to deal with resistance include:

- Outline the process of developing, distributing, analysing, and reporting results for the survey, and the resources required for each stage.
- Include both senior and local manager representatives as co-investigators, seeking their feedback and making reasonable modifications at their request. (Apa et al., 2012)
- Be clear about what the survey can realistically achieve.
- Discuss strategies for dealing with feedback from employees and managing employee expectations.
- Develop strategies for managing competing interests of different managers, for example, by emphasising mutual goals and benefits or engaging a professional facilitator.

In addition to senior and local managers, it may be necessary to obtain the endorsement of relevant unions. Involving unions, in addition to managers and employee representatives, increases the likelihood that survey outcomes will be actioned appropriately within the organisation (Dollard and Metzer, 1999). Dollard and Winefield (1994), for example, discuss a study commissioned by the South Australian Government that used a survey to identify sources of stress experienced by Australian correctional officers. The researchers engaged in a consultative process to develop research methods and subsequent recommendations: specifically, a committee was formed that included managerial, employee, and union representatives. The success of the research was attributed to the researchers' attempts to gain an understanding of the research context, consultation with stakeholders prior to and throughout the research, and reciprocal education regarding important issues that occurred as a result of the consultation.

Finally, obtaining the support and involvement of employees, who usually comprise the research sample, is invaluable: without it, meaningful assessment and organisational change cannot be accomplished (Church and Waclawski, 2001). Some strategies to engage front-line employees include:

- Market the survey effectively to enhance awareness of the survey's objectives and expected outcomes, as well as its relevance to employees' work situations. For example, conducting information sessions that provide opportunities to ask questions and meet researchers can be beneficial.
- Allow employees to have input in the process. For example, conduct focus groups to identify issues of importance to the employees or establish a steering committee, comprising representatives from different employee groups, to help oversee the process (Church and Waclawski, 2001).
- Uphold the ethical conduct of the survey, particularly the voluntary and confidential nature of the research, as any actual or suspected breach of confidentiality will limit the survey's credibility and validity (Church and Waclawski, 2001).
- Understand and abide by the rules and procedures, which may vary slightly at each facility. Having a local contact within each facility can assist with this (Apa et al., 2012; Wakai et al., 2009).
- Plan research activities in a manner that avoids disrupting or overburdening employees. Within criminal justice occupations, this is not limited to actual research participation but includes additional demands such as the provision of security for researchers when undertaking on-site visits (Wakai et al., 2009).
- Since participating in research generates an expectation that change will occur, communicate realistically the anticipated outcomes and limitations to avoid building unrealistic expectations (Church and Waclawski, 2001).

Overall, it is important to effectively manage the involvement and participation of multiple stakeholders throughout the research process. It needs to be emphasised, however, that stakeholder involvement should be balanced with the need for a scientifically valid and reliable research process. For example, it may be important to negotiate upfront that researchers will retain ultimate responsibility for technical aspects of the survey content, to ensure that the psychometric integrity of measures is maintained.

Step 3: survey design

The quality of data collected and organisational initiatives based on the results is largely dependent on the quality of the survey instrument (Rogelberg *et al.*, 2004). Below we discuss some key considerations for survey design, including (a) selecting measures, (b) including open-ended questions, (c) integrating occupation and generic questions, and (d) continuity and flexibility of survey content.

Selecting measures

Measures are either sourced from existing literature or developed specifically for the research. The legitimacy of the findings may be undermined if measures are included that have not been subjected to psychometric testing, which is the process undertaken to establish whether the measure is valid and reliable (Ginty, 2013). A measure is valid if it accurately measures the construct it is intended to measure and reliable if it consistently produces the same result each time it is administered (Carmines and Zeller, 1979). Therefore, it is preferable to draw on existing measures, which have already undergone psychometric testing, unless organisational researchers possess the skills and resources to develop scientifically robust new measures (Kelley *et al.*, 2003). The following guidelines can assist with selecting measures for inclusion in the survey:

- Conduct a literature search to identify established measures relevant to the survey (Kelley *et al.*, 2003).
- Consider the psychometric properties of the measures, including their reliability and validity.
- Check that items are specific, clear, and concise, appropriate for the research sample, and free of jargon and bias (Church and Waclawski, 2001).

It is also recommended that pilot testing with a small sample of employees be conducted in order to identify errors, especially if new questions were developed for the survey (Kelley *et al.*, 2003).

Including open-ended questions

Surveys predominantly contain close-ended questions, in which employees are instructed to select the most relevant option from a list of predetermined responses (Mrug, 2010). Close-ended questions are easy to administer, code, and analyse, and enable comparisons with established norms (Kelley *et al.*, 2003; Mrug, 2010). However, it can be useful to supplement close-ended questions with a small number of open-ended questions, which allow people to respond 'from their own unique perspective instead of being forced into the response options that are driven by the paradigm of the survey practitioner or design team' (Church and Waclawski, 2001, p. 66). Open-ended questions can be general or specific (e.g. 'Do you have any additional concerns that have not been covered in this survey?'), and are particularly useful when there is a need to clarify perceptions of specific workplace issues or to generate novel solutions to unique/new issues. Qualitative responses to these questions are coded using similar methods to those discussed in Chapter 8.

Occupation-specific and generic measures

It may be beneficial to measure perceptions of *generic* aspects of work applicable to a wide range of occupations in addition to *unique* work characteristics experienced by criminal justice employees (i.e. occupation-specific measures). Studies conducted in criminal justice occupations have demonstrated the value of measuring both generic and occupation-specific perceptions of work (Biggs, 2011; Brough and Biggs, 2015). In her Australian survey research with correctional employees, for example, Biggs (2011) found that both generic work demands (e.g. problem-solving and monitoring job demands) and occupation-specific stressors (e.g. fear of allegations by offenders) predicted levels of employee work engagement, burnout, and psychological strain. Furthermore, job resources (high levels of support and job control) attenuated the effect of occupation-specific stressors on work-related outcomes, but did not reduce the negative effect of generic stressors. As noted above, it is preferable to draw on existing measures that have been subjected to psychometric testing, and several measures have been established for criminal justice occupation-specific stressors. It may be necessary to develop new measures when existing measures are not suitable, however, and it is recommended that this process be conducted in collaboration with appropriately skilled researchers.

Striking a balance between consistency and flexibility

When collecting data on a regular basis, maintaining some consistency in the questions over time is recommended. This provides baseline data for monitoring purposes and enables the detection of significant changes in employee perceptions. At the same time, it is advisable to allow some flexibility over the content, in order for emerging issues to be evaluated, such as the introduction of new processes, policies, or technology. Biggs *et al.* (2014b) adopted this approach in their research investigating the impact of a natural disaster on police officers' levels of psychological health and well-being. The natural disaster occurred in the month prior to an annual organisation-wide survey, and Biggs *et al.* included additional questions in what effectively became the 'post-disaster' survey. Due to the consistency of measures on work characteristics and well-being assessed annually, in addition to allowing some flexibility to integrate new items, the researchers were able to evaluate the impact of involvement in the disaster relief effort on well-being and performance, *while controlling for baseline values of these measures*. The ability to control for baseline or prior levels of well-being and performance allowed a comparison between post-disaster levels of these outcomes compared to pre-disaster values of these outcomes, which were measured under more 'normal' circumstances. This provided a much stronger test of causality for observing the effects of exposure to a natural disaster, demonstrating the value of balancing consistency with flexibility of measures and pre- and post-research designs. The value of pre- and post-research designs for evaluation purposes is discussed in greater detail in Chapter 7.

Step 4: survey distribution

Sample size

Determining the required sample size relies on several factors including: (a) availability of resources; (b) research purpose; and (c) planned statistical analysis (Kelley *et al.*, 2003). The number of surveys to be distributed can then be calculated based on the required sample size, taking into account the proportion of drop-out or non-response that is expected. Research within criminal justice organisations typically generates response rates of approximately 30 per cent (Biggs *et al.*, 2014a, 2014b, 2014c, 2014d), so a distribution of three times the required *respondent* sample size is generally recommended.

Distribution methods

Surveys can be distributed via post, online, in person, or by telephone, with advantages and disadvantages associated with each method (see Kelley *et al.*, 2003; Mrug, 2010). Electronic surveys are now commonly used, and numerous software options are available to develop them. Although earlier research indicated that electronic methods produced lower response rates in comparison to traditional paper-based surveys, more recent research has shown that disparate response rates are now infrequent, as computer literacy and access have improved. For example, Saunders (2012) reported that response rates for electronic surveys were greater than paper-based surveys (49.1 per cent and 33.5 per cent respectively), even after taking into account the higher rate of partially completed and abandoned responses for the electronic surveys.

Electronic surveys, therefore, provide an effective and resource-efficient method for conducting research in large populations of employees (Saunders, 2012; Trau *et al.*, 2013). Electronic surveys automate many research processes, including data entry and some basic reporting, and also provide additional information that paper-based surveys cannot, such as rates of partial completions and time spent completing the survey. They are particularly suited to research conducted in geographically remote worksites, such as rural police stations and correctional facilities. Recommendations for using electronic surveys in criminal justice occupations include:

- Use electronic surveys only when employees are sufficiently computer literate and all staff have computing access at work.

- Liaise with internet and computing staff to ensure the organisation's spam filters are not set to reject emails containing survey links and that employees are able to access external websites hosting the survey software.
- Non-response is likely to occur if employees fail to notice survey invitations in their inbox, which commonly occurs in workplaces with a high volume of emails. Saunders (2012) recommends promoting the survey so employees know to expect it, ensuring the subject line for electronic survey invitations stands out, and avoid distributing survey invitations from email addresses that routinely send 'all staff' emails.
- Data collected via online survey software is likely to be stored on servers of the company owning the survey software. It is essential to consider who will have access to the data, how the data will be stored, who will own the data, and how participants' privacy will be protected.
- As many organisations monitor internet usage, and online software usually records IP addresses, survey respondents may be concerned about their anonymity (Trau *et al.*, 2013). This concern will be exacerbated if employees also mistrust the organisation's intentions for collecting data. These concerns can undermine the validity and accuracy of the data and should be carefully considered (Saunders, 2012).
- Avoid using forced response options, so that employees are free to skip questions they do not wish to answer them all.

Number and timing of survey distributions

Surveys can be conducted on a single occasion (cross-sectional) or repeated on multiple occasions (longitudinal). Cross-sectional surveys are useful for quickly assessing attitudes towards a particular work-related event or issue, testing a measure's psychometric properties, and establishing prevalence/incidence rates. For most organisational purposes, however, it is preferable to conduct longitudinal surveys:

- Organisational researchers are usually interested in understanding dynamic, cyclical processes, for example, how job demands impact on well-being, and how well-being in turn affects future working conditions. Longitudinal surveys are more suitable for accurately measuring dynamic processes as they involve several points of data collection (Edwards, 1992).
- Longitudinal surveys clarify whether a variable is a predictor or outcome; this distinction is important because correctly identifying predictors and outcomes informs the type of intervention required, ultimately determining the intervention's effectiveness (Eatough and Spector, 2013).
- Longitudinal surveys provide an indication of whether employee attitudes are within a normal range or are unusually positive or negative as a result of temporary or atypical circumstances (de Lange *et al.*, 2003; Edwards, 1992).
- Longitudinal surveys detect stability and change in perceived working conditions, which is useful for evaluating interventions (Eatough and Spector, 2013). Chapter 7 discusses evaluations in further detail.

The timing of survey distributions and the interval between the survey distributions should be carefully considered to avoid over-surveying employees, while still accurately measuring processes of interest to organisational researchers (Biggs and Brough, 2015b).

Step 5: data analysis

The most appropriate data analytic method depends on the design of the survey and the type of data collected (Kelley *et al.*, 2003). For qualitative data obtained from open-ended questions, techniques such as content analysis may be used (see Chapter 8). For quantitative data obtained from close-ended questions, there are many analytic strategies available. For example:

- Descriptive statistics can be used to observe the frequencies of responses to questions compared to established norms (e.g. the proportion of employees who report high compared to very low work engagement).
- Differences across employee subgroups can be calculated with an analysis of variance (e.g. it may be of interest to compare level of work engagement across police functions).
- The impact of several independent variables on a single dependent variable can be compared using multiple hierarchical regression analysis (e.g. examining the relative impact of job demands and job resources on work engagement, while controlling for personality.

There are many more analytic strategies available; a detailed discussion of these is beyond the scope of this book, and several resources have been provided at the end of this chapter. It is recommended that statistical experts are consulted from the outset of the research to assist with analysing the data.

Step 6: reporting and taking action

Participation in research requires an investment of organisational and individual resources, and failure to report results, take action, or explain inaction is considered to be unethical and detrimental to future research endeavours (Rogelberg *et al.*, 2004). Usually, a top-down approach for reporting results is adopted, starting with senior managers, followed by middle-level managers, employee representative groups (e.g. HRM and unions), and employees. It is particularly important that the participants themselves have access to feedback of the outcomes of research, to show that the time they spent completing the survey resulted in tangible outcomes. Results can be communicated in a variety of formats, including presentations, meetings, hard-copy reports, electronic reports, or newsletters. It is important to emphasise that results are based on grouped data, and results for any sub-group of employees (e.g. comparisons between police stations) will only be reported when sufficient responses are provided in order to prevent individual identification (e.g. ten officers per station). Any organisational initiatives or actions taken as a result of the survey should be clearly communicated to stakeholders (Rogelberg *et al.*, 2004). Furthermore, the effect of any new initiatives or changes should be evaluated to determine their impact.

Survey difficulties and misuses

The accuracy and utility of organisational research is often undermined by the misuse and overuse of surveys, particularly those requiring employees to provide information regarding *their own* work-related opinions and experiences (i.e. self-report (SR) surveys; Eatough and Spector, 2013). Criticisms frequently focus on the sole use of SR surveys to assess aspects of the external work environment (Eatough and Spector, 2013). First, data collected from a single source (e.g. employee) using a single method (e.g. SR survey), can lead to biased results by overestimating the causal relationship between predictors (e.g. demands) and outcomes (e.g. strain). Second, information obtained from SR surveys is often treated as an accurate and objective report of the external work environment, rather than a collection of individual perceptions *which the respondents are willing to reveal* (Eatough and Spector, 2013).

Strategies to overcome these criticisms include: (a) supplementing SR surveys with data from other sources (e.g. colleagues, supervisors, subordinates, clients, organisational records); (b) using alternative methods of data collection (e.g. job analysis to assess demands, physiological measures of strain); and (c) collecting longitudinal data (e.g. Eatough and Spector, 2013; Spector *et al.*, 2000). Drawing on multiple sources/methods will either provide evidence consistent with SR data that strengthens conclusions, or contradict results, suggesting conclusions should be interpreted cautiously. In addition, when interpreting and reporting SR survey results, remember the data reflects individual perceptions that may deviate from reality (Eatough and Spector, 2013).

Finally, low response rates compromise the quality and impact of survey results, as they reduce the likelihood that results reflect the opinions of the wider organisational population (Baruch and Holtom, 2008; Kelley *et al.*, 2003; Saunders, 2012). Low response rates are especially concerning when non-response is linked to aspects of work that are specifically measured by the survey. For example, if only employees with low work demands respond to a survey about the effect of job demands on strain, the results are likely to be biased. Therefore, it is important to aim for higher response rates to maximise the accuracy and utility of the survey's findings. Specific strategies include:

- Consider a non-coercive incentive for participation, such as a small incentive for all respondents, a random prize draw, or collective incentives for workgroups/regions with the highest response rates. Lambert and Paoline (2008), for instance, obtained a response rate of 70 per cent by providing correctional personnel with a monetary incentive and conducting multiple face-to-face survey administrations to cover all shifts.

- Avoid scheduling surveys when a high volume of staff are likely to be absent from work or during periods of intense work demands (e.g. end of financial year). Ghaddar *et al.* (2008), for instance, noted a high rate of non-response coincided with a period in which 28 per cent of correctional personnel were absent.
- Clearly communicate the purpose and relevance of the survey, and report results back to stakeholders in a timely manner.
- Keep surveys brief to avoid overloading employees.
- Develop a strategic organisational survey plan to avoid conducting multiple surveys. Many organisations conduct multiple surveys containing overlapping content, which could be combined to reduce the volume of surveys.
- Offer employees the opportunity to complete the survey during work hours. It may be necessary to provide frontline employees with a break from duties for this purpose.
- Send out survey completion reminders.
- Maintain high ethical standards, especially in relation to confidentiality.
- Draw on existing infrastructure to assist with distributing surveys and collecting data. For example, Neveu (2007) obtained a response rate of 57 per cent by enlisting the support of medical teams who worked directly with, and were highly trusted by, correctional employees. The medical teams distributed and collected the surveys from officers when they attended for routine medical check-ups.

Conclusion

Surveys are a useful means for collecting data from large, representative samples of employees. This chapter outlined a systematic approach to administering surveys in criminal justice occupations, and provided suggestions for avoiding common pitfalls. Surveys are particularly effective when the focus of the research is assessing employee perceptions of their working environment. Drawing on additional sources of data and utilising alternative data collection methods to supplement self-report surveys is recommended, however, when the purpose of the research is to assess more objective features of the work environment (Eatough and Spector, 2013).

References

Apa, Z.L., Bai, R., Dhritiman, V.M., Herzig, C.T.A., Koenigsmann, C., Lowy, F.D., and Larson, E.L. (2012) Challenges and strategies for research in prisons. *Public Health Nursing*, 29(5): 467–472. doi:10.1111/j.1525–1446.2012.01027.x.

Baruch, Y., and Holtom, B.C. (2008) Survey response rate levels and trends in organizational research. *Human Relations*, 61(8): 1139–1160. doi:10.1177/0018726708094863.

Biggs, A. (2011) *A longitudinal evaluation of strain, work engagement, and intervention strategies to address the health of high-risk employees.* Doctoral Thesis, Griffith University, Brisbane.

Biggs, A., and Brough, P. (2015a) Challenges of intervention acceptance in complex, multifaceted organizations: the importance of local champions. In Karanika-Murray, M. and Biron, C. (eds) *Derailed organizational stress and well-being interventions: confessions of failure and solutions for success.* London: Springer (pp. 151–158).

Biggs, A., and Brough, P. (2015b) Explaining intervention success and failure: what works, when, and why? In Karanika-Murray, M. and Biron, C. (eds) *Derailed organizational stress and well-being interventions: confessions of failure and solutions for success.* London: Springer (pp. 237–244).

Biggs, A., Brough, P., and Barbour, J.P. (2014a) Enhancing work-related attitudes and work engagement: a quasi-experimental study of the impact of a leadership development intervention. *International Journal of Stress Management,* 21(1): 43–68. doi:10.1037/a0034508.

Biggs, A., Brough, P., and Barbour, J.P. (2014b) Exposure to extraorganizational stressors: impact on mental health and organizational perceptions for police officers. *International Journal of Stress Management,* 21(3): 255–282. doi:10.1037/a0037297.

Biggs, A., Brough, P., and Barbour, J.P. (2014c) Relationships of individual and organizational support with engagement: examining various types of causality in a three-wave study. *Work and Stress,* 28(3): 236–254. doi:10.1080/02678373.2014.934316.

Biggs, A., Brough, P., and Barbour, J.P. (2014d) Strategic alignment with organizational priorities and work engagement: a multi-wave analysis. *Journal of Organizational Behavior,* 35(3): 301–317. doi:10.1002/job.1866.

Brough, P., and Biggs, A. (2015) Job demands x job control interaction effects: do occupation-specific job demands increase their occurrence? *Stress and Health,* 31(2): 138–149. doi:10.1002/smi.2537.

Brown, J., Campbell, E.A., and Fife-Shaw, C. (1995) Adverse impacts experienced by police officers following exposure to sex discrimination and sexual harassment. *Stress and Health,* 11(1): 221–228. doi:10.1002/smi.2460110137.

Carmines, E.G., and Zeller, R.A. (1979) *Reliability and validity assessment.* Thousand Oaks, CA: SAGE.

Church, A.H., and Waclawski, J. (2001) *Designing and using organizational surveys: a seven-step process.* San Fransisco, CA: Jossey-Bass.

de Lange, A.H., Taris, T.W., Kompier, M.A.J., Houtman, I.L.D., and Bongers, P.M. (2003) 'The *very* best of the millennium': longitudinal research and the demand-control-(support) model. *Journal of Occupational Health Psychology,* 8(4): 282–305. doi:10.1037/1076–8998.8.4.282.

Dollard, M.F., and Metzer, J.C. (1999) Psychological research, practice, and production: the occupational stress problem. *International Journal of Stress Management,* 6(4): 241–253. doi:10.1023/A:1021988204290.

Dollard, M.F., and Winefield, A.H. (1994) Organizational responses to recommendations based on a study of stress among correctional officers. *International Journal of Stress Management,* 1: 81–101.

Dollard, M.F., and Winefield, A.H. (1998) A test of the demand-control/support model of work stress in correctional officers. *Journal of Occupational Health Psychology,* 3(3): 243–264.

Eatough, E.M., and Spector, P.E. (2013) Quantitative self-report methods in occupational health psychology research. In Sinclair, R.R., Wang, M., and Tetrick, L.E. (eds) *Research methods in occupational health psychology: measurement, design, and analysis.* New York: Routledge (pp. 248–267).

Edwards, J.R. (1992) A cybernetic theory of stress, coping, and well-being in organizations. *Academy of Management Review,* 17: 238–274.

Ghaddar, A., Mateo, I., and Sanchez, P. (2008) Occupational stress and mental health among correctional officers: a cross-sectional study. *Journal of Occupational Health*, 50: 92–98.

Ginty, A. (2013) Psychometric properties. In Gellman, M. and Turner, J.R. (eds) *Encyclopedia of behavioral medicine*: New York: Springer (pp. 1563–1564).

Hough, M., and Roberts, J. (1998) *Attitudes to punishment: findings from the British Crime Survey*. London: Home Office.

Kelley, K., Clark, B., Brown, V., and Sitzia, J. (2003) Good practice in the conduct and reporting of survey research. *International Journal for Quality in Health Care*, 15(3): 261–266. doi:http://dx.doi.org/10.1093/intqhc/mzg031.

Lambert, E.G., and Paoline, E.A., III. (2008) The influence of individual, job, and organizational characteristics on correctional staff job stress, job satisfaction, and organizational commitment. *Criminal Justice Review*, 33(4): 541–564.

Mrug, S. (2010) Survey. In Salkind, N.J. (ed.) *Encyclopedia of research design*. Thousand Oaks, CA: SAGE. http://dx.doi.org.libraryproxy.griffith.edu.au/10.4135/9781412961288.n449.

Neveu, J. (2007) Jailed resources: conservation of resource theory as applied to burnout among prison guards. *Journal of Organizational Behaviour*, 28: 21–42.

Rogelberg, S.G., Church, A.H., Waclawski, J., and Stanton, J.M. (2004) Organizational survey research. *Handbook of research methods in industrial and organizational psychology*. Malden, MA: Blackwell Publishing (pp. 141–160).

Saunders, M.N.K. (2012) Web versus mail: The influence of survey distribution mode on employees' response. *Field Methods*, 24(1): 56–73. doi:10.1177/1525822X11419104.

Sollund, R. (2005) Obstacles and possibilities in police research. *Outlines. Critical Practice Studies*, 7(2), 43–64. http://ojs.statsbiblioteket.dk/index.php/outlines/article/view/2103.

Spector, P.E., Zapf, D., Chen, P.Y., and Frese, M. (2000) Why negative affectivity should not be controlled in job stress research: don't throw out the baby with the bath water. *Journal of Organizational Behavior*, 21(1): 79–95.

Trau, R.N.C., Härtel, C.E.J., and Härtel, G.F. (2013) Reaching and hearing the invisible: organizational research on invisible stigmatized groups via web surveys. *British Journal of Management*, 24: 532–541. doi:10.1111/j.1467–8551.2012.00826.x.

Wakai, S., Shelton, D., Trestman, R.L., and Kesten, K. (2009) Conducting research in corrections: challenges and solutions. *Behavioral Sciences and the Law*, 27: 743–752. doi:10.1002/bsl.894.

Additional resources

Field, A.P. (2013) *Discovering statistics using IBM SPSS statistics: and sex and drugs and rock 'n' roll*. Los Angeles: SAGE.

Tabachnick, B.G., and Fidell, L.S. (2013) *Using multivariate statistics*. Boston: Pearson.

11 Delphi technique

Introduction

As uncertainty increases decision-making becomes more difficult. Previous chapters of this book have argued that criminal justice agencies are subject to economic stringencies and face reform pressures exerted by governments. Chief officers and senior managers, under conditions of crisis, often have short planning horizons and may formulate strategies that serve themselves rather than the public's best interests (Linstone, 2002). While the range of solutions to be considered can be large, chief officers can reduce their attentional focus and resort to trusted and tried solutions, thereby narrowing down and avoiding more creative possibilities. The Delphi technique offers a decision-making method to dispel uncertainty and increase consideration of a wide range of alternatives. Developed in the late 1940s by the RAND Corporation, the Delphi method is a way to solicit expert opinion and achieve a consensus. In essence there are a series of sequential questionnaires or 'rounds' interspersed by controlled feedback that seek agreement from a group of experts (Powell, 2003). There are four key features of the method:

1 anonymity of the expert participants in order that they may freely express their opinions;
2 ability to refine views in the light of information received;
3 receipt of controlled feedback to inform participants of the collective's views; and
4 statistical collation of responses.

Informal methods attempting to gain some unanimity of view are prone to domination by powerful individuals or bias through particular personality traits or seniority. The Delphi method avoids these pitfalls and has been adopted many thousands of times on a whole range of problem areas, particularly in the health sector (Powell, 2002). Criminal justice applications are exemplified by:

- effects of a declining economy on crime and the criminal justice system (Wright, 1982);

- strategic policy development in the police (Loo, 2002);
- future developments in crime trends (Loyens *et al.*, 2011);
- improving the care of aging prisoners (Patterson *et al.*, 2014);
- identification of key professionals who can undertake case formulation of personality disorder offenders (Völlm, 2014).

In this chapter we briefly describe the Delphi technique, draw attention to its strengths and weakness, and present a detailed case study examining how in practical terms the police service can instil organisational justice regimes in the workplace.

The Delphi technique

The name Delphi was taken from Greek mythology referring to the consulting of the oracle to forecast the future (Loo, 2002). Developed by the RAND Corporation as a way to use expert opinion to improve policy making, the Delphi method was originally employed to forecast the Soviet Union's policy in order to estimate the number of atomic bombs the USA would need for its defence. The method structures and facilitates communication between experts who focus on a problem and come to a view about the best options for future development. The method comprises six key components:

1   A sample of experts representing a broad range of opinion on the topic at issue is identified to make up a panel.
2   The participants remain unknown to each other as the consultation is conducted remotely.
3   A moderator (often the researcher) constructs a series of questionnaires which are sent individually to the panel members and who …
4   Collates feedback from the answers to the first questionnaire from which the next questionnaire is developed and sent back to the panel.
5   Several rounds of the questionnaire responses are collated and sent to the participants.
6   The outcome is usually in the form of a report which forecasts a policy direction with recommendations to management and often includes an implementation plan.

Advantages and disadvantages

The Delphi approach provides a means of generating objective and authoritative solutions (Loo, 2002; Powell, 2002). Its main advantage is that a high level of agreement is reached in areas of uncertainty or where there is a lack of empirical evidence. It is a relatively quick (there are no co-ordination problems of trying to get the relevant people together in the same place and at the same time) and cheap method (travel and subsidence costs are unnecessary), and it offers an efficient way to combine the knowledge and abilities of a group of experts (by means of an iterative process). As Loo (2002) declared, Delphi virtually eliminates interpersonal conflicts and power plays because the panel members do not interact. Indeed, Delphi has been referred to as a method of last resort when dealing with complex problems for which there is no obvious or available solution (Linstone, 2002). Anonymity reduces the risk of reaching an artificial consensus and protects participants from social conformity pressures so that they give their opinions freely without fear of criticism and provides an opportunity to offer divergent views (Loyens *et al.*, 2011).

The technique does require a degree of resilience from the panel members (Linstone, 2002) as the rounds can become quite onerous. Respondents may be under time constraints to answer quickly without adequate thought. The outcomes are only as good as the expertise of the panel members and these may not always be chosen appropriately. Anonymity can be a disadvantage as well as an advantage, as the source of the statement is what gives it its authority (see Chapter 5 on the principles of good communication). Some experts may wish to have personal recognition for their contribution and be unwilling to participate in an exercise that does not reveal their identity. The exercise may not be run well and there can be a poor interaction between the moderator and participants. The original problem formulation may be 'sloppy'. If the problem is either over-specified or too vague, the information produced by the experts may be compromised. Linstone also suggested a potential weakness lies with superficial analysis of responses, or an over-selling of the power of the analysis.

Powell (2002) explained that Delphi methodologies do not use conventional scientific criteria of reliability and validity. Instead evaluation is made through 'goodness' criteria such as the clarity of the decision trail to defend the appropriateness of applying the method and choice of experts. Face validity can be applied in terms of the usefulness and applicability of the recommendations. Collection of parallel data and triangulation with the expert views presents an evaluation option.

The proof of the efficacy of Delphi forecasting is in its usefulness and success. The Delhi forecast made in the Wright (1982) study predicting the direction of the economy and its implications for crime did remarkably well both as a short- and long-term forecast. The experts in this case were pessimistic about the economy and that there would be low growth and significant unemployment. They thought personal crime would result in a small but significant increase. They were wrong in their prediction that property crime would increase in times of recession. They also thought pressures wrought by a downturn in the economy would have an adverse impact on the criminal justice agencies abilities to deliver services, especially public defenders, probation, and parole officers. They predicted a decrease in the use of probation and increases in incarceration rates. Overall, Delphi has proven to be a useful and flexible tool to aid decision-making and policy development under conditions of uncertainty. Clayton (1997) concluded that, notwithstanding some of its limitations, Delphi offers a viable means to harness expert opinion, results in a tangible set of recommendations, and helps focus dissent as well as agreement.

A case study

Background

As part of the work of the Independent Police Commission (2011–2013) chaired by Lord Stevens (a former Commissioner of the London's Metropolitan Police Service) it was felt important to offer a tangible programme for action. The Commission had identified organizational procedural justice – the extent to which supervisors and senior managers treat staff with dignity and respect, explain their decisions, act in a neutral and transparent manner and allow staff an input into decision-making processes – as a key influence not only on 'staff-satisfaction', but also in relation to people's readiness to work on behalf of organizations, comply with rules and regulations, and their attitudes towards those they serve (Independent Police Commission, 2013).

The Commission carried out a survey of police officer and police support staff in England and Wales in October 2012 and March 2013 respectively. A suite of questions probing the respondent's sense of procedural and other aspects of organisational justice were included in the two surveys administered to 15,554 police officers and $N=5,455$ police staff respectively. Results from the procedural justice survey questions are shown in Table 11.1. A range of opinions were

Table 11.1 Responses to procedural justice items

Organisational issues	Experienced little/none of the time – police officers (%)	Experienced little/none of the time – police staff (%)
Promotion being achieved purely on merit	65	50
Have the sense you can influence decisions	62	70
Good quality communication within the organisation	57	50
Explanations for decisions made by managers	53	49
Equal distribution of work such that no one is carrying an unfair load	44	30
Openness and honesty in way managed	41	38
Fair, consistent, and impartial decision making	39	34
Fair and respectful interpersonal contact amongst officers and staff	18	15

reported, with officers least happy with the fairness of promotion exercises, whilst police support staff were most exercised about not having a voice in decision–making processes.

Our further analyses found that police officers who felt their organisation behaved in a just and fair manner were more likely to think their police service concentrates on doing the right things, are more likely to rate themselves as close to their force's values, and less likely to have considered leaving the service. The statistical effects were both significant and substantively quite large, most notably, officers who felt they experienced more organisational justice at work were also more likely to be supportive of new arrangement for the democratic oversight of policing.

For police staff it was found that respondents who felt fairly treated by their managers were more likely to believe that their organization was legitimate. Second, when these respondents believed that the public received fair treatment, they were also more likely to believe the police service 'did the right thing', was free of corruption, and did a good job overall. Police staff respondents who reported unfair relationships between staff were more likely to think that there were higher degrees of corruption within the organisation. It seems that difficult relationships between staff may indeed, at times, damage the legitimacy of the organisation. When police staff do not feel fairly treated there is a greater sense that it is time to change one's job. Equally, feeling unsupported by managers, co-workers and others makes employees afraid for their jobs, whether they wish to leave them or not. In the light of these survey findings, it was felt important to present some solutions in helping to make the police working environment a fairer one and also to explore a positive framework within which change can take place. This is a relatively new area and as yet, little research has been published either describing how to inculcate a procedurally fair regime or evaluate its effects once implemented within policing (but see Bradford *et al.*, 2014). Accordingly a Delphi consultation was undertaken.

Administering the Delphi rounds

In the first instance there is a requirement to focus on the research problem. In the present consultation this can be stated in two parts as:

a   identification of processes and procedures to create a fair working environment for police officer and police staff; and
b   formulation of a framework in which change can take place effectively.

The research problem derived from the procedural justice literature (see Chapter 2 for a summary) and the empirical findings of the two surveys (an extract from which is reported in Table 11.1). In essence this Delphi procedure focused on how the police could create greater fairness around promotion, distribution of workloads, flexible working, participation in decision-making, and being given explanations for decisions made. A sample of experts was approached from specialists who were members of the Police reference group from the Chartered Institute of Personnel Development (CIPD). The requirements for expert selection were:

- knowledge of and expertise in the issues under investigation;
- capacity and willingness to participate;
- sufficient time to participate;
- effective communication skills.

A total of eight experts were recruited to take part. Table 11.2 describes their areas of expertise.

The data collection was undertaken through a series of steps.

Table 11.2 Expertise of panel members in Delphi consultation

Experts	Area of expertise
Expert 1	HR generalist, culture and change management, employee engagement, internal communication
Expert 2	Organisational design, leadership development, change management
Expert 3	Strategic HR, change management, structural and cultural, employee relations, learning and development, performance management
Expert 4	All areas of HR and learning and development, resourcing and recruiting, learning and development, HR Systems, performance and talent management, business transformations and culture change
Expert 5	Change management, business transformation, strategy, leadership
Expert 6	Head of change, organisational development, service improvement and performance
Expert 7	Employee relations, change management, employee engagement, workforce planning
Expert 8	Learning and development, occupational health, organisational development, change design

Step 1: sending a communication (in this case an email) to each volunteer from the expert group with the round one questionnaire

This comprised a brief rationale for the project, an explanation of the procedure and a request to complete a series of open-ended questions asking their views about a range of procedural organisational justice items solicited from the survey of police officers and staff. The questions asked were as follows.

1   How can the police create a working environment where people feel they are treated fairly in respect of:

   a   positive attitudes to flexible working arrangements?
   b   ensuring equal distribution of workloads?

c   ensure fair and impartial decision-making by managers?
d   encourage managers to explain their decision-making?
e   engage the workforce to participate in decision-making?

2   What are the qualities necessary for:

a   design of effective change?
b   implementation of change?
c   consolidation of change?

3   What would a service look like if it was a truly learning organisation?
4   What features need to be in place to make the police service more professional?
5   What is the best way to embed practice skills?

Step 2: analysis of open ended responses

A qualitative content analysis was devised to reduce the complexity of individual answers and create a usable number of units of response. These broad themes represented the experts' opinions about what parameters should be deployed in creating a procedurally just working environment. The identified themes were:

- communication
- leadership
- values
- process
- engagement
- delivery
- training/competence
- accountability/empowerment.

Step 3: creation of questionnaire for round two

The number of individual suggestions within each theme were reduced to make the next round more manageable. A criterion was established whereby an item was selected if it was mentioned by at least four of the eight participants. Once the questions had been reduced, a copy of a new questionnaire was sent to the experts (round two survey). The experts were asked to rate items in terms of importance of its contribution to procedural fairness, and to the creation of an organisationally just workplace. As an example, our experts were asked to rate the importance of their earlier suggestions in relation to encouraging managers to explain the basis of their decisions to staff (as shown in Figure 11.1).

Thus the experts thought that reducing the macho style as a feature of the working culture and showing greater availability and visibility were key to encouraging explanations of decisions made. Management target setting was thought to be the least helpful. Other key questions asked in round two included

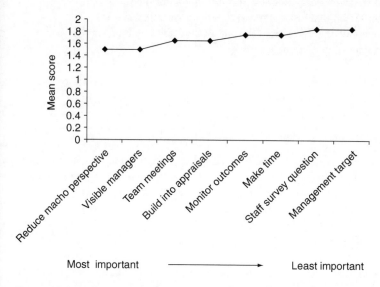

Figure 11.1 Rating importance of items encouraging managers to explain the basis of their decision-making.

Note
The lower the score the greater the rated importance.

identifying the factors that were felt most important when designing fair promotion processes, equitable distribution of workloads, and better decision-making consultation. The experts indicated effective communication, strong leadership, and alignment of values between the organisation and its staff was crucial in managing organisational change.

When asked to indicate what features must be in place to make the police a truly learning organisation, their responses were, in order of importance, as follows:

1   an organisation that is brave enough to admit when it is wrong;
2   making change the norm;
3   a visible performance system that accommodates learning from experimentation but is intolerant of repeated errors and errors of judgement;
4   systems and models that facilitate continuous improvement;
5   a culture of turning mistakes and errors into true learning;
6   fully signing up the newly elected Police and Crime Commissioners (PCC) to the changes;
7   post-implementation review and acceptance of learning thereby gained;
8   better networking with partners;
9   greater sharing of knowledge and information;
10   fewer ad hoc initiatives;
11   buy in to shared goals;

12   all staff to be encouraged to be professionally curious;
13   an organisation that reflects the diversity of those it serves;
14   consistency of short-term and long-term goal setting and tasking;
15   continuous evaluation and re-design.

Key here are the concepts of honesty, transparency, evidence-based practice, and continual professional development.

Step 4: post-Delphi data collection

Once the survey responses from the experts had been collated and rank ordered, the most strongly endorsed items were chosen and a questionnaire comprising these items were then sent to a further sample of serving police officers ($N = 8,738$). The evaluation respondents were asked to make was in terms of how effective they thought the listed suggestions devised by the experts would be in creating a fairer workplace and also factors necessary to permit constructive organisational change. The responses of both the experts and the officers to factors critical in changing their organisation are illustrated in Figure 11.2.

The experts rated investment in training and publishing outcomes as key to organisational change. This is in marked contrast to the workforce who identified effective communication and strong leadership as the most critical elements in orchestrating change. The implication of this finding is that the workforce be involved in designing the means by which change processes can be effectively implicated.

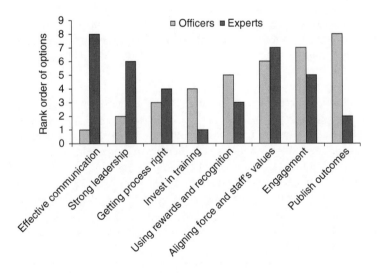

Figure 11.2 Ordering of officers' and experts' rankings of critical factors in organisational change.

Consequently, police officer respondents were asked how effective they thought the experts' suggestions would be in encouraging people to accept change. Their answers are ranked in order:

- acknowledging when things go wrong (50.2 per cent)
- attempting to understand the issues of people who resist change (39.4 per cent)
- creating an environment where people feel it is safe to change (31.7 per cent)
- show the positive sides of the change (25.7 per cent)
- visible leadership modelling the desired behaviours (24.1 per cent)
- having open discussions in which to challenge the views of those who do not accept the change (20.7 per cent)
- creating a positive picture about the future (18.1 per cent)
- send a strong internal message about the reasons for change (14.5 per cent)
- indicate the costs of not changing (14.3 per cent)
- reward those who accept the change (12.3 per cent)
- involve the fence-sitters at an early stage (9.5 per cent)
- find appropriate role models to sway the fence-sitters (7.5)
- use those who accept change as change champions (3.7 per cent).

The figures in brackets are the percentage of respondents who thought these were very effective means to help people accept change. As can be seen, most thought that admitting when things have gone wrong as being most effective, and this relates to a later question in which honesty is felt to be critical in creating a framework in which change takes place. As one respondent commented:

> Clear and honest messages keeping all those involved up to date with changes and decisions. Involving those directly involved in decision-making and/or explanations as to why decisions had to be made without involving those effected.

Some of the experts' suggestions were not met with enthusiastic endorsement, particularly the utilising of change champions or role models. It is important to note these reactions from the workforce rather than simply promoting change mechanisms as thought appropriate by experts. This may mean explaining more carefully what is meant by the term 'change champion', as they may simply be seen as management 'stooges' or modify their use and involve the workforce in their selection. The follow-up survey also asked police officer respondents to endorse those items they felt might be most effective in helping to create a fairer working environment. Table 11.3 lists the top three endorsed activities in each area of work practice.

The police respondents were also asked to endorse the experts' suggestions as to which features would characterise the Police Service as a truly learning organisation. The rank orders of their judgements are compared to those of the experts

Table 11.3 Police officers' views about how to create a procedurally just working environment

Creating fairness in promotion procedures	Training for those involved in the promotion process
	Giving ethical feedback to both successful and unsuccessful candidates
	Mentoring
Flexible working	Managing expectations balancing personal need against those of the organisation
	Making decisions without fear of discrimination claims
	Training for senior managers in flexible working
Distribution of workloads	Better management of poor performers
	Mangers ensuring they make time to monitor and evaluate workloads
	Use of a transparent workload allocation model
Impartial decision-making	Monitoring outcomes and making decisions transparent
	Investing in management/leadership training
	Building decision-making style into a managers appraisal
Explain decisions	Making time for briefings and de-briefings
	Team meetings
	Reduce macho perspective that managers know all the answers
Participate in decision-making	Supporting people who make mistakes
	Have good induction and development programmes for managers
	Build trust

with the result shown in Figure 11.3. Again, whilst there was some overlap, there were some important differences. Interestingly, the experts thought that remaining professionally curious was a key ingredient to being a learning organisation, an attribute not as well endorsed by officers themselves. They thought having change, i.e. continuous improvement, as the norm as crucial. Both experts and officers thought having greater diversity in the workforce was also critical to continuous learning.

Process of change

In the Delphi round a set of questions were asked about the process of change itself: designing, implementing, and consolidating change. It became apparent from the expert's ratings that the change process involves different elements of these three phases of change. What became clear was that the conceptual distinction between the phases was endorsed by the workforce survey participants who, similarly to the experts, recognise and agree that there are different qualities associated with the design, implementation, and consolidation of change (Table 11.4). This is a representation of the workforce's endorsement of the experts' suggestions.

Critical and central to change are inspiring leadership, support for staff, and transparency. At the outset when designing change there must be an honesty of purpose and truth telling to the workforce. During the design phase it is important

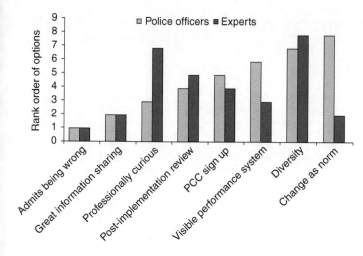

Figure 11.3 Police and experts' rank-ordering of options thought to be needed to make the police a learning organisation.

to develop a range of options, some of which may not be implemented. Identifying the crucial skills and looking for them in people who may not be currently employed in the organisation is also a key preliminary step. Good communication and rapid response is also critically important as is the need to respond quickly to challenges and provide feedback. Appointing people to key roles in implementing change, a willingness to involve staff from all levels and using positive stories to encourage change were all identified as activities likely to achieve change. Having a clear plan and identifying impactful levers were also thought to be ingredients for success. At the consolidation phase, continuous support and training as follow through, as well as humane response to those who may be disadvantaged by the changes, were thought to be the most important.

Conclusion

The Delphi method offers a flexible and relatively quick means to canvas expert opinion, especially in relation to complex or novel problems for which there is relatively little available evidence or information. The case study described in this chapter was drawn from work undertaken on behalf of the Independent Police Commission. The rationale was to develop a concrete set of proposals to help construct a procedurally just workplace for police officers and support staff. Loyens *et al.* (2011) advised several necessary conditions for successful applications of the Delphi method:

- the quality and reputation of the participating experts, i.e. need for a well considered selection phase with appropriate range and reputation of experts;

Table 11.4 Strategies associated with different stages of a change process

	Presumptions	Tools	Response and adjustment
Design	Honest belief in purpose of the change Provision of an honest rationale Key drivers for change identified Desired outcomes clearly stated	Fast response to challenges Good communication	Generate range of options Identify needed skills Secure right people (from outside if necessary) Provide honest feedback
Implement	Right people appointed to key roles	Identify quick wins Clear plan with bite size achievable goals Identify levers having most impact	Willingness to involve all levels of staff in change Use positive stories about value of change and achievements
Consolidate	Good change management systems introduced Personalise solutions found for individuals going through change Constant review and response to change	Use influencing skills of leaders Create sense of urgency about the need to change	Treat people who may be disadvantaged fairly and humanely On-going development of individuals and managers Continuous re-enforcement of positive outcomes

- treat opinions with caution and preferably verify through some form of triangulation;
- high levels of motivation of experts, which can be increased by a face-to-face workshop or by naming the experts in the final report;
- clear communication of ground rules in the several Delphi rounds;
- specification of the maximum duration of each round.

As long as it is remembered that the Delphi method represents informed opinion rather than empirically established fact, it does provide a useful scoping technique especially under conditions of uncertainty. Also, it is important to consult the workforce as well as experts and to be flexible in adjusting processes in the light of feedback.

References

Bradford, B., Quinton, P., Myhill, A., and Porter, G. (2014) Why do 'the law' comply? Procedural justice group identification and officer motivation in police organisations. *European Journal of Criminology*, 11: 110–131.

Clayton, M. (1997) Delphi; a technique to harness expert opinion. *Educational Psychology*, 17: 373–387.

Independent Police Commission (2013) *Policing for a better Britain*. London: The Commission.

Linstone, H.A. (2002) Eight basic pitfalls: a checklist. In Turoff, M. and Linstone, H.A. (eds) *The Delphi method: techniques and applications*. http://is.njit.edu/pubs/delphibook/ accessed 22 January 2015.

Loo, R. (2002) The Delphi method: a powerful tool for strategic management. *Policing: An International Journal of Police Strategies and Management*, 25: 762–769.

Loyens, K., Maesschalck, J., and Bouckaert, G. (2011) Delphi in criminal justice policy: a case study on judgmental forecasting. *Qualitative Report*, 16: 1477–1495.

Patterson, K., Newman, C., and Doona, K. (2014) Improving the care of older persons in Australian prisons using the policy Delphi method. *Dementia*, 13. doi:10.1177/1471301214557531.

Powell, C. (2003) The Delphi technique: myths and realities. *Journal of Advanced Nursing*, 41: 376–382.

Wright, K. (1982) A Delphi assessment of the effects of a declining economy on crime and the criminal justice system. *Federal Probation*, 46: 36–40.

Völlm, B. (2014) Case formulation in personality disordered offenders: a Delphi survey of professionals. *Criminal Behaviour and Mental Health*, 24: 60–80.

Part III

Organisational problems and solutions

12 Sustaining environments
Work–life balance

Introduction

There are a number of reasons why the ability to adequately balance work and family (life) demands (i.e. work–life balance) is an increasingly pertinent issue both for many workers and for employers. For workers regularly employed on shift-work schedules, work–life balance is often especially difficult to achieve, although as we shall see in this chapter, shift-work can also be the *solution* for achieving work–life balance for some employees. In this chapter we describe the key reasons why work–life balance is of increasing concern for criminal justice workplaces. We also examine some innovative practices which some criminal justice workplaces have adopted in an attempt to improve the work–life balance experiences for their employees.

Work–life balance: reasons for due consideration

Over the past three decades, there has been increasing interest in the issue of work–life balance (Brough and O'Driscoll, 2015; O'Driscoll *et al.*, 2006). Reasons for this interest are diverse, and include:

- increased numbers and proportions of women engaging in employment globally;
- changing family structures and orientations toward parenthood;
- newer technologies which have to some extent dissolved work and family boundaries;
- changing employer expectations concerning worker availability and work engagement; and
- shifts in personal values towards a better 'balance' between work responsibilities and non-work commitments and activities.

Consequently, although in previous years it may have been possible for workers to compartmentalise their work and family (non-work) lives into distinct domains, it is clear that this is often no longer viable or, indeed, desirable.

In Chapter 16 we discuss the specific issue of workplace diversity and discrimination within criminal justice workplaces. The issue of work–life balance overlaps with these discussions because work–life balance was initially regarded as a work problem primarily for *female* employees (Brough *et al.*, 2008). For example, numerous organisations commonly introduced 'maternity' leave provisions before the concept of 'paternity' or simply 'parental' leave policies were considered. Importantly, discrimination in this area occurs despite legal guidelines and is commonly attributed to perceptions that an employee who accesses parental leave provisions is fundamentally less committed to work. Common experiences include, for example, dismissal (especially of pregnant women), delays in career advancement, allocation to inferior job roles or responsibilities, unexpected changes to work hours, and hostility from co-workers (Brough and O'Driscoll, 2010; O'Driscoll *et al.*, 2007).

The prevalence of these incidents remains surprisingly high and indeed countries such as the UK, USA, and Australia have recently recorded *increased* rates of discrimination against pregnant women (Morgan *et al.*, 2013; Salihu *et al.*, 2012). For example, in the USA there was a reported 40 per cent increase in pregnancy-bias complaints brought against employers over the 1997–2007 period, with a distinct spike reported in the recent years (EEOC, 2007). Similarly, a UK Equal Opportunities Commission (EOC) report revealed a marked increase in the dismissal of pregnant women and new parents, equating to approximately 30,000 annual job losses (EOC, 2005). The EOC noted that becoming mothers was *the most influential cause of women's inequality in the (UK) labour market*. Pregnancy discrimination in Australia constitutes approximately 20 per cent of submitted sexual discrimination cases, again with observed increases in recent years (Charlesworth and Macdonald, 2007). These statistics draw attention to the reality of work–life *im*balance experienced by some employees.

It is pertinent to acknowledge that work–life balance has now generally become an employment provision more equally sought by *both* male and female workers and, as stated above, this recognition (as well as national employment legislation) has influenced its increased importance in employers' human resource management policies. Indeed, some of the current discussions describe how employee gender differences in relation to the impact of work–life balance are now notably decreasing and, in some cases, are no longer observed (Brough and O'Driscoll, 2015). Thus, both male and female employees are increasingly recognising the benefits of being able to spend time pursuing non-work activities whether family, volunteering, study, sporting, or leisure commitments (Brough *et al.*, 2014).

Organisational benefits of work–life balance

The social and financial benefits to organisations that provide adequate work–life balance human resource policies are well documented. The negative impact of unbalanced multiple life roles upon work attendance and performance, attitudes to work (for example, job commitment and job satisfaction), and work-related health and well-being have been clearly established (for recent reviews see: Brough, O'Driscoll, Kalliath, Cooper, and Poelmans, 2009; Eby, Casper, Lockwood, Bordeaux, and Brinley, 2005). Reports acknowledge that increasing numbers of both male and female employees place a high importance upon the ability to access adequate work–life balance employment provisions and many workers will regularly move to a different organisation which better suits their needs (Brough, O'Driscoll, and Biggs, 2009; O'Driscoll *et al.*, 2011; Eby *et al.*, 2005). Thus both the basic recruitment and retention of employees is significantly influenced by having adequate and accessible work–life balance employment policies.

Work performance is also directly impacted by work–life balance policies which are perceived by an employee to be inadequate and/or inaccessible. One of the main performance consequences is an employee's negative attitudes, typically expressed by job dissatisfaction, work disengagement, and withdrawal behaviours (e.g. lateness, absenteeism; O'Driscoll *et al.*, 2011). Chronically 'toxic' employees who consistently publicise their negative work attitudes produce negative work performance outcomes both for themselves and for their immediate colleagues, including new recruits they may be supervising, as we discussed in Chapter 4.

The specific culture of an organisation, and especially the perceived supportiveness of immediate supervisors, has also been found to influence levels of employee performance and work–life balance. In this respect, workplace culture can be described as being either *supportive* or *hindering* (Dikkers *et al.*, 2004). A supportive culture values workers' non-work responsibilities and seeks to accommodate the multiple needs of workers (for instance, by recognizing the importance of work–life balance to individuals' health and well-being) so that they will be psychologically present for work tasks. In contrast, a hindering culture requires workers to prioritise work over their non-work responsibilities. This can take the form of expectations that workers will put extra time into ensuring that work will be completed or norms where workers get a clear message that prioritising personal needs will have negative consequences for their career progression (O'Driscoll *et al.*, 2011).

Finally, related to organisational culture are the specific attitudes of supervisors and their role as 'gate-keepers' enabling employees to access organisational policies (Brough *et al.*, 2008; Thompson *et al.*, 2006). Workers with supervisors who are unsupportive to work–life balance issues can be deterred from accessing work–life balance polices due either to a direct lack of policy information being disseminated by supervisors and/or due to perceived repercussions for their personal careers (O'Driscoll *et al.*, 2011). Male employees especially often still report a stigma being attached to their requests for accessing work–life balance policies such as paid parental leave following the birth of a child (Brough, O'Driscoll, Kalliath, *et al.*, 2009). In an assessment of work-based support for work–life balance in a sample of Canadian police employees, Tremblay *et al.*, (2011) noted that for various reasons formal supervisors in general did not provide sufficient support to their subordinates. Instead, colleagues were relied upon for support provisions, primarily via the swapping of shifts and work days. Tremblay *et al.* also noted that organisational support provisions significantly influenced (voluntary) work relocations to other stations or departments; relocations did not occur where supervisior support was considered to be inadequate or unsympathetic to work–life balance demands. Research generally supports these observations; the demands of work–life balance is one explanation for the lack of senior promotion applications from female employees (Agocs *et al.*, 2015; Dick and Cassell, 2004; Moen, 2015).

Work–life balance organisational policies and programmes

The increase in the number of female workers seeking full-time employment in criminal justice workplaces from the 1980s onwards created challenges to traditional human resource management policies. New policies which addressed employee demands for parental/carers leave, part-time employment, flexible working hours, and temporary deployment away from frontline operational roles were introduced and continue to be modified today. Most organisational work–life balance human resource policies focus on four key aspects: (1) provision of employee services such as health and fitness centres, on-site childcare, and dry-cleaning services; (2) provision of employee benefits such as paid parental leave and spouse/partner benefits; (3) job restructuring such as part-time work and flexible work hours; and (4) organisational development initiatives such as supportive leadership development and diversity training (Harrington and James, 2006). In a more recent review of evidence-based work–life balance organisational programmes, Brough and O'Driscoll (2010) noted the common occurrence of three main types of programmes: those that address working time and/or working hours; collaborative action research focused on improving workplace equity and performance levels; and programmes to embed work–life balance within organisational cultures. Brough and O'Driscoll (2010) described how the most common workplace work–life programmes involved changes to working time and/or working hours, such as compressed work week or flexible work hours. Compressed work weeks enable employees to experience concentrated periods of family and/or leisure time. These concentrated periods are commonly sought by workers with specific social-economic situations such as paid childcare, child access arrangements, sporting fixtures, and study requirements.

Whilst the nature of police, corrections, and judicial employment commonly limits opportunities for flexible work time arrangements, some trials of programmes addressing working hours for frontline staff have been undertaken. For example, in the 1990s several US police services trialled a programme of compressed work weeks for operational police officers. A trial of a three-day (40-hour) compressed work week occurred for some Texan police officers and they were compared to a control group who worked a traditional five-day week. Pre- and post-evaluations were conducted across both groups. It was reported that work attitudes, work–life balance, and productivity (measured by the volume of bookings and arrests) all improved for officers in the compressed work week group. Furthermore, no differences in levels of fatigue or stress were reported by the officers working the three-day week (Vega and Gilbert, 1997). The main disadvantage for officers working a three-day week was the need for additional communications concerning the progression of cases when they began their work shift. A year-long trial of a four-day (40-hour) compressed work week with a sample of Illinois police officers is also reported to have produced similar positive results (Moore and Morrow, 1987). While the popularity of compressed working week employment options is currently exhibiting a general resurgence (Brough and O'Driscoll, 2010), further reports of implementations within criminal justice workplaces, especially involving frontline operational staff, are rare.

An alternative to implementing any changes to human resource policies or resources is to improve the skills and abilities of individual employees to better manage their work–life balance demands. Placing the responsibility upon individual employees is, of course, the 'easier' option for employers, but is rarely sufficient on its own. For example, a recent assessment of experiences of work–life balance with a sample of UK police employees focused on 'self-management' solutions, defined as what employees actually do in practice to manage their own individual levels of work–life balance (McDowall and Lindsay, 2014). Boundary management, for example, was reported to be a common self-management work–life balance practice, and included behaviours focused on keeping work and personal/family lives separate (e.g. no discussing work with friends, avoiding taking work home, clearly compartmentalising work and family lives). The value of employees focusing upon these self-management techniques typically has a minimal long-term impact in isolation. This is particularly true if both the organisational culture and formal policies do not offer direct support for work–life balance initiatives.

The difficulties of achieving work–life balance within the legal professions, including the recognition of the adverse consequences for personal careers when accessing parental leave entitlements, continues to be discussed (Bacik and Drew, 2006; Brough and O'Driscoll, 2010; Patton, 2004). A rare trial of an evidence-based work–life balance programme for lawyers was reported by Bailyn *et al.* (2006). The programme introduced flexible working practices which were responsive to changing individual employee needs and, importantly, also focused on changing the organisational culture to remove the stigma associated with accessing these employment options. The authors reported that the programme was successful with uptake by both male and female employees and was also directly associated with an improved rate of retention of female lawyers within this law practice.

Conclusions

This chapter has discussed the issue of work–life balance and the difficulties experienced by many criminal justice employees of achieving an adequate balance between their work and non-work lives. The chapter described the reasons why work–life balance is of increasing importance, including the somewhat surprising current rates of pregnancy discrimination and how becoming a mother can still have direct disadvantages for female career progression, especially within criminal justice agencies. The chapter also discussed the common formal organisational work–life balance policies and informal supports accessible to employees. The role of the supervisor as a 'gate-keeper' controlling access to formal work–life balance polices was identified; the importance of this supervisor being 'supportive' is paramount for new parents especially.

This chapter also reviewed innovative examples of work–life balance practices trialled by some criminal justice organisations to provide improved working conditions for their employees. These included trials of compressed working weeks (40 hours work in three days) undertaken by US police officers, and a successful organisational culture change to remove the stigma associated with accessing flexible working options by a law firm. It remains concerning that having caring responsibilities (children, elderly parents, ill spouses and relatives) still remains to a significant extent a 'gender issue', which is particularly noticeable in the (relative lack) of female career progression within many criminal justice agencies. The work to install an organisation culture which is tolerant of diversity, including flexible employment practices, remains a significant challenge, but this is clearly the solution for improving levels of work–life balance and other employment conditions for all criminal justice workers.

References

Agocs, T., Langan, D., and Sanders, C.B. (2015) Police mothers at home: police work and danger-protection parenting practices. *Gender and Society*, (29)2: 265–289.

Bacik, I., and Drew, E. (2006) Struggling with gender: gender and work/life balance in the legal professions. *Women's Studies International Forum*, 29(2): 136–146.

Bailyn, L., Bookman, A., Harrington, M., and Kochan, T.A. (2006) Work–family interventions and experiments: workplaces, communities, and society. In Pitt-Catsouphes, M., Kossek, E.E., and Sweet, S. (eds) *The work and family handbook: multidisciplinary perspectives, methods, and approaches*. Mahwah, New Jersey: Lawrence Erlbaum Associates (pp. 651–683).

Brough, P., and O'Driscoll, M. (2010) Organizational interventions for balancing work and home demands: an overview. *Work and Stress*, 24: 280–297. doi:10.1080/0267837 3.2010.50680.

Brough, P., and O'Driscoll, M.P. (2015) Integrating work and personal life. In Burke, R.J., Page, K.M., and Cooper, C.L. (eds) *Flourishing in life, work, and careers: individual wellbeing and career experiences*. Cheltenham, UK: Edward Elgar Publishing (pp. 377–394).

Brough, P., Holt, J., Bauld, R., Biggs, A., and Ryan, C. (2008) The ability of work–life balance policies to influence key social/organisational issues. *Asian-Pacific Journal of Human Resources*, 46: 261–274. doi:10.1177/1038411108095758.

Brough, P., O'Driscoll, M., and Biggs, A. (2009) Parental leave and work-family balance among employed parents following childbirth: an exploratory investigation in Australia and New Zealand. *Kotuitui: New Zealand Journal of Social Sciences Online*, 4: 71–87. doi:10.1080/1177083X.2009.9522445.

Brough, P., O'Driscoll, M., Kalliath, T., Cooper, C.L., and Poelmans, S. (2009) *Workplace psychological health: current research and practice*. Cheltenham, UK: Edward Elgar.

Brough, P., Timms, C., O'Driscoll, M., Kalliath, T., Siu, O.L., Sit, C., and Lo, D. (2014) Work–life balance: a longitudinal evaluation of a new measure across Australia and New Zealand workers. *International Journal of Human Resource Management*, 25(19): 2724–2744. doi:10.1080/09585192.2014.899262.

Charlesworth, S., and Macdonald, F. (2007) *Hard labour? Pregnancy, discrimination and workplace rights*. Melbourne: Centre for Applied Social Research, RMIT University.

Dick, P., and Cassell, C. (2004) The position of policewomen: a discourse analytic study. *Work, Employment and Society*, 18(1): 51–72.

Dikkers, J., Geurts, S., den Dulk, L., Peper, B., and Kompier, M. (2004) Relations among work-home culture, the utilization of work-home arrangements, and work-home interference. *International Journal of Stress Management*, 11(4): 323–345.

Eby, L.T., Casper, W.J., Lockwood, A., Bordeaux, C., and Brinley, A. (2005) Work and family research in IO/OB: content analysis and review of the literature (1980–2002). *Journal of Vocational Behavior*, 66: 124–197.

EEOC (2007) Pregnancy discrimination charges EEOC and FEPAs combined: FY1997–FY2006. www.eeoc.gov/stats/pregnanc.html.

EOC (2005) *EOC's investigation into pregnancy discrimination: summary final report*. London: Equal Opportunities Commission.

Harrington, B., and James, J.B. (2006) The standards of excellence in work–life integration: from changing policies to changing organizations. In Pitt-Catsouphes, M., Kossek, E.E., and Sweet, S. (eds) *The work and family handbook: multi-disciplinary perspectives, methods and approaches*. Mahwah, NJ: Lawrence Erlbaum (pp. 665–683).

McDowall, A., and Lindsay, A. (2014) Work–life balance in the police: the development of a self-management competency framework. *Journal of Business and Psychology*, 29(3): 397–411.

Moen, P. (2015) An institutional/organizational turn: getting to work–life quality and gender equality. *Work and Occupations*, 42(2): 174–182.

Moore, D.T., and Morrow, J.G. (1987) Evaluation of the four/ten schedule in three Illinois Department of State Police Districts. *Journal of Police Science and Administration*, 15: 107–108.

Morgan, W.B., Walker, S.S., Hebl, M.M.R., and King, E.B. (2013) A field experiment: reducing interpersonal discrimination toward pregnant job applicants. *Journal of Applied Psychology*, 98(5): 799–809.

O'Driscoll, M., Brough, P., and Biggs, A. (2007) Work–family balance: concepts, implications and interventions. In Houdmont, J. and McIntyre, S. (eds) *Occupational health psychology: European perspectives on research, education and practice*. Portugal: ISMAI Publishers (pp. 193–217).

O'Driscoll, M.P., Brough, P., and Haar, J. (2011) The work–family nexus and small-medium enterprises: implications for worker well-being. In Kelloway, E.K. and Cooper, C.L. (eds) *Occupational health and safety for small and medium sized enterprises*. Cheltenham, UK: Edward Elgar (pp. 106–128).

O'Driscoll, M.P., Brough, P., and Kalliath, T. (2006) Work–family conflict and facilitation. In Jones, F., Burke, R., and Westman, M. (eds) *Work–life balance: a psychological perspective*. Hove: Psychology Press (pp. 117–142).

Patton, P.A. (2004) Women lawyers, their status, influence, and retention in the legal profession. *William and Mary Journal of Women and the Law*, 11(2): 173.

Salihu, H.M., Myers, J., and August, E.M. (2012) Pregnancy in the workplace. *Occupational medicine*, 62(2): 88–97.

Thompson, B., Brough, P., and Schmidt, H. (2006) Supervisor and subordinate work-family values: does similarity make a difference? *International Journal of Stress Management*, 13: 45–63. doi:10.1037/1072–5245.13.1.45.

Tremblay, D.-G., Genin, E., and di Loreto, M. (2011) Advances and ambivalences: organisational support to work–life balance in a police service. *Employment Relations Record*, 11(2): 75–93.

Vega, A., and Gilbert, M.J. (1997) Longer days, shorter weeks: compressed work weeks in policing. *Public Personnel Management*, 26(3): 391–402.

13 Toxic environments
Occupational stress

Introduction

There is no doubt that working within the criminal justice workplace can be a demanding experience. Many employees self-select out of this occupation when the demands of the job become apparent, and this is illustrated, for example, by the relatively high turnover of new police and prison officers. Working within most criminal justice workplaces is compounded by the stigma of being 'tough enough to handle the job' which includes being able to successfully manage its associated stressors. Thus many staff prefer to deny or avoid acknowledging their experiences of stress (at least within their work environment), primarily in order to avoid being labelled as weak or otherwise stigmatised (Brough, 1998). For many criminal justice employees, admitting to experiencing work stress would, they believe, seriously hinder their personal reputations and negatively impact on their future work opportunities.

In countries including the UK, EU member states, New Zealand, and Australia, workplace health and safety legislation effectively holds employers responsible for both the physical and the *psychological* health of employees (i.e. duty of care). Proven breaches of this employer responsibility have resulted in employee's stress compensation claims and/or litigation. The costs of health insurance premiums associated with such claims are a significant proportion of annual budgets for many agencies. There are, therefore, a number of pertinent internal and external reasons for agencies to effectively manage occupational stress. This chapter reviews the key issues and identifies some pertinent best practices adopted by agencies for the effective management of occupational stress within criminal justice workplaces.

Overview of occupational stress

Figure 13.1 illustrates the key causes and consequences of stress for employees within criminal justice workplaces. The following text discusses these issues in further detail.

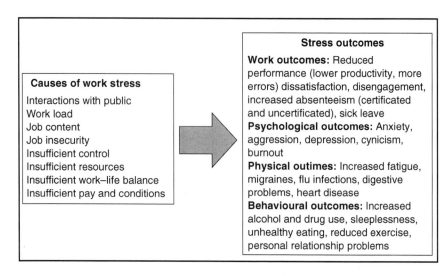

Figure 13.1 Overview of occupational stress.

Key causes of occupational stress

As can be seen in Figure 13.1, the main causes of occupational stress for employees within criminal justice workplaces can be classified into eight broad categories (Brough and Biggs, 2010). We briefly describe these eight key occupational stressors here:

1 **Interactions with people:** negative interactions with people at work. This includes bullying, harassment, intimidation, and risk of violence (e.g. by the public and/or prisoners). Workplace harassment and discrimination remains one of the leading causes of occupational stress for criminal justice employees (Brough and Biggs, 2010). The absence of *positive* supportive relationships, e.g. with supervisors and work colleagues, can significantly exacerbate the presence of other stressors (e.g. work demands) and can increase overall stress experiences (Biggs, Brough and Barbour, 2014a).

2 **Job content:** nature of the work performed. Criminal justice employees who work directly with the public typically experience both types of work content stress: *operational stressors* such as managing traumatic and violent incidents, and dealing with death and bereavement; and *organisational stressors* such as interacting with bureaucratic systems, managing organisational paperwork and reporting requirements, dealing with the court and criminal justice systems, training requirements. Long-term (chronic) exposure to operational stressors, in particular, has been demonstrated to have a detrimental impact upon these workers, specifically when paired with inadequate training, recovery and support facilities (Brough and Biggs, 2010; Brown and Campbell, 1990).

3 **Workload:** workload and time pressures. Having too many or too few work demands and/or insufficient time to complete work to the required standards is a key cause of work stressors for workers in all occupations. The legal implications of the work performed by criminal justice employees increases the pressure to ensure job tasks are completed competently. Regularly finishing work late, missing meal breaks, and working overtime have all been linked to increased perceptions of occupational stress, especially when these incidents are forced upon the worker (Brough *et al.*, 2009).

4 **Insufficient control:** a perceived lack of control in regards to key work characteristics is a widely recognised cause of occupational stress for employees in all occupations. As criminal justice workers work within highly regulated, bureaucratic environments, many perceive they have low levels of influence over most of their work processes, decision-making, work teams, the timing of job tasks, and their work hours (including accessing part-time working options; Brough and Biggs, 2015).

5 **Job insecurity:** uncertainty about the future of one's position within an organisation is a common work stressor for many workers. While many policing and prison agencies have typically offered workers 'a job for life', the rationalising of these departments in the current tight economic climate is increasingly being experienced. Recent examples include, for example, the removal of specific job ranks/levels, dissolution of work teams/departments, and the increased outsourcing of roles. In addition, due to the nature of their work, many criminal justice employees work with a constant threat of removal from their duties due to internal disciplinary systems. In some agencies the overuse of internal disciplinary systems to resolve relatively minor interpersonal workplace conflicts is a recognised problem (Brough and Biggs, 2010; Brown and Campbell, 1990).

6 **Insufficient resources:** a common complaint which causes significant work stress for many criminal justice employees is inadequate or malfunctioning equipment, a general lack of resources, and ineffective communication processes. For some policing agencies in particular, a lack of vehicles (and/or the location of the keys to vehicles) is a recognised problem significantly impacting on work performance. The introduction of new/updated computer systems often has long-term benefits but the increase in delays and errors in the short-term is a recognised stressor for workers in all occupations (Biggs *et al.*, 2014b).

7 **Work–life balance:** while inadequate work–life balance is a problem for many workers, especially shift-workers in most occupations, this issue is often exacerbated by the nature of criminal justice work. Thus, for example, the discussion of work at home to elicit social support is often prohibited. Similarly the contrasting behaviours commonly demanded by work (authoritarian, cynical, suspicious) and family (gentle, loving, communicative) are also recognised as stressors. The shiftwork requirements for operational employees can also be a stressor in itself and patterns of rostering which aim to minimise fatigue and improve work–life balance have been assessed

(Brough and O'Driscoll, 2015). Chapter 12 examined the issue of work–life balance experienced within criminal justice workplaces in more detail.

8   **Insufficient pay and conditions:** this final stressor is also experienced in many occupations and is certainly not specific to criminal justice workplaces. A perceived or objective inadequacy of remuneration and other tangible benefits is a widely recognised stressor. In most self-report surveys most employees rate their rate of pay as being 'unsatisfactory' and believe their work performance is worthy of a higher salary. For some police and prison workers this issue has become especially pertinent due to the increase in non-sworn (staff member) employees being employed to do tasks that were previously categorised as sworn/officer roles. Equal access to job roles which are associated with promotion also occurs in this category. In the past the 'sidelining' of staff based on gender and/or racial demographic characteristics into job roles which had limited career advancement opportunities blatantly occurred within criminal justice workplaces. This issue is less apparent now, although recent reports have identified issues such as parenting and the taking of stress leave as having a negative impact upon career advancement in policing and corrections agencies (Brough and Biggs, 2010; Brown and Campbell, 1990).

Most criminal justice work commonly includes all of these key causes of occupational stress, and is commonly identified as being a 'high risk of stress' occupation. The experience of occupational stress can also be exacerbated by organisational systems that are overly bureaucratic, punitive of staff, strictly managed, and experiencing restructuring or organisational change (Brough and Biggs, 2015). A recent review of the common occupational stressors experienced by correctional officers for example, identified five key categories: stressors intrinsic to the job, job role, rewards at work, supervisory relationships at work, and the organizational structure and climate (Finney *et al.*, 2013). Importantly, Finney *et al.* (2013) concluded that the organizational structure and climate had the strongest impact upon correctional officer's levels of stress and burnout. Similarly, the *Correctional Officer Job Demands* measure, which assesses common occupational stressors such as lack of decision-making, understaffing, formal complaints, and management support, was associated with adverse psychological health and low job satisfaction for Australian correctional officers (Brough and Biggs, 2015; Brough and Williams, 2007). Similar results are reported elsewhere, with the importance of both organisational culture (see Chapter 2) and the related issue of supportive supervisory relationships also being identified as the key work characteristics which impact upon occupational stress experienced by prisons, police, and other criminal justice employees (Biggs *et al.*, 2014b, 2014c; Brough and Biggs, 2015; Garland *et al.*, 2012; Hartley *et al.*, 2013; Stinchcomb and Leip, 2013). Police and prison services have recognised this impact of occupational culture to varying extents, and some have made attempts to 'soften' the traditional culture, primarily by increasing the diversity of staff, expanding training and promotion programmes, and flattening the hierarchical structure by reducing some levels of management (Brough and Biggs, 2010).

The effective management of occupational stress within criminal justice workplaces

Two useful systems for categorising occupational stress interventions are those developed by Murphy (1988) and DeFrank and Cooper (1987). Murphy's tripartite model describes *primary prevention* (elimination of stressors from the work environment to prevent stress), *secondary prevention* (detecting stress and providing stress management skills), and *tertiary prevention* (rehabilitation of stressed workers). DeFrank and Cooper's classification system focuses on the target of the interventions, and comprises interventions directed at *individuals* (equipping individuals with skills to manage stress, e.g. relaxation), the *individual/organisational interface* (interactions between individuals and their workplace, e.g. decision-making authority), and *organisations* (the organisational context, e.g. job design). The majority of criminal justice workplaces commonly use individual-level secondary and tertiary interventions; usually peer-support officers or trained professionals, to internally manage stress, although failing to modify the stressful work environment tends to be ineffective at producing long-term outcomes (Brough and Biggs, 2010). One of the most common stress management strategies is the *Critical Incident Stress Management* (CISM).

Critical Incident Stress Management (CISM)

Critical Incident Stress Management (CISM) usually involves the provision of support services to prepare staff who are at risk of exposure to traumatic events, minimise the impact of the trauma, or promote recovery after exposure to a critical incident (Brough and Biggs, 2010). Thus a detailed CISM programme consists of an integrated, multi-component crisis intervention incorporating the pre-crisis, acute crisis, and post-crisis stages (Hurley *et al.*, 2014). A primary goal of CISM is the protection and/or recovery of the health and well-being (and work performance) of an employee exposed to a critical incident, especially in terms of the prevention or management of maladaptive responses caused by the incident.

Critical Incident Stress Debriefing (CISD)

Critical Incident Stress Debriefing (CISD) is one commonly used component of CISM and is conducted individually and/or in small groups using therapeutic discussion methods. CISD aims to reduce symptomology and to encourage effective coping responses to manage/reduce the impact of the critical incident. CISD is based on the premise that the voicing of personal thoughts, feelings, and emotions arising from the incident will reduce the psychological impact of the critical incident (and will, therefore, avoid or reduce experiences of post-traumatic stress disorder (PTSD)). CISD has become a widely used technique, especially for groups of workers who experienced the same critical incident.

The actual value of CISD is difficult to demonstrate empirically. Some research indicates that the timely provision of CISD (i.e. within 24–72 hours post-incident) is effective in reducing PTSD symptomology (Campfield and Hills, 2001). The value of group-based debriefing sessions, compared to individual counselling, has also been noted, primarily due to the perception of social support elicited from the group members (Hurley *et al.*, 2014). However, other research has raised some concerns over the use of CISD, especially when CISD is used alone without any other CISM components (Choe, 2005). The mandatory use of CISD (as opposed to voluntary attendance) succeeded in overcoming the stigma associated with individuals who attended these debriefing sessions, but also exposed individuals with no identifiable symptoms to reliving the incidence and potentially to experience PTSD and other negative responses.

In an assessment of US male police officers, Pasciak and Kelley (2013) noted that CISD was largely incompatible with the characteristics of these officers and suggested instead that other forms of (peer support and training) interventions were preferable. Similarly, Jahnke *et al.*'s (2014) investigation with samples of (predominately male) US firefighters also reported on their negative views of CISD and identified their preference for peer support programmes that 'were more ecologically embedded in their organisational contexts and cultures' (p. 122). Thus some organisations, including those within the criminal justice arena, who once experienced psychological stress litigation due to the *absence* of organisational psychological health support facilities (i.e. CISM), may now experience complaints and/or litigation from employees for the provision of *inadequate* or *harmful* psychological debriefing programmes (Devilly *et al.*, 2006).

Practical implications for the effective management of occupational stress within criminal justice workplaces

The experience of occupational stress arising from multiple sources, and of both the bureaucratic hassle and traumatic incident types, is an unavoidable characteristic of most criminal justice work. Considerable efforts have been made by employers to manage these negative experiences so as to enhance staff health and job performance. A summary of the key best management approaches was described by Biggs (2011) from her occupational stress research with both police and correctional workers (see Figure 13.2). It can be seen from Figure 13.2 that Biggs (2011) described the following four key stages involving the development, implementation, and evaluation of an occupational stress intervention.

1   **Development of the intervention protocol:** based on a comprehensive evaluation of needs identifying the job-specific and/or occupational-specific workplace stressors experienced by the workers. Biggs and Brough (2015, p. 4) emphasised the importance of this stage: 'This will ensure that a theoretically driven intervention protocol that is tailored to meet the needs of the specific work context will be achieved and that changes will be genuinely

beneficial for the organization and its employees'. The gaining of input and commitment of stakeholders at all organisational levels is also a vital component of this first stage, albeit often difficult to achieve in practice. The development of the intervention strategies will be most successful if broader 'macro' organisational factors are also carefully considered. Thus intervention relevance, importance, and quality; motivations to undertake change and support for change; availability of intervention resources; and consideration of previous successful and unsuccessful interventions should be assessed.

2 **Implementation of both intervention and organisational change:** assessments and feedback gained during the intervention implementation should ensure that participant's views of the quality of the intervention, their transfer of training back into their workplace, and the facilitation of their feedback to the organisation are enabled and actioned. Assessments of the resulting organisational change should also occur, although in practice this latter point is rarely assessed.

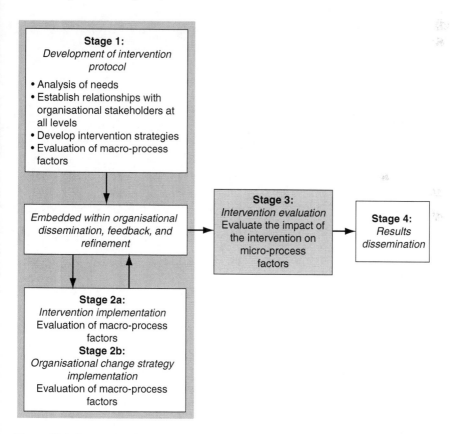

Figure 13.2 Occupational stress intervention development, implementation, and evaluation (source: adapted from Biggs (2011)).

3   **Evaluation of the intervention:** it is essential that a formal objective evaluation of the implementation be undertaken. Such evaluations should be focused on the resulting changes which can be directly attributed to the intervention; that is both individual employee changes in terms of reduced stress experiences and improved levels of health and work performance, and also organisational improvements such as reduced overtime, sickness leave, and other staffing costs and improved levels of productivity.

4   **Results dissemination:** dissemination of the results of the interventions both within the organisation to other employees and externally to interested stakeholders (e.g. unions, government agencies) is recommended to ensure that the spread of best practices occur and to prevent the 'reinvention of the wheel' for the development of subsequent occupational stress interventions (see also Biggs and Brough, 2015).

Conclusion

Working in the police or prison services is typically a rewarding but demanding role. The dual demands of regular exposure to operational (often traumatic) stressors, and a highly regulated bureaucratic organisational system, defines police and prison work as 'high-stress' occupations. Individual susceptibility to occupational stress experiences can be heightened by both organisational and individual factors such as culture, support, gender, and age. Similarly, improving individual levels of 'stress resilience' can also be approached from both an individual and an organisational level, with the most effective results emerging from a joint approach. Thus, organisational efforts to prevent or manage occupational stress necessitate effective training, education, resources, and supports. Individual efforts entail stress recognition, active coping strategies, and help-seeking. The nature of police and prison work ensures that occupational stress is a permanent job risk; designing and implementing practices to *reduce* this risk most effectively should be the focus of both service managers and researchers.

Most agencies are proficient in the four key management process for high risk of stress employees:

1   *preparing employees for stress experiences*, through training and the provision of clear guidelines for incident management;

2   *minimising the risk of stress exposure*, by reducing environmental risks, changing culture and work practice, reducing job demands and effective resourcing of employees, and encouraging healthy employees (through the promotion of effective fatigue management, coping skills, and stress resilience);

3   *providing support for exposed employees*, including acknowledging the need for support without any associated stigma, providing both informal support networks (e.g. peer support, supportive supervisors) and formal support systems (e.g. CISM and counselling programmes); and

4   *evaluating the working environment*, including the critical review of expo-
     sure and work practices and the willingness to learn and change the environ-
     ment to further reduce risk.

This chapter explored these four people management issues in some depth and
described a four-stage best-practice framework for occupational stress intervention development, implementation, and evaluation.

References

Biggs, A.J. (2011) *A longitudinal evaluation of strain, work engagement, and intervention strategies to address the health of high risk employees.* Unpublished Doctoral
Thesis, Griffith University, Brisbane.

Biggs, A., & Brough, P. (2015). Explaining intervention success and failure: What works,
when, and why?. In: M. Karanika-Murray and C. Biron (Editors.). *Derailed organizational stress and well-being interventions: Confessions of failure and solutions for
success.* (pp 237–244). Springer, UK.

Biggs, A., Brough, P., and Barbour, J.P. (2014a) Enhancing work-related attitudes and
work engagement: a quasi-experimental study of the impact of an organizational intervention. *International Journal of Stress Management,* 21(1): 43–68.

Biggs, A., Brough, P., and Barbour, J.P. (2014b) Relationships of individual and organizational support with engagement: examining various types of causality in a three-
wave study. *Work and Stress,* 28(3): 236–254. doi:10.1080/02678373.2014.934316

Biggs, A., Brough, P., and Barbour, J.P. (2014c) Exposure to extraorganizational stressors: impact on mental health and organizational perceptions for police workers. *International Journal of Stress Management,* 21(3): 255–282. doi:10.1037/a0037297

Brough, P. (1998) The utility and value of in-service police welfare provision. *Police
Research and Management,* 2: 27–34.

Brough, P., and Biggs, A. (2010) Occupational stress in police and prison staff. In Brown,
J. and Campbell, E. (eds) *The Cambridge handbook of forensic psychology.* Cambridge: Cambridge University Press (pp. 707–718).

Brough, P., and Biggs, A. (2015) Job demands × job control interaction effects: do
occupation-specific job demands increase their occurrence? *Stress and Health,* 31(2):
138–149. doi:10.1002/smi.2537.

Brough, P., and O'Driscoll, M.P. (2015) Integrating work and personal life. In Burke,
R.J., Page, K.M., and Cooper, C.L. (eds) *Flourishing in life, work, and careers: individual wellbeing and career experiences.* Cheltenham, UK: Edward Elgar Publishing
(pp. 377–394).

Brough, P., and Williams, J. (2007) Managing occupational stress in a high-risk industry:
measuring the job demands of correctional officers. *Criminal Justice and Behavior,* 34:
555–567. doi:10.1177/0093854806294147.

Brough, P., O'Driscoll, M., Kalliath, T., Cooper, C.L., and Poelmans, S. (2009) *Workplace
psychological health: current research and practice.* Cheltenham, UK: Edward Elgar.

Brown, J.M., and Campbell, E.A. (1990) Sources of occupational stress in the police.
Work and Stress, 4(4): 305–318.

Campfield, K.M., and Hills, A.M. (2001) Effect of timing of critical incident stress
debriefing (CISD) on posttraumatic symptoms. *Journal of traumatic stress,* 14(2):
327–340.

Choe, I. (2005) The debate over psychological debriefing for PTSD. *The New School Psychology Bulletin*, 3(2): 71–82.

DeFrank, R., and Cooper, C. (1987) Worksite stress management interventions: their effectiveness and conceptualisation. *Journal of Managerial Psychology*, 2: 4–10.

Devilly, G.J., Gist, R., and Cotton, P. (2006) Ready! Fire! Aim! The status of psychological debriefing and therapeutic interventions: in the work place and after disasters. *Review of General Psychology*, 10(4): 318–345.

Finney, C., Stergiopoulos, E., Hensel, J., Bonato, S., and Dewa, C.S. (2013) Organizational stressors associated with job stress and burnout in correctional officers: a systematic review. *BMC Public Health*, 13: 82–95. doi:10.1186/1471–2458–13–82.

Garland, B., Hogan, N.L., and Lambert, E.G. (2012) Antecedents of role stress among correctional staff: a replication and expansion. *Criminal Justice Policy and Review*, 24(5): 527–550. doi:10.1177/0887403412451445.

Hartley, D.J., Davila, M.A., Marquart, J.W., and Mullings, J.L. (2013) Fear is a disease: the impact of fear and exposure to infectious disease on correctional officer job stress and satisfaction. *American Journal of Criminal Justice*, 38: 323–340. doi:10.1007/s12103–012–9175–1.

Hurley, D., Ferreira, S., Briseau, M., and Pain, C. (2014) Critical incident stress management. In Csiemik, R. (ed.) *Workplace wellness: issues and responses*. Ontario: Canadian Scholars' Press (pp. 243–257).

Jahnke, S.A., Gist, R., Poston, W.S.C., and Haddock, C.K. (2014) Behavioral health interventions in the fire service: stories from the firehouse. *Journal of Workplace Behavioral Health*, 29(2): 113–126.

Murphy, L.R. (1988) Workplace interventions for stress reduction and prevention. In Cooper, C.L. and Payne, R. (eds) *Causes, coping, and consequences of stress at work*. New York: Wiley (pp. 301–339).

Pasciak, A., and Kelley, T. (2013) Conformity to traditional gender norms by male police officers exposed to trauma: implications for Critical Incident Stress Debriefing. *Applied Psychology in Criminal Justice*, 9(2): 137–156.

Stinchcomb, J.B., and Leip, L.A. (2013) Expanding the literature on job satisfaction in corrections: a national study of jail employees. *Criminal Justice and Behavior*, 40(11): 1209–1227. doi:10.1177/0093854813489667.

14 Transforming environments
Leadership development

Introduction

As we discussed in Chapter 4, leadership has a profound capacity to shape the culture of an organisation, impacting on employees' well-being and performance, role-modelling appropriate behaviours, and influencing the quality of the service provided by the organisation. Although earlier perspectives considered leadership ability to be innate, most contemporary perspectives consider that effective leadership can be developed, contingent upon appropriate learning opportunities and supportive organisational culture and policies. An ongoing challenge for criminal justice organisations is to support leadership development at all levels throughout the organisation. This chapter will discuss the need for leadership development in criminal justice organisations, in addition to common challenges and barriers to developing effective leaders in these organisational contexts. We then discuss a best-practice approach to conducting leadership development programmes. Finally, the chapter will conclude with an example of a successful leadership development programme conducted in an Australian police service. While Chapter 4 provided an overview of leaders and managers, this chapter examines in detail the key issues for the development of effective leaders in criminal justice workplaces.

Leadership development in criminal justice organisations

As discussed in Chapter 4, it is increasingly recognised that in order for criminal justice organisations to provide a high quality of service and successfully meet emerging challenges, a change in culture and practice is required. In order to navigate these changes, strong leadership and management are simultaneously needed. The practice of selecting and developing leaders and managers in criminal justice organisations has been subjected to much criticism, debate, and attempted reform, particularly within police services (Winsor, 2012). Two primary areas of concern will be discussed: (a) strategic investment in leadership development programmes; and (b) alignment of leadership development with Human Resource Management (HRM) strategies, such as talent management and succession planning.

Leadership development programmes

There is ample evidence to demonstrate that leadership development programmes successfully improve leadership capabilities of individuals, teams, and organisations (Kelloway and Barling, 2010); stimulate organisational culture change; improve the well-being and motivation of followers; and strengthen the organisation's strategic direction (Biggs *et al.*, 2014a, 2014b, 2014c). Bass (1990), for example, discussed an experiment conducted in prison industrial shops, in which shop supervisors worked with groups of prisoners to produce products for sale outside the prison. Supervisors were allocated to four conditions: (a) transformational training and pre- and post-surveys; (b) transactional training and pre- and post-surveys; (c) pre- and post-surveys only; and (d) post-surveys only (this 'quasi-experimental' research design was discussed in detail in Chapter 7). Bass reported that the performance of both trained groups improved, although the transformational leadership group reported the greatest improvement in productivity, absenteeism, and citizenship behaviours amongst prisoners, and won more respect from prisoners.

Despite the promising effects of leadership development on an array of outcomes, organisations typically fail to commit adequate resources to develop organisational leadership as part of their business strategy (Leskiw and Singh, 2007). According to Bass (1990, p. 25) 'many executives still feel that leadership is like the weather – something to talk about, but about which not much can be done.' This trend is also reflected within criminal justice organisations, where relatively few leadership development programmes exist and barriers to instigating such programmes are common.

First, resourcing for frontline services and mandatory training tends to be prioritised over non-essential training, including leadership development programmes (Stojkovic *et al.*, 2012). For instance, Stojkovic *et al.* (2012) discussed a successful leadership development programme conducted for approximately ten years in a US Corrective Service agency, which was ultimately removed due to cost-cutting measures, rather than issues with quality. The programme in question 'was viewed as a luxury that could be ended when compared to other pressing needs facing the department' (Stojkovic *et al.*, 2012, p. 190). When resources are limited, there is strong pressure on administrators to commit those resources to frontline operations and withdraw from areas such as training. Focus groups conducted with criminal justice employees reflected this sentiment: participants consistently repeated the theme that levels of management and administration within the organisation need to be streamlined in order to commit more human and economic resources to frontline operations (Biggs, 2011).

Second, existing leadership development programmes emphasise managerial skills, with insufficient focus on leadership (Stojkovic *et al.*, 2008; Winsor, 2012). As discussed in Chapter 4, effective leadership is linked with the ability to: combine authentic transformational and contingent reward (transactional) leadership; role-model competent and ethical practices; encourage participation in decision-making; and adapt styles to suit the context (Campbell and Kodz,

2011). It has been recommended that contemporary understandings of leadership effectiveness need to be embraced in leadership development programmes: for example, the UK Police Leadership Development Board have endorsed the need to integrate transformational leadership within learning and development training (Dobby *et al.*, 2004).

Third, a greater focus on ethical behaviour is needed in criminal justice leadership development programmes. As discussed in Chapter 4, recent research has demonstrated the importance of authentic and ethical practice amongst leaders (Burgess and Hawkes, 2013; Hannah *et al.*, 2011). Research in criminal justice settings has also emphasised the importance of leaders role-modelling competent and ethical behaviours to set the standard of behaviour required in their subordinates (Neyroud, 2011).

Finally, leadership development programmes need to be supported by the organisation's culture and infrastructure (Leskiw and Singh, 2007). Several aspects of the organisational culture, structure, and policies in criminal justice organisations that represent significant barriers for leadership development, particularly for authentic, transformational leadership, were discussed in Chapter 4. These included the existence of strong organisational cultures that are resistant to change, which is problematic as leadership development requires a degree of organisational change in order to support new styles of leadership.

Aligning leadership development with HRM strategies

It is not sufficient to conduct leadership development training programmes; they also need to be aligned with HRM strategies, such as systems that assess leadership capabilities and identify development opportunities for employees at all levels, succession planning, and performance management and promotion processes (Dobby *et al.*, 2004; Neyroud, 2011). Leadership development programmes tend to be reserved for executive leaders located at the top of the organisation's hierarchy, despite the recognised necessity of building leadership capacity at multiple levels throughout the organisation (Bass, 1990; Neyroud, 2011). This is especially relevant for criminal justice employees, such as police officers and correctional officers, who are responsible for managing and/or leading members of the public and using authority to command situations, regardless of their organisational level (Neyroud, 2011; Stojkovic *et al.*, 2012). The challenge for criminal justice organisations, therefore, is to develop the leadership capacity of the entire organisation, rather than focusing on the development of a small number of senior leaders (Neyroud, 2011).

Developing leaders at lower levels of the organisation is also important for succession planning (Leskiw and Singh, 2007; Stojkovic *et al.*, 2012). Leskiw and Singh (2007, p. 449) noted 'best-practice organizations do not necessarily select the same level, position, or type of employee as the target of leadership development,' and emphasised the need to connect succession planning and leadership development to identify and prepare future leaders. This is particularly important, as leadership development in criminal justice organisations tends to be undermined by the high level of change amongst managers and leaders. This is due to turnover, transfers, and a substantial proportion of employees acting in managerial roles for shorter periods of time. The latter is particularly problematic if employees acting in leadership roles are excluded from development opportunities.

An additional point supporting leadership development throughout the organisational hierarchy is research revealing that the effectiveness of leadership development programmes targeting lower-, middle-, and higher-level managers is greater for those programmes aimed at lower leadership levels (Avolio *et al.*, 2009). This is likely due to the greater interaction between followers and their immediate supervisors: this effect further reinforces the need to conduct leadership development at multiple levels in hierarchical organisations. In fact, we recommend a top-down approach, in which senior leaders undergo development first, followed by leaders at lower levels of the organisation's hierarchy. This approach was successfully conducted in an Australian police service (Biggs *et al.*, 2014a; Brough *et al.*, 2012).

Finally, in order to develop leadership and management capability within criminal justice organisations, it may be necessary to modify recruitment, selection, and promotion systems to enable multiple entry points to senior leadership positions (Winsor, 2012). The traditional practice of appointing senior leaders based on experience within the organisation, rather than leadership capability, is still widespread (Stojkovic *et al.*, 2008; Villiers, 2009). However, it has long been evident that such an approach is limited and alternate strategies are needed (Winsor, 2012). A review commissioned by the Home Department (Winsor, 2012), investigating UK police remuneration and conditions, recommended multiple-point entry into senior police leadership in order to:

- expand the pool of future potential leaders;
- diversify the skills and experience of senior leaders, enriching leadership;
- implement positive cultural change; and
- address the under-representation of women and minority group officers in senior ranks.

Drawing on several sources, the Winsor (2012) review also acknowledged several difficulties with multiple-point entry to senior leadership positions:

- Effective leaders in other organisational contexts may not be effective police leaders.
- Effective police management and leadership requires expertise in operational decision-making, which is difficult to attain without on-the-job experience.
- Appointment to senior leadership positions, without frontline experience, may result in a lack credibility and respect from subordinates.
- The authority of leaders may be undermined if they are perceived to have been promoted for diversity reasons rather than on the basis of merit.

Another review, also conducted within the UK police (Neyroud, 2011), acknowledged that despite recommendations for multiple-point entry to senior leadership, there is continuing and overwhelming resistance against the idea. This sentiment was also observed by Biggs (2011) in a sample of correctional officers:

- Generally, there tends to be lower acceptance of senior leaders who did not achieve their position through the culturally accepted route of internal promotion through the ranks.
- Such leaders tend to be viewed as 'out of touch' due to perceptions that they have had no direct experience with frontline operations, have no idea about the issues faced by employees at 'the coal face' of the organisation, and are, therefore, incapable of making effective decisions about how the service is run.
- Finally, these leaders also tend to be perceived as 'career public servants' with little vested interest in the department itself, who wish to initiate unnecessary changes and programmes purely to boost their CV.

Despite acknowledging this resistance, Winsor (2012) still recommended multiple-point entry as a means to progress leadership development, noting 'I do not accept that every officer must start as a constable and work his way through every rank before reaching the highest ranks' (p. 20). To minimise resistance, he recommended that: leadership development programmes include a balance between internal and external recruits; development programmes and advancement opportunities be better aligned; and all external entrants join as constables to attain some experience in the rank prior to promotion:

> This does not need to be a lengthy process, but officers do need experience of what it means to be on the streets. They should have used the powers of a constable, and understand how serious it is to make a decision to arrest a suspect, subject an unwilling person to a search, and to use reasonable force. They should have faced danger.
>
> (Winsor, 2012, p. 147)

Summary

This chapter discussed just a few of the challenges for developing leaders in criminal justice organisations. However, to ensure the future success of these organisations, it is critical to overcome these barriers, particularly the idea that leadership development is a non-essential function. As noted by Leskiw and Singh (2007), organisations committed to fostering effective leadership development and adopting strategic plans to align leadership development with HRM strategies will more effectively address emerging challenges. Failing to adequately develop leadership capabilities throughout the hierarchies within criminal justice organisations has an adverse effect on every aspect of organisational functioning, including the capacity to perform front-line duties adequately (Stojkovic *et al.*, 2012). Inadequate resourcing and focus on leadership development results in 'the quality of leader who will make decisions that do not reflect the best possible practices; communities will ultimately suffer and waste an enormous number of resources' (Stojkovic *et al.*, 2012, p. 190).

Leadership development programme framework

As with any form of organisational change or intervention, a systematic approach to conducting leadership development is highly recommended. Leskiw and Singh (2007) conducted a review of best-practice leadership development initiatives, and identified six principles for systematically conducting leadership development:

1   Undertake a needs assessment by (a) outlining the objectives of the leadership development programme, which need to be aligned with the overall organisational strategy, and (b) assessing existing strengths as well as gaps between current and ideal leadership.
2   Identify appropriate targets for leadership development (i.e. who the participants will be).
3   Consider whether the organisational context will support leadership development and address factors that are likely to impede upon the success of the programme. In order for these programmes to be successful, they need to be supported by appropriate organisational policies and the organisational culture (Bass, 1990; Walumbwa and Wernsing, 2012). Examples of the factors discussed by Leskiw and Singh (2007) include:

   a   Alignment with strategic priorities and embedded within the organisation's culture, to increase perceived support and relevance of the programme.
   b   Involvement of senior leadership in the programme.
   c   Support of the programme by employees at all levels, from senior leaders to frontline employees.
   d   Cultural acceptance of learning and development. For instance, leaders need sufficient levels of autonomy to practice and successfully implement newly acquired skills; furthermore, the existence of a learning culture, where feedback is accepted and collective growth and development is encouraged, complements leadership development programmes to a greater extent than a punitive culture focusing on fault-finding and punishment.
   e   Shared responsibility for leadership development across departments and functions, as opposed to viewing it purely as a HRM function.
   f   Clear accountability frameworks. When multiple levels of hierarchy exist within the organisations, a single employee may have multiple leaders, making leadership accountability unclear. This may undermine

the effectiveness of leadership development and it may be necessary to clarify these frameworks so job incumbents understand who they report to and who reports to them.

4   Plan programme content, blending formal training, action learning opportunities, and ongoing developmental relationships. Meaning of the training will be enhanced if the content is applicable to the context. Action-learning activities, such as case-studies or mini projects, 'provide the opportunity to apply and improve the application of the new learning' (Leskiw and Singh, 2007, p. 453). Development opportunities include coaching, mentoring, and 360-degree performance reviews. This point is especially pertinent, given the criticism that leadership development in policing organisations has typically heavily relied on classroom-based training, which is not only expensive but inconsistent with best-practice training in other contexts that emphasise blended learning and ongoing developmental opportunities (Neyroud, 2011).

5   Evaluate leadership development programmes to determine whether they achieved the objectives outlined in the needs assessment phase. We discussed the importance of programme evaluations in Chapter 7. However, evaluating leadership development programmes also requires consideration of two additional points. First, while the programme is designed to improve the leadership capacity of the participants, the intention of the intervention is to positively impact organisational performance or the well-being and performance of followers. Second, the effect of leadership development may be delayed due to these indirect effects, requiring a longer delay for the post-programme evaluation in order for any effect to be observed (Kelloway and Barling, 2010).

6   Maintain an ongoing commitment to continuous improvement and reward successes. This involves making use of the information obtained in the evaluation to continually inform the development of leadership development programmes.

Many of these best-practice principles are integrated in the leadership development example conducted in an Australian state police service, discussed in the next section.

Leadership development example: *Healthy Workplaces Project*

The Healthy Workplaces Project (Biggs *et al.*, 2014a, 2014b, 2014c; Brough *et al.*, 2012) is a multifaceted workplace intervention programme designed to maintain optimal health and performance of criminal justice employees. A component of this project is a senior leadership and management development programme conducted with senior leaders of a large Australian police service. The leadership development programme was integrated in the project, in response to the needs analysis that identified:

1   The supportiveness of the work culture and quality of relationships between senior managers and frontline police was a significant factor in predicting work engagement, psychological strain, and employee attitudes.
2   A desire to build leadership capability within the organisation.
3   A requirement for ongoing development, support, and resources for senior leaders.

Furthermore, it was recognised that including a senior leader development programme would signal the commitment of the leaders to the project, promoting acceptance of the broader programme of interventions throughout the organisation's hierarchy.

Leadership development programme elements

The leadership development programme aimed to develop awareness of leadership practices and skills, and was based on an existing programme tailored to ensure its relevance in a policing context (Pollard, 2010). The programme was implemented within two police geographic regions. Participants were invited to attend if they were classified in a rank equivalent to Sergeant and above and if their day-to-day activities involved people-management responsibilities. The programme consisted of three primary components: (a) 270-degree leadership review; (b) action-learning workshops; and (c) executive coaching. These elements were delivered in an action-learning framework, enabling participants to engage with the material in a manner that was meaningful to their working context and allowed opportunities for vicarious learning through shared experiences.

270-degree leadership review

Prior to Workshop 1, participants were asked: (a) to complete a pre-workshop evaluation; (b) to complete a leadership styles questionnaire for the 270-degree review process; and (c) to nominate up to 20 followers and one supervisor, who were also invited to complete a survey as part of the review process. The survey assessed transformational and transactional leadership behaviours, employee well-being, attitudes, and performance. All followers' responses were amalgamated so that the reports included only the grouped data. Alternatively, supervisors were provided with the option of their results being presented separately (and, therefore, being identifiable), or presented within the grouped data (remaining anonymous). This information was used to compile confidential reports for each leader, which was provided to the executive coaches for coaching purposes and the participating leaders only.

The 270-degree leadership review aimed to provide participants with an opportunity: to reflect on their own leadership styles and behaviours; to obtain direct (anonymous) feedback of other employees' perceptions of their leadership styles and behaviours; to observe the degree of correspondence between the leader's and others' feedback; and to enhance the leaders' awareness of their own leadership styles/strengths and the impact of their leadership on the performance and well-being of their followers.

Action-learning workshops

All the leaders attended a series of action-learning workshops. Workshops were conducted over five days, with the first four workshops being presented over a one- or two-week block, and the fifth workshop being held approximately six months later as a follow-up session after completion of the executive coaching component. These workshops were presented in an action-learning mode, following a common framework:

- presentation of a leadership concept or theory and its application in the workplace;
- development of individual plans for practical application of the knowledge to the workplace, which were then reviewed in the larger group;
- participants' taking back to the workplace an amalgamation of their own work/ideas and those of colleagues; and
- discussion of the impact (positive and negative) of each leader's action plan and a review of (group) lessons learnt from each leader's experience.

Therefore, the programme presented principles of organisational and strategic leadership, synthesising contemporary leadership perspectives (Pollard, 2010). The combination of action learning and theory is consistent with best-practice approaches to leadership development, which complements training with opportunities to practice skills in real-world environments (Leskiw and Singh, 2007).

Executive coaching

Individual coaching sessions were conducted during the programme to provide personalized feedback of the 270-degree review process and enable participants to discuss any difficulties experienced while implementing newly developed leadership skills.

Evaluation of leadership development programme

As discussed in Chapter 7, a detailed evaluation of this leadership programme was purposefully designed. Two forms of evaluation were conducted to determine whether the leadership development programme was effective. First, a short participant evaluation survey was completed by participants prior to the commencement of the programme (pre-workshop evaluation) and immediately upon completing the programme (post-workshop evaluation). These evaluations assessed satisfaction with various aspects of the programme, improvements in levels of knowledge and confidence surrounding pertinent leadership issues, and suggestions for programme improvement. These evaluations were distributed to participants electronically. The majority of participants (76 per cent) found the programme to be valuable, and significant improvements in confidence and knowledge regarding leadership abilities were observed (e.g. leading employees with diverse work styles, enacting sustainable organisational change, and cultivating a work environment where creativity and innovation are encouraged). These results are also presented in graph form in Chapter 7. According to the participants, the most valuable aspects of the programme were the group discussions, case studies, executive coaching, strategies for dealing with employees, and education about varying leadership styles and how they impact communication and behaviour.

The second form of evaluation included a quasi-experimental research design (Biggs *et al.*, 2014a). Data on perceptions of work characteristics and well-being were assessed via surveys administered before and after the leadership development programme. Pre- and post-data were compared for employees who were identified as direct reports of intervention participants compared to other employees in the region. Improvements were noted for work culture support, strategic alignment, work engagement, and job satisfaction.

Conclusion

A significant current and future challenge for criminal justice administrators is to successfully transform organisational leadership and culture in order to maintain success in contemporary criminal justice contexts. The nature of crime is rapidly evolving, creating unprecedented demands that require innovative procedures and practices. In order to meet this challenge, effective criminal justice leadership and management is required at all organisational levels. This is conditional upon creating organisational infrastructure that supports leadership development and greater recognition of the need to invest resources into leadership development and cultural change. Furthermore, more research is required in criminal justice settings to more precisely define the nature of effective leadership in these contexts and provide greater clarity as to how leadership can be developed (Dobby *et al.*, 2004).

References

Avolio, B.J., Richard, R.J., Hannah, S.T., Walumbwa, F.O., and Chan, A. (2009) A meta-analytic review of leadership impact research: experimental and quasi-experimental studies. *The Leadership Quarterly*, 20: 764–784. doi:10.1016/j.leaqua.2009.06.006.

Bass, B.M. (1990) From transactional to transformational leadership: learning to share the vision. *Organizational Dynamics*, 18(3): 19–31. doi:10.1016/0090–2616(90)90061-S.

Biggs, A. (2011) *A longitudinal evaluation of strain, work engagement, and intervention strategies to address the health of high-risk employees.* Doctoral Thesis, Griffith University, Brisbane.

Biggs, A., Brough, P., and Barbour, J.P. (2014a) Enhancing work-related attitudes and work engagement: a quasi-experimental study of the impact of a leadership development intervention. *International Journal of Stress Management*, 21(1): 43–68. doi:10.1037/a0034508.

Biggs, A., Brough, P., and Barbour, J.P. (2014b) Relationships of individual and organizational support with engagement: examining various types of causality in a three-wave study. *Work and Stress*, 28(3): 236–254. doi:10.1080/02678373.2014.934316.

Biggs, A., Brough, P., and Barbour, J.P. (2014c) Strategic alignment with organizational priorities and work engagement: a multi-wave analysis. *Journal of Organizational Behavior*, 35(3): 301–317. doi:10.1002/job.1866.

Brough, P., Biggs, A., and Barbour, J.P. (2012) *Healthy Workplace Project: final report.* Brisbane: Griffith University.

Burgess, M., and Hawkes, A. (2013) *Authentic leadership and affective, normative and continuance commitment: the mediating effects of trust in leadership and caring ethical climate.* Paper presented at the Proceedings of the 10th Industrial and Organisational Psychology Conference, Perth.

Campbell, I., and Kodz, J. (2011) *What makes great police leadership? What research can tell us about the effectiveness of different leadership styles, competencies and behaviours: A rapid evidence review.* London: National Policing Improvement Agency.

Dobby, J., Anscombe, J., and Tuffin, R. (2004) *Police leadership: exectations and impact.* London: Research, Development and Statistics Directorate, Home Office.

Hannah, S.T., Walumbwa, F.O., and Fry, L.W. (2011) Leadership in action teams: team leader and members' authenticity, authenticity strength, and team outcomes. *Personnel Psychology*, 64: 771–802. doi:10.1111/j.1744–6570.2011.01225.x.

Kelloway, E.K., and Barling, J. (2010) Leadership development as an intervention in occupational health psychology. *Work and Stress*, 24(3): 260–279. doi:10.1080/026783 73.2010.518441.

Leskiw, S., and Singh, P. (2007) Leadership development: learning from best practices. *Leadership and Organization Development Journal*, 28(5): 444–464. doi:http://dx.doi. org/10.1108/01437730710761742.

Neyroud, P. (2011) *Review of police leadership and training.* London: Home Office.

Pollard, F. (2010) *Leadership development program.* Brisbane.

Stojkovic, S., Kalinich, D., and Klofas, J. (2008) *Criminal justice: administration and management*, 4th edn. Belmont, CA: Thompson Wadsworth.

Stojkovic, S., Kalinich, D., and Klofas, J. (2012) *Criminal justice organizations: administration and management*, 5th edn. Belmont, CA: Wadsworth.

Villiers, P. (2009) *Police and policing: an introduction.* Hook, UK: Waterside Press.

Walumbwa, F.O., and Wernsing, T. (2012) From transactional and transformational leadership to authentic leadership. In Rumsey, M.G. (ed.) *The Oxford handbook of leadership.* New York: Oxford University Press. doi:10.1093/oxfordhb/978019539879 3.013.0023.

Winsor, T.P. (2012) *Independent review of police officer and staff remuneration and conditions.* London: HMSO.

15 Dangerous environments

Bullying and harassment

Introduction

Workplace bullying and harassment are specific forms of aggression that cause harm and disrupt organisational processes. Workers' compensation statistics indicate that workplace bullying and harassment are a leading cause of expensive mental health compensation claims and prolonged work absences (Safe Work Australia, 2013). The substantial economic and psychological costs arise not only from actual or vicarious exposure to bullying and harassment, but also as a result of perceived mismanagement or ignorance of such incidents by organisational leaders (Brough *et al.*, 2009; Galanaki and Papalexandris, 2013). Despite increased awareness and legislation, bullying and harassment are still significant workplace problems and effective interventions are needed to minimise their adverse consequences and fulfil the organisation's obligations to provide a safe work environment. Specific best-practice strategies will be discussed in this chapter, including developing effective policy and training, risk assessment, and creating positive organisational cultures.

Understanding bullying and harassment

Clearly defining bullying and harassment supports the development of effective policy and training, equipping employees to detect problematic behaviours, allowing them to intervene early and minimising harmful outcomes (Branch, 2008; Rayner and Lewis, 2011). Most conceptualisations of bullying emphasise the core components reflected in the following definition:

> Bullying at work means harassing, offending, socially excluding someone or negatively affecting someone's work tasks. In order for the label bullying (or mobbing) to be applied to a particular activity, interaction or process it has to occur repeatedly and regularly (e.g. weekly) and over a period of time (e.g. about six months). Bullying is an escalating process in the course of which the person confronted ends up in an inferior position and becomes the target of systematic negative social acts. A conflict cannot be called bullying

if the incident is an isolated event or if two parties of approximately equal 'strength' are in conflict.

(Einarsen *et al.*, 2003, p. 15)

Bullying, therefore, involves a pattern of **enduring and repetitive** behaviours that **escalate over time**, distinguishing it from isolated acts of violence and aggression (Branch, 2008). Although some definitions specify the frequency and minimum timeframe required in order to be classified as bullying, this has been contested as 'there is no real reason why people should endure bullying behaviour for six months in order to meet a (relatively) arbitrary criterion when it is obvious that the behaviour is harming them much earlier' (Caponecchia and Wyatt, 2009, p. 440). This criterion is also difficult to apply when bullying is not strictly episodic, for example, when a single extreme incident or a hostile work environment produces an ongoing cognitive threat (Branch, 2008; Branch *et al.*, 2013; Einarsen *et al.*, 2011).

Bullying also involves a **power imbalance**, where the target feels powerless to defend themselves. This power imbalance may exist prior to the bullying or occur as a result of the bullying, as the target becomes progressively disempowered (Branch *et al.*, 2013; Einarsen *et al.*, 2011; Zapf *et al.*, 1996). Power imbalances may result from formal organizational power structures, as is the case when managers perpetrate bullying, or informal power sources such as knowledge, experience, and access to influential people (Branch *et al.*, 2013; Einarsen *et al.*, 2011).

Most definitions consider bullying to involve any **inappropriate or unreasonable action**, unwanted by the target, that produces humiliation, distress, or offence (Branch, 2008; Einarsen *et al.*, 2011). This 'all encompassing' approach is a common organisational practice to prevent policies becoming outdated (Branch *et al.*, 2013). However, the use of broad definitions is less useful for employees seeking to understand unacceptable behaviours (Rayner and Lewis, 2011). Definitions often also **specify what bullying is not**, such as reasonable managerial actions conducted in a lawful manner (WorkCover Queensland, 2014).

Finally, the definition of bullying provided above references harassing behaviour, which leads us to consider the conflicting use of these terms in policy and research. Workplace harassment is typically considered to involve intimidating, insulting, or humiliating behaviours directed at a person on the basis of personal characteristics covered by anti-discrimination or human rights legislation (e.g. sex and ethnicity; Australian Human Rights Commission, 2010). Some key differences between bullying and harassment have been noted:

- Bullying behaviours follow a repetitive and escalating trajectory, while harassment can occur in an isolated incident (Branch, 2008; Nielsen *et al.*, 2010).
- Both harassment and bullying involve an imbalance of power between targets and perpetrators. Bullying involves an imbalance in formal and/or

informal power structures created *within the work environment*. In contrast, harassment directed towards a target based on their affiliation with a marginalised social group reflects *wider societal power imbalances* (Branch, 2008; Fox and Stallworth, 2009).

•   Options for addressing bullying and harassment differ, as harassment is generally covered by anti-discrimination legislation, whereas bullying is usually represented in workplace health and safety policy (McKay, 2013).

Within criminal justice occupations, sexual harassment is the form of harassment most frequently discussed. Dowler and Arai (2008, p. 125), for example, drew attention to sexual harassment as a 'serious and disturbing element of police work and subculture' and noted that sexual harassment of female police officers is a 'particularly virulent type of gender bias.' Similarly, Belknap (2007) reviewed research on sexual harassment experienced by female lawyers, which indicated that it is a major issue, particularly in private practice. The sexual harassment experienced by the female lawyers was perpetrated by male lawyers, clients, judges, and other legal staff, demonstrating the array of potential sources of sexual harassment in criminal justice occupations.

The confusion in the terms lies in the tendency for 'workplace bullying' being used as an umbrella term comprising a range of negative behaviours, including harassment. It has been recommended that a distinction be made between bullying and specific forms of harassment (e.g. sexual harassment) within organisational policies, in recognition of the uniqueness of the concepts (Branch, 2008). For example, Worksafe Queensland cites bullying as distinct from isolated incidents of unlawful discrimination, vilification, or sexual harassment. Despite these noted differences, bullying and harassment are often treated interchangeably in research, as there is considerable overlap in the precursors and consequences of harmful interpersonal behaviours (Einarsen *et al.*, 2011; Tuckey *et al.*, 2012).

Prevalence of bullying and harassment

Prevalence rates of bullying and harassment are important for understanding the scope of the problem, but are difficult to obtain due to (a) inconsistent conceptualisations of the terms, (b) lack of research with representative samples, and (c) varying individual perceptions of what does and does not constitute bullying and harassment. For example, an Australian study on sexual harassment demonstrated that 22 per cent of respondents who initially reported 'they had not experienced sexual harassment' had actually experienced behaviours that conformed to legal definitions of sexual harassment (Australian Human Rights Commission, 2008). Therefore, prevalence figures should be treated with caution.

International studies have reported rates of workplace bullying between 10 and 20 per cent, depending on the measure of bullying employed (Nielsen *et al.*, 2010). Zapf *et al.* (2011) calculated prevalence rates between 10 and 15 per cent.

In a large Australian sample of the working population, 6.8 per cent of respondents indicated they had experienced workplace bullying, with approximately half of those (representing 3.5 per cent of the total sample) experiencing bullying for longer than six months (Dollard *et al.*, 2012). These Australian figures were based on a stricter conceptualisation of bullying, focusing on targets only, excluding employees who witnessed bullying.

Prevalence statistics also indicated that female employees experience higher rates of bullying and most forms of harassment. A study of 2,005 Australians indicated 22 per cent of women and 5 per cent of men had experienced sexual harassment in the workplace in their life time. Approximately 12 per cent also indicated they had witnessed sexual harassment (Australian Human Rights Commission, 2008). In another Australian study (Dollard *et al.*, 2012), females experienced more bullying than males, and the duration of bullying was longer on average. Furthermore, females reported significantly higher rates of unwanted sexual advances, humiliation, and unfair treatment due to gender, while males reported higher rates of physical violence and verbal abuse (i.e. being yelled or sworn at; Dollard *et al.*, 2012). Workers' compensation statistics also indicated that the rate of claims for bullying and harassment between 2009 and 2012 made by women were three times higher than those made by men (Safe Work Australia, 2014).

Comparisons in prevalence rates between occupations typically suggests that bullying and harassment are more prevalent in tough work cultures and organisations with greater power differentials between organisational levels, as is evident in criminal justice occupations (Ilies *et al.*, 2003). A comparison of 13 occupations indicated that security guards and police officers were included in the top five occupations with highest mean risk of co-worker aggression (LeBlanc and Kelloway, 2002). Australian workers' compensation statistics for 2009–2012 also indicated that prison officers and police officers had the first and third highest respective frequency rates of claims due to bullying and harassment (Safe Work Australia, 2014). Female employees within these occupations are particularly vulnerable. Belknap (2007) reported that females were four times more likely to suffer gender-related incivility during federal litigation than men, while female Swedish police officers reported higher rates of sexual harassment in comparison to male police officers (Svedberg and Alexanderson, 2012).

Precursors of bullying and harassment

Understanding individual, social, and organisational precursors of bullying and harassment is necessary to develop effective policies and interventions (Bond *et al.*, 2010; Einarsen *et al.*, 2011; Salin, 2003). Research has examined **individual precursors**, including personality traits of the target and perpetrator, coping strategies, and the target's response to bullying (Einarsen *et al.*, 2011). **Dyadic and social group dynamics** between perpetrators and targets have also been examined, such as personality clashes and interpersonal conflict (Einarsen *et al.*, 2011). As they are seldom isolated or private phenomena, however, recent research has focused to a greater extent on **organisational factors** that 'provide normative permission' to perpetrate bullying and harassment (Fox and Stallworth, 2009, p. 225).

To synthesise this research, Salin (2003) identified three categories of organisational risk factors:

- **Enabling factors** are organisational conditions that provide a fertile environment for bullying and harassment, by creating power imbalances and reducing consequences for perpetrators (Salin, 2003, 2008). These include non-existent or poorly implemented policies, organisational structure and culture, ineffective leadership, and job stress.
- **Motivating factors** are aspects of the work environment that reward bullying behaviour. For example, the promotion of employees who perpetrate bullying may encourage others to 'get ahead' by acting aggressively (Tuckey *et al.*, 2012).
- **Precipitating factors** are events that trigger bullying and harassment, such as downsizing, restructuring, and group composition changes. Downsizing, for example, may result in increased competition for resources and positions.

Recent research has discussed enabling and motivating factors within criminal justice organisations. For instance, the bureaucratic and paramilitary structure results in a strong adherence to hierarchy, intensifying power imbalances between employees of higher and lower ranks (Bond *et al.*, 2010; McKay, 2013). This is further exacerbated by features of the organisational culture, including solidarity and authority, which emphasise loyalty to colleagues, respect for the chain of command, and conformity (Archer, 1999; McKay, 2013). Speaking out against fellow employees, especially leaders, violates these norms (McKay, 2013). Formal complaints processes are also often perceived negatively by employees as they bypass the appropriate chain of command and threaten camaraderie.

The cultural value placed on masculine characteristics, such as toughness, is an additional challenge for managing bullying and harassment in criminal justice occupations. Seeking support or complaining about bullying often results in punitive reactions and stigmatisation of the target, as it violates normative expectation that you need to be tough in order to work with offenders. A joking culture also exists within many criminal justice occupations, in which making inappropriate jokes and playing pranks is viewed as an acceptable form of socialisation and coping (McKay, 2013). It is very easy for jokes and banter to escalate into bullying and harassment, if the target is unable to defend themselves or 'take it like a man' [*sic*] (Salin, 2003). Again, the perceived inability to take a joke conflicts with the perception of toughness needed to work in criminal justice occupations, and complaining about bullying or banter may result in greater scrutiny of the target's suitability as an employee than the actions of the perpetrator (McKay, 2013).

The value of traditional masculine characteristics combined with a lack of diversity in workforce composition has also been linked to sexual harassment (e.g. Willness *et al.*, 2007). McDonald (2012) noted that sexual harassment is most likely to occur in organisations where there are clearly demarcated power differentials, gender dominated environments and occupational cultural norms sanctioning sexual bravado, sexual posturing, and the denigration of females (such as the police). Female officers may experience greater social exclusion and harassment if they are deemed to be lacking the qualities required to perform their role or fit within the work culture and are subsequently viewed as intruders who disrupt male camaraderie (Bond *et al.*, 2004). For example, gender equality was predictive of lower bullying and harassment, while greater social exclusion predicted greater bullying and harassment over a period of six months in a sample of correctional officers (Biggs, 2011; Biggs and Brough, 2014).

The 'high stress' nature of criminal justice occupations is an additional risk factor for bullying and harassment (e.g. Brough and Biggs, 2010). Job stress increases frustration, inhibits impulse control, and impedes effective conflict resolution, culminating in aggression enacted towards colleagues (Tuckey *et al.*, 2012). Insufficient psychological and tangible resources in particular have been linked to bullying and harassment. For example, high levels of job control and support coincided with lower perceptions of bullying and harassment in a sample of correctional officers (Biggs and Brough, 2014). Furthermore, insufficient tangible resources (e.g. budget, people, vehicles, and equipment) were important precursors of bullying and harassment in a sample of police officers, likely due to competition and conflict over limited resources (Tuckey *et al.*, 2012).

Modern criminal justice organisations are making progress in increasing ethical conduct, diversity, and professionalism amongst employees. However, components of the organisational structure that reinforce power imbalances are still deemed necessary for the provision of effective public services, and some aspects of the culture remain deeply entrenched and resistant to change. This creates ongoing challenges for addressing bullying and harassment in criminal justice occupations.

A final precursor of bullying that has seldom been discussed is whistleblowing. Whistleblowing involves the disclosure by organisational members of employers' wrongdoing to organisational leaders or external authorities (Matthiesen *et al.*, 2011). 'Because it can lead to the discovery and rectification of wrongdoing, whistleblowing is widely acknowledged as having potentially positive effects – for organisations and for society at large' (Brown and Donkin, 2008, p. 1). Despite seldom being studied together, there is substantial overlap between bullying and whistleblowing: effective whistleblowing systems can uncover wrongdoing associated with bullying and harassment, and bullying and harassment are likely outcomes of poorly handled instances of whistleblowing (Bjørkelo *et al.*, 2011). The reactions to whistleblowing are important, especially the response of managers, and it is in the organisation's best interest to create policies and systems that protect whistleblowers from retaliation and bullying.

Outcomes of bullying and harassment

Economic costs associated with bullying and harassment are incurred due to performance deficits, litigation, workers' compensation, long-term absenteeism, and increased turnover (Bond *et al.*, 2010). For instance, Australian workers' compensation statistics show that claims associated with bullying and harassment are amongst the most costly, with a median direct cost of $18,100 per claim and median time loss of 8.4 working weeks (Safe Work Australia, 2014). The US Equal Opportunity Commission reported costs related to charges and resolutions of sexual harassment of US$52.3 million for the 2011 financial year, which excluded monetary benefits obtained through litigation (US Equal Employment Opportunity Commission, n.d.).

Psychological costs include poor morale, disengagement, and ill-health, and are not only experienced by direct targets of bullying, but also by witnesses to the bullying and harassment (i.e. vicarious bullying). Consequences of bullying, identified in a meta-analysis (Nielsen and Einarsen, 2012), included: mental ill-health (i.e. anxiety and depression); post-traumatic stress; physical ill-health; burnout; psychological strain; absenteeism; intention to leave, job dissatisfaction; and reduced organisational commitment. Criminal justice-specific research has also noted a range of consequences of bullying and harassment including post-traumatic stress symptoms within Australian police officers (Bond *et al.*, 2010); psychotropic drug use within Canadian correctional officers (Lavigne and Bourbonnais, 2010); and sickness absence within Swedish police officers (Svedberg and Alexanderson, 2012). Furthermore, a longitudinal study with Australian police demonstrated current exposure to negative workplace behaviours was significantly associated with psychological strain, while past exposure (12 months prior) was associated with poor cardiovascular health (Tuckey *et al.*, 2010). Finally, bullying from supervisors predicted lower work engagement and higher burnout, while bullying from colleagues predicted higher social exclusion and lower perceptions of equal opportunities, over a six month period within Australian correctional officers (Biggs and Brough, 2014).

Best-practice examples of dealing with bullying and harassment

Prevention and intervention strategies primarily revolve around risk assessment, policy development, and training. To a lesser extent, broader approaches aiming to promote positive organisational cultures are also implemented. As with any organisational intervention, the development, implementation, and evaluation of strategies equally require consideration, and the lack of evaluations in particular presents a significant barrier. This is especially pertinent given poorly executed strategies may actually exacerbate bullying and harassment (Bingham and Scherer, 2001). These issues will be discussed in the following paragraphs.

Risk assessment and monitoring

Regular assessment of the occurrence, precursors, and consequences of bullying and harassment assists with early identification of emerging problems, policy development, training needs assessment, and evaluation (Fox and Stallworth, 2009). Assessment may involve annual surveys (Chapter 10), interviews, or focus groups (Chapter 8). A comprehensive approach comprises the following components:

1   **Assessment of direct or vicarious exposure to bullying and harassment.** Two forms of measurement are commonly incorporated in organisational surveys (Galanaki and Papalexandris, 2013; Nielsen *et al.*, 2010). First, the *self-identification* method asks employees to indicate whether they have experienced bullying/harassment according to an accompanying definition (drawn from organisational policy). Second, the *behavioural method* asks employees to indicate whether they have experienced or witnessed any actions from a list of negative acts commonly associated with bullying and harassment. Incorporating both forms of measurement is recommended.

2   **Assessment of risk factors and consequences of bullying and harassment.** Pertinent risk factors may be drawn from existing theory and research, and also from organisational records of previous complaints or interviews/focus groups conducted with staff.

3   **Assessment of proxy indicators of bullying and harassment.** Existing organisational data (e.g. sickness absences and disciplinary infractions) can be assessed for specific commands, ranks/levels, or departments within the organisations, to identify if there are 'hot spots' where levels seem higher than average. Any spikes in such organisational data may warrant further investigation as potential indicators of bullying. Paradoxically excessively high performance returns may also be indicative of oppressive management or bullying.

Policy

Organisations commonly implement anti-bullying policy to set acceptable behavioural standards, help redress power imbalances, and clarify informal and formal complaints processes (Salin, 2008). Policy development should be approached with a clear conceptualisation of bullying and harassment, precursors, and consequences, which may be informed by legislation, empirical research, and the results of risk assessment (Rayner and Lewis, 2011). The policy should comply with legislation whilst also being tailored to meet the needs of the organisation. Replication of generic policy is a common practice that limits its effectiveness, as it is less likely to consider the organisation's specific needs and resources or obtain the support, commitment, and awareness of employees (Salin, 2008). Finally, effective policy development involves the commitment and involvement of senior managers, personnel involved in enacting the policy (e.g. HRM), and the broader employee community, to increase awareness and acceptance of the policy throughout the organisation (Salin, 2008).

The actual content of policy should be clear, easy to read, and include the following components (Pate and Beaumont, 2010; Rayner and Lewis, 2011; Salin, 2008):

- A statement communicating the organisation's zero-tolerance stance towards bullying and harassment.
- Clear definitions and examples of bullying and harassment.
- Informal resolution processes, including details of relevant contact people. The first point of contact is often the immediate supervisor, although other independent sources of assistance should be listed for instances where the immediate supervisor is the alleged perpetrator.
- Formal resolution processes, including time-frames, roles, and responsibilities of various stakeholders (e.g. employees, managers, HR); potential consequences for perpetrators; and general recommendations for all involved parties.
- A statement detailing monitoring and review processes.

Bullying and harassment still occur, despite the existence of formal written policy, pointing to a gap between the intended and actual implementation of policies (Pate and Beaumont, 2010; Woodrow and Guest, 2014). Guidelines for closing the gap include: promoting the policy to employees in multiple formats; incorporating policy in training and promotion materials; providing adequate training for contact people; and conducting investigations in a timely manner, keeping all involved parties well informed of the investigation's progress (Rayner and Lewis, 2011). Policies need to be continually evaluated to ensure they maintain their effectiveness, adhere to current legislative requirements, are regarded positively by employees, and are up-to-date with the continually evolving nature of bullying and harassment. Pate and Beaumont (2010) recommended policies be evaluated against multiple criteria, drawing on official organisational records (e.g. official complaints); employee's perceived experience of bullying and harassment; and broader organisational factors, such as trust in managers and group cohesion. Finally, a change in organisational culture may be needed to reduce stigmatisation surrounding reporting bullying and harassment, in order for policies to be effective (see Chapter 12 for a case study in creating a procedurally just workplace.)

Training and education for supervisors

Leader's unwillingness or incapacity to intervene in interpersonal matters and toxic leadership, in which leaders actually role-model inappropriate behaviour, are important precursors of bullying and harassment. Leadership training and support is, therefore, a key strategy for reducing these phenomena at work (Salin, 2003, 2008). Training should aim to enhance a leader's (a) ability to identify early signs of aggression, (b) capacity to intervene competently, and (c) understanding of their responsibility for managing bullying and harassment. Furthermore, as leaders shape the organisational culture and set the tone for acceptable behaviour at work, training to reduce toxic leadership behaviours and encourage effective conflict resolution skills, role-modelling of appropriate behaviour, and positive interpersonal interactions with subordinates is also recommended (Salin, 2003, 2008). Training in equity issues, bullying/harassment, and interpersonal skills should be integrated within promotion processes, and repeated periodically to account for the high level of changeover of leaders in criminal justice occupations. Our evaluation of leadership development programmes for police leaders has demonstrated the positive effect of providing training to increase leader's capacity to manage people effectively, for example, through increasing skills for providing positive and constructive performance feedback (Biggs *et al.*, 2014a).

Education for employees

Education for employees of all levels is also recommended to increase awareness of organisational policies, establish joint responsibility for maintaining a safe and fair workplace, improving interpersonal skills, and reducing stigma (Salin, 2008). The latter benefit is particularly pertinent for criminal justice occupations, where targets are deterred from seeking support or raising issues for fear of ridicule, punishment, job insecurity, and diminished promotion opportunities. In focus groups conducted with correctional officers, for example, we noted a divide in opinion amongst participants, with some viewing formal complaints processes positively, and others viewing complaints as a form of 'snitching' (Biggs, 2011).

Face-to-face discussions about bullying and harassment may be confronting for employees, and creative solutions for broaching the subject in a non-threatening manner may be required. Strandmark and Rahm (2014), for example, developed a card-based activity, consisting of 20 playing cards, each containing different scenarios, along with five possible solutions. Focus group participants drew a card and everyone in the group discussed suitable solutions and procedures for dealing with the scenario. This activity was effective in stimulating reflection and reducing fear of publically discussing bullying in a focus group context. A further strategy we have used with correctional officers is to provide a summary of results from a risk assessment survey, which included items about workplace bullying, harassment, and violence, and ask group participants to comment on the findings and suggest possible solutions (Biggs, 2011). This strategy was effective, as it provided a non-threatening means of broaching the topic of bullying, stimulated reflection and conversation, and also helped the discussion remain on topic.

Promoting positive work cultures

Approaches discussed to this point attempt to increase individual agency without sufficiently addressing facets of the organisation's structure and culture that perpetuate bullying and harassment (McKay, 2013). This is particularly challenging in criminal justice occupations, as many acknowledged structural and cultural risk factors are also functional in ensuring safe and effective delivery of services to the community. For example, cultural norms emphasising obedience of authority are functional during critical incidents but can be detrimental when they result in abuses of power (McKay, 2013). In addition, attempts to reduce levels of hierarchy may exacerbate bullying and harassment by fostering competition for promotions, which would also be counterproductive (McKay, 2013).

Nonetheless, recent Australian research has suggested that adopting a broader approach focusing on fostering a healthy and positive culture within criminal justice workplaces is likely to reduce bullying and harassment. For example, the existence of a supportive work culture was one of the most important long-term predictors of bullying, harassment, engagement, and strain experienced by police officers (Biggs and Brough, 2014; Biggs *et al.*, 2014b). Psychosocial safety climate (PSC), referring to employees' beliefs regarding their organisation's commitment to protecting their psychological safety and well-being, has also been shown to predict bullying, harassment, and psychological outcomes (e.g. PTSD symptoms; Bond *et al.*, 2010).

According to Bond *et al.* (2010), organisations with high levels of PSC have leaders who are committed to creating and enacting policies that protect employees' well-being and are willing to take corrective action to ensure bullying and harassment are neither ignored nor rewarded. Furthermore, a consultative approach to dealing with matters of well-being is adopted, in which people are free to speak up without fear of punishment or stigma. Involving employees has an additional benefit of enhancing the relevance and utility of strategies. Strandmark and Rahm (2014), for instance, discussed an intervention to increase awareness of bullying and harassment amongst employees and enhance humanistic cultural values of respect, empathy, and tolerance, which was developed and evaluated using focus groups of employees.

Finally, job stress, a known precursor of bullying and harassment, occurs when available resources are not matched to the demands of the job. Tuckey *et al.* (2012, p. 292) noted that 'harassment may have its genesis in lack of resources (e.g. budget, time, people, vehicles, computers, office equipment, training and operational equipment) at the micro level' and an important tactic for minimising bullying and harassment is ensuring employees have sufficient tangible resources they need to counteract their unique operational demands. Job stress tends to be lower in organisations with high levels of PSC, because work is designed and managed to ensure employees possess the psychological and tangible resources to manage their demands (Bond *et al.*, 2010).

Treatment of employees within informal and formal complaints systems

An organisation's capacity to respond fairly and appropriately to formal complaints is often discussed but seldom formally evaluated. Specific concerns relating to formal complaints processes include punitive or ignorant responses (e.g. being told to toughen up) and arduous and prolonged formal processes. These factors deter targets from lodging complaints early, resulting in an escalation of the bullying or harassment (Tuckey *et al.*, 2012). For example, an Australian study found that only 16 per cent of people who experienced sexual harassment, and 35 per cent who witnessed sexual harassment, made a formal complaint (Australian Human Rights Commission, 2008). In addition, Biggs and Brough (2014) recently evaluated confidence in the organisation's response to bullying and harassment in a sample of more than 5,000 criminal justice employees. Just over half of the sample (60 to 61 per cent) strongly agreed or agreed that 'managers would act on the complaint in an appropriate way' and 'employees would be supported if they reported being the target of bullying'. Nonetheless, a substantial proportion of the sample (approximately 40 per cent) did not feel confident this would be the case. Furthermore, perceived confidence in the organisation's capacity to respond fairly and appropriately was a stronger predictor of strain and work engagement over a 12-month period than actual bullying experiences.

Overall, these concerns highlight two issues. First, *a lack of confidence in organisational processes* suggests a need for more effective policy and processes, embedded within a supportive organisational culture. Our research within criminal justice organisations (Biggs and Brough, 2014) demonstrated that supportive work cultures, supervisor support, group cohesion, and high morale predicted greater confidence in organisational processes: strategies to promote positive and supportive work cultures are thus likely to promote greater confidence in formal policy and processes. The second issue is *fear of repercussions for making a complaint*. The Australian Human Rights Commission (2008) noted that it was critical that employers provide avenues for targets and witnesses of bullying and harassment to make formal complaints without fear of punishment or retaliation. Protecting those lodging bullying complaints from experiencing further victimisation is akin to the goal of whistleblowing systems that aim to protect whistleblowers from experiencing retaliation and bullying. Reporting genuine organisational wrongdoing, including bullying and harassment, is an important initial step in rectifying the wrongdoing, and is recognised as an important mechanism for promoting positive organisational change (Matthiesen *et al.*, 2011). As a result, it is in the organisation's best interest to create policies and systems that protect whistleblowers from retaliation and bullying.

Concerns regarding the fair treatment of alleged perpetrators have also been raised in our criminal justice research, including the uncertainty for alleged perpetrators due to overly arduous and intrusive investigations, and the use of internal investigators who may not be sufficiently independent (Biggs, 2011). Apprehension about vexatious claims were also discussed: 24 per cent of participants indicated they were worried about vexatious complaints being made against them, particularly by offenders and members of the public, and the resultant damage to reputations that persists despite a claim being unsubstantiated. Therefore, while it is important to ensure that policies and procedures are not so arduous that genuine targets are dissuaded from speaking up, it is also important to consider strategies to discourage malicious claims.

Conclusion

Bullying and harassment are not limited to particular sectors or occupational groups. However, there are aspects of the work environment within criminal justice organisations that are linked to an increased risk of bullying and harassment, including: the hierarchical and bureaucratic organisational structure; emphasis on authority and solidarity; homogeneity of employees; value attached to traditionally masculine characteristics; and the existence of a joking culture. Policies are most often developed to address bullying and harassment (Salin, 2008), although they are likely to be insufficient when used in isolation. A comprehensive approach to managing bullying and harassment was discussed in this chapter, including the provision of leader and employee training, positive cultural change, and fair treatment of participants involved in formal complaints processes. An important next step is to evaluate the effects of policy, training, and programmes to provide evidence-based examples of what works in reducing bullying and harassment in criminal justice organisations.

References

Archer, D. (1999) Exploring 'bullying' culture in the para-military organisation. *International Journal of Manpower*, 20(1/2): 94–105. doi:http://dx.doi.org/10.1108/01437729910268687.

Australian Human Rights Commission (2008) *Sexual harassment: serious business. Results of the 2008 Sexual Harassment National Telephone Survey*. Sydney: Australian Human Rights Commission.

Australian Human Rights Commission (2010) What is workplace discriminaion and harassment? www.humanrights.gov.au/what-workplace-discrimination-and-harassment.

Belknap, J. (2007) *The invisible woman: gender, crime and justice*, 3rd edn. Belmont, CA: Thompson Wadsworth.

Biggs, A. (2011) *A longitudinal evaluation of strain, work engagement, and intervention strategies to address the health of high-risk employees*. Doctoral Thesis, Griffith University, Brisbane.

Biggs, A., and Brough, P. (2014, July) *Bullying and harassment in 'tough' work cultures*. Paper presented at the 28th International Congress of Applied Psychology, Paris.

Biggs, A., Brough, P., and Barbour, J.P. (2014a) Enhancing work-related attitudes and work engagement: a quasi-experimental study of the impact of a leadership development intervention. *International Journal of Stress Management*, 21(1): 43–68. doi:10.1037/a0034508.

Biggs, A., Brough, P., and Barbour, J.P. (2014b) Relationships of individual and organizational support with engagement: examining various types of causality in a three-wave study. *Work and Stress*, 28(3): 236–254. doi:10.1080/02678373.2014.934316.

Bingham, S.G., and Scherer, L.L. (2001) The unexpected effects of a sexual harassment educational program. *The Journal of Applied Behavioral Science*, 37(2): 125–153. doi:10.1177/0021886301372001.

Bjørkelo, B., Einarsen, S., Nielsen, M.B., and Matthiesen, S.B. (2011) Silence is golden? Characteristics and experiences of self-reported whistleblowers. *European Journal of Work and Organizational Psychology*, 20(2): 206–238. doi:10.1080/13594320903338884.

Bond, M.A., Punnett, L., Pyle, J.L., Cazeca, D., and Cooperman, M. (2004) Gendered work conditions, health, and work outcomes. *Journal of Occupational Health Psychology*, 9(1): 28–45.

Bond, S.A., Tuckey, M.R., and Dollard, M.F. (2010) Psychosocial safety climate, workplace bullying, and symptoms of posttraumatic stress. *Organization Development Journal*, 28(1): 37–56.

Branch, S. (2008) You say tomatoe and I say tomato: can we differentiate between workplace bullying and other counterproductive behaviours? *International Journal of Organisational Behaviour*, 13(2): 4–17.

Branch, S., Ramsay, S., and Barker, M. (2013) Workplace bullying, mobbing and general harassment: a review. *International Journal of Management Reviews*, 15: 280–299. doi:10.1111/j.1468–2370.2012.00339.x.

Brough, P., and Biggs, A. (2010) Occupational stress in police and prison staff. In Brown, J. and Campbell, E. (eds) *The Cambridge handbook of forensic psychology*. Cambridge: Cambridge University Press (pp. 707–718).

Brough, P., O'Driscoll, M., Kalliath, T., Cooper, C.L., and Poelmans, S. (2009) *Workplace psychological health: current research and practice*. Cheltenham, UK: Edward Elgar.

Brown, A.J., and Donkin, M. (2008) Introduction. In Brown, A.J. (ed.) *Whistleblowing in the Australian public sector: enhancing the theory and practice of internal witness management in public sector organisations*. Canberra: ANU E-Press (pp. 1–22).

Caponecchia, C., and Wyatt, A. (2009) Distinguishing between workplace bullying, harassment and violence: a risk management approach. *Journal of Occupational Health and Safety – Australian and New Zealand*, 25(6): 439–449.

Dollard, M.F., Bailey, T., McLinton, S., Richards, P., McTernan, W., Taylor, A., and Bond, S. (2012) *The Australian Workplace Barometer: report on psychosocial safety climate and worker health in Australia*. South Australia: Safe Work Australia.

Dowler, K., and Arai, B. (2008) Stress, gender and policing: the impact of perceived gender discrimination on symptoms of stress. *International Journal of Police Science and Management*, 10(2): 123–135. doi:10.1350/ijps.2008.10.2.81.

Einarsen, S., Hoel, H., Zapf, D., and Cooper, C.L. (2003) The concept of bullying at work: the European tradition. In Einarsen, S., Hoel, H., Zapf, D. and Cooper, C.L. (eds) *Bullying and emotional abuse in the workplace: international perspectives in research and practice*. London: Taylor & Francis (pp. 3–30).

Einarsen, S., Hoel, H., Zapf, D., and Cooper, C.L. (2011) The concept of bullying and harassment at work: the European tradition. In Einarsen, S., Hoel, H., Zapf, D., and Cooper, C.L. (eds) *Bullying and harassment in the workplace: developments in theory, research, and practice*, 2nd edn. Boca Raton, FL: CRC Press (pp. 3–39). http://site. ebrary.com.libraryproxy.griffith.edu.au/lib/griffith/docDetail.action?docID=10417857.

Fox, S., and Stallworth, L.E. (2009) Building a framework for two internal organizational approaches to resolving and preventing workplace bullying: alternative dispute resolution and training. *Consulting Psychology Journal: Research and Practice*, 61(3): 220–241. doi:10.1037/a0016637.

Galanaki, E., and Papalexandris, N. (2013) Measuring workplace bullying in organisations. *The International Journal of Human Resource Management*, 24(11): 2107–2130. doi:10.1080/09585192.2012.725084.

Ilies, R., Hauserman, N., Schwochau, S., and Stibal, J. (2003) Reported incidence rates of work-related sexual harassment in the United States: using meta-analysis to explain reported rate disparities. *Personnel Psychology*, 56(3): 607–631. doi:10.1111/j.1744–6570.2003.tb00752.x.

Lavigne, E., and Bourbonnais, R. (2010) Psychological work environment, interpersonal violence at work and psychotropic drug use among correctional officers. *International Journal of Law and Psychiatry*, 33: 122–129. doi:10.1016/j.ijlp. 2009.12.005.

LeBlanc, M.M., and Kelloway, E.K. (2002) Predictors and outcomes of workplace violence and aggression. *Journal of Applied Psychology*, 87(3): 444–453.

Matthiesen, S.B., Bjørkelo, B., and Burke, R.J. (2011) Workplace bullying as the dark side of whistleblowing. In Einarsen, S., Hoel, H., Zapf, D., and Cooper, C.L. (eds) *Bullying and harassment in the workplace: developments in theory, research, and practice*, 2nd edn. Boca Raton, FL: CRC Press (pp. 301–324).

McDonald, P. (2012) Workplace sexual harassment 30 years on: a review of the literature. *International Journal of Management Reviews*, 14(1): 1–17. doi:10.1111/j.1468–2370.2011.00300.x.

McKay, R.B. (2013) Confronting workplace bullying: agency and structure in the Royal Canadian Mounted Police. *Administration and Society*. doi:10.1177/0095399713509245.

Nielsen, M.B., and Einarsen, S. (2012) Outcomes of exposure to workplace bullying: a meta-analytic review. *Work and Stress*, 26(4): 309–332. doi:10.1080/02678373.2012.7 34709.

Nielsen, M.B., Matthiesen, S.B., and Einarsen, S. (2010) The impact of methodological moderators on prevalence rates of workplace bullying: a meta-analysis. *Journal of Occupational and Organizational psychology*, 83: 955–979. doi:10.1348/096317909X481256.

Pate, J., and Beaumont, P. (2010) Bullying and harassment: a case of success? *Employee Relations*, 32(2): 171–183. doi:10.1108/01425451011010113.

Rayner, C., and Lewis, D. (2011) Managing workplace bullying: the role of policies. In Einarsen, S., Hoel, H., Zapf, D., and Cooper, C.L. (eds) *Bullying and harassment in the workplace: developments in theory, research, and practice*, 2nd edn. Boca Raton, FL: CRC Press (pp. 327–340).

Safe Work Australia (2013) *The incidence of accepted workers' compensation claims for mental stress in Australia*. Canberra: Safe Work Australia.

Safe Work Australia (2014) *Psychosocial health and safety and bullying in Australian workplaces*. Canberra: Safe Work Australia.

Salin, D. (2003) Ways of explaining workplace bullying: a review of enabling, motivating and precipitating structures and processes in the work environment. *Human Relations*, 56(10): 1213–1232. doi:10.1177/00187267035610003.

Salin, D. (2008) The prevention of workplace bullying as a question of human resource management: measures adopted and underlying organizational factors. *Scandinavian Journal of Management*, 24: 221–231. doi:10.1016/j.scaman.2008.04.004.

Strandmark, M., and Rahm, G. (2014) Development, implementation and evaluation of a process to prevent and combat workplace bullying. *Scandinavian Journal of Public Health*, 42: 66–73. doi:10.1177/1403494814549494.

Svedberg, P., and Alexanderson, K. (2012) Associations between sickness absence and harassment, threats, violence, or discrimination: a cross-sectional study of the Swedish police. *Work*, 42: 83–92. doi:10.3233/WOR-2012-1333.

Tuckey, M.R., Chrisopoulos, S., and Dollard, M.F. (2012) Job demands, resource deficiencies, and workplace harassment: evidence of micro-level effects. *International Journal of Stress Management*, 19(4): 292–310. doi:10.1037/a0030317.

Tuckey, M.R., Dollard, M.F., Saebel, J., and Berry, N.M. (2010) Negative workplace behaviour: temporal associations with cardiovascular outcomes and psychological health problems in Australian police. *Stress and Health*, 26: 372–381. doi:10.1002/smi.1306.

US Equal Employment Opportunity Commission (n.d.) Sexual harassment charges EEOC and FEPAs combined: FY1997–FY2011. www.eeoc.gov/eeoc/statistics/enforcement/sexual_harassment.cfm.

Willness, C.R., Steel, P., and Lee, K. (2007) A meta-analysis of the antecedents and consequences of workplace sexual harassment. *Personnel Psychology*, 60: 127–162. doi:10.1111/j.1744–6570.2007.00067.x.

Woodrow, C., and Guest, D.E. (2014) When good HR gets bad results: exploring the challenge of HR implementation in the case of workplace bullying. *Human Resources Management Journal*, 24(1): 38–56. doi:10.1111/1748–8583.12021.

WorkCover Queensland (2014) *Workplace bullying information tool*. www.worksafe.qld.gov.au/injury-prevention-safety/workplace-hazards/workplace-harassment-and-bullying/workplace-harassment-or-bullying-information-tool#definition.

Zapf, D., Escartín, J., Einarsen, S., Hoel, H., and Vartia, M. (2011) Empirical findings on prevalence and risk groups of bullying in the workplace. In Einarsen, S., Hoel, H., Zapf, D., and Cooper, C.L. (eds) *Bullying and harassment in the workplace: developments in theory, research, and practice*, 2nd edn. Boca Raton, FL: CRC Press (pp. 75–105).

Zapf, D., Knorz, C., and Kulla, M. (1996) On the relationship between mobbing factors, and job content, social work environment, and health outcomes. *European Journal of Work and Organizational Psychology*, 5(2): 215–237. doi:10.1080/13594329 608414856.

16 Diverse environments
Discrimination

Introduction

This chapter addresses the issues of discrimination and equality in the workplace and begins with some definitions. In most jurisdictions, criminal justice agencies tend to have an unbalanced workforce, being dominated for the most part by men, although other demographic characteristics such as ethnicity and sexuality are also under-represented. The exception is probation where the gender balance is tipped in favour of women (Mawby and Worrell 2013). There are adverse consequences suffered by visible minority groups working within policing, probation, prisons, and the court system, as well as potential detriments to the services offered and in the perceived legitimacy of the administration of justice. Most developed countries have equality legislation in place to try and protect certain groups from discriminatory practices. This chapter reviews evidence about the persistence of discrimination and charts the rationale for, and progress made in, achieving greater diversity in CJS workplaces. We also describe the barriers that are still in place and present some remedies for overcoming these.

Definitions

Diversity in the context of work tends to describe the range of both visible and non-visible differences between individual members of an organisation. Jackson *et al.* (2003) described this as the distribution of personal attributes that can be readily detected such as demographic characteristics (age, gender, and ethnicity) and underlying attributes which become evident on knowing the person (such as values, personality, and knowledge). Rather than this more diluted version of diversity, for the purposes of this chapter, consideration is given to 'protected' characteristics. These are aspects of a person that have been subject to equality legislation that prohibits discrimination on the grounds of age, disability, ethnicity, religion, and sexuality. Kandola and Fullerton (1998) suggested there are some crucial differences between the concepts of equality and diversity:

- Diversity is internally driven whereas equality is externally initiated.
- Diversity tends to be driven by business need, whereas equality is legally driven.

- Diversity is designed to improve organisational outcomes, whereas equality is about improving access to and increasing numbers of disadvantaged groups in occupations.
- Diversity is aimed at pluralism, whilst equality assumes assimilation objectives.
- Diversity is concerned with all differences between people, whilst equality focuses on protected characteristics.

Diversity is about recognising difference and creating organisational cultures and practices that respect and harness the value of differences. Equality is about trying to create a fairer society in which everyone can participate and fulfil their full potential. Legislation defines areas at work which may be the subject of unequal or discriminatory treatment such as recruitment, career advancement (promotion and access to specialisms) training opportunities, access to part-time working, and being subjected to disciplinary proceedings. A framework for considering potential areas of discrimination within CJS sites is represented in Figure 16.1.

The case for diversity and equality

The pursuit of talent has been a frequently cited argument for increasing diversity at work (Robinson and Dechant, 1997). In making a pragmatic business case

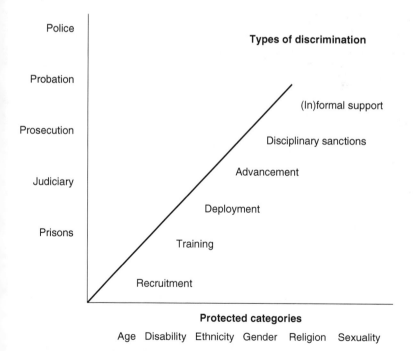

Figure 16.1 The discrimination matrix.

the rationale for promoting diversity is that it improves understanding of the organisation's actual and potential clientele, enhances the breadth of supervisory and leadership skills, engenders greater creativity and increases problem-solving capacity. The agencies of the criminal justice system are in a competitive market for new members and the present fiscal climate of austerity gives greater urgency to recruiting able people from the widest pool of talent.

More particularly, the case for diversity within the CJS has been made on the grounds of legitimacy. With respect to the police, the Council of Canadian Academies (2014) stated that having a service that is representative of the population served is generally held to be important for legitimacy and police effectiveness whereby greater community co-operation with officers is induced, as well as inculcating less fearfulness amongst citizens, especially the marginalised. Davenport (2006) presented a rationale for developing a diverse and a more representative police service based on the principle of policing by consent. Central to this premise are notions of trust and confidence. She argued that in a contemporary democracy, the citizen must be able to recognize the values of the police service and to feel that it is accountable. The means to evaluate the performance of the police is through a participative engagement between police and community and for the citizen to be policed by officers who look like themselves. Key to achieving legitimacy is transparent accountability and visible identification. This resonates with ideas of procedural justice we discussed in Chapter 2. The central idea of procedural justice is that people care about being treated fairly because this both generates and reinforces a sense of shared group membership with the police and the social groups it represents. This can be thrown out of balance without a representation of the community members being policed. Lack of such representation undermines people's sense of identification and is less likely to engender a moral alignment with the purposes of policing or engage the public's co-operation and compliance with policing tasks (Loader, 2014).

In respect to the courts, Malleson (2013, p. 481) suggested there is 'now a clear consensus ... that a diverse judiciary is an indispensable requirement of any democracy'. Similarly, Rackley (2013, p. 503) declared 'that the judiciary – particularly in its upper echelons – should be more diverse has in recent years become a truth almost universally acknowledged'. Tyler (2010) extended the arguments about legitimacy to correctional settings, and that a procedural justice focus may assist in the aim of prevention and in the creation of an environment that releases less alienated prisoners back into the community.

There is also a transformational argument (Cockburn, 1989). Such a project for equal opportunities is intended to examine the purposes of an organisation, and throw light on and change the processes through which some have power over others and the way in which these processes are reproduced, and the impact this has on the objectives of the organisation and how these are achieved. Thus Rackley (2013), in commenting about the judiciary, a transformative diversity seeks to create a new environment that allows for difference in substance and style, bringing different perspectives to judging and in turn better justice.

Rabe-Hemp (2008) argued that bringing more women into policing (in the USA) would help to establish a less aggressive and more calming style to conflict resolution. A report by ACPO, APA, and the Home Office, (2001) maintained there is a clear link between internal workplace diversity and external service provision in policing, arguing that a more diverse workforce will result in:

- a broader range of information for decision-making and a wider range of possible solutions;
- a greater willingness to challenge established ways of thinking and consider new options;
- improvements in the overall quality of the team;
- better staff management, leading to improvements in staff satisfaction;
- a reduction in the number of employees leaving the service;
- fewer grievances and complaints; and
- better relationships with the community, resulting in a more effective service and better quality services, leading to increased public confidence.

A recent UN report on justice concluded that 'employing women on the front line of justice service delivery can help to increase women's access to justice. Data show that there is a correlation between the presence of women police officers and reporting of sexual assault' (UN Women, 2012, point 5). Belknap (2007) discussed the presence on women in corrections as contributing to a normalisation of the environment relaxing tension and bringing about improvements in inmates behaviour and language.

Transformational equal opportunities are presented as an alternative to the liberal and radical approaches. The aim of the former is to remove barriers that inhibit fulfilment of potential and create distortions in the labour market that prevent the best person being appointed (i.e. letting more people in). The radical approach seeks more direct intervention into working practices to achieve an equitable distribution of rewards, i.e changing the organisational culture. Liberal policies are more likely located in the business case and are procedural in emphasis, whilst the radical approach is based on some moral criterion and focuses on outcomes. The latter has a political agenda and seeks to accelerate the achievement of equality, which potentially undermines strict application of the merit principle. The use of quotas and positive discrimination are controversial because they permit a member of an under-represented group, who is not necessarily the best candidate, to be appointed.

Diversity audit

As suggested in the introduction, for the most part, the CJS is dominated by white men. The Council of Europe (2012) undertook a review of their 47 member states' justice systems. Overall they found that 52 per cent of judicial appointments were held by men and 48 per cent by women, but that there was considerable disparity between states. For example, in Slovenia 78 per cent of judges were women, compared to 23 per cent in the UK. The figure for Australia was 33 per cent (Australian Women Lawyers, 2013).

The Council of Europe report also looked at the percentage of women prosecutors. Out of the 28 states they were able to collect data for, a majority (15) indicated that there are more women than men prosecutors practicing in lower courts, but that the trend is reversed before the appeal courts, with even more disparity before the Supreme Court. In England and Wales about a third of all barristers are women and 7 per cent are from an ethnic minority (MOJ, 2014).

Prenzler and Sinclair (2013) examined the representation of women in policing. Of the 16 jurisdictions they looked at, India had the lowest (5 per cent) and Northern Ireland the highest (27 per cent). The average for Australia was 24 per cent and for Canada 20 per cent. The most recently available data for England and Wales shows the percentage of women to be 27.9 per cent. It is also instructive to look at the percentage share of rank for women in the police. In England and Wales 17 per cent of women hold supervisory rank compared to 17 per cent in Canada and 12 per cent in Australia. In Australia 30 per cent of men hold supervisory rank and in England and Wales the percentage is 25 per cent. Van Ewijk (2011) showed that as rank of officer increases levels of diversity diminishes within police forces in Europe. Rates of representation of women, homosexuals, and persons having a migrant background generally are lower than representation in European society as a whole, although ratios have improved over time. Dowler and Arai (2008) reported research showing that most women officers believe that male domination and discrimination impedes career advancement. In their own study of the Baltimore police they found that women officers thought they were held to a higher standard compared to men. Intriguingly, their male counterparts thought that women were actually treated more leniently by police administrators, itself a source of irritation. This study also indicated the lack of family-friendly policies, including issues of childcare, parental leave, and part-time working options that added to the stress burden of women officers. A similar finding was relayed by the Independent Police Commission (2013) reporting the results of a large survey of police officers and civilian support staff serving in England and Wales.

Prenzler et al. (2010) found a disproportionately high number of policewomen in administration and a lower proportion in specialist areas such as counter-terrorism. Brown et al. (2014) also show gender segregation in that women were more likely to be deployed in areas of uniformed community policing and less likely to hold specialist roles such as dog handling or firearms officers.

As the majority of prisoners are male, then male prison officers predominate. Belknap (2007) reported that about one in four corrections officers in the United States were women. In England and Wales the ratio is about 3 : 1 men to women serving as officers. The policy of cross-posting means that either gender can serve in both male and female prison establishments (Tait, 2008). Thus in the ten women's prison establishments in England and Wales there are 440 male officers (40 per cent) compared to 640 women officers. Tait (2008) suggested women prisoners felt an overall benefit from having male officers, whom they found to be less punitive and petty than women officers in their dealings with inmates. Women officers working in male establishments experience more resistance from male colleagues than from inmates, partly because of the perception that the presence of women disrupts officer solidarity.

The National Probation Service in England and Wales has a greater number of women (74 per cent) possibly due to the Probation Service's past association with social work. In England and Wales, Probation and Prison Services are combined into the National Offender Management Service. Overall white heterosexual males dominate (there were 44 per cent women, 8.5 per cent ethnic minorities, and 14.5 per cent self-declared lesbian/gay/bi-sexual (LGB) staff in the workforce (MOJ, 2014).

The probation service in England and Wales actually has more women than men with the latest figures available from the Ministry of Justice showing there to be 71.7 per cent women and 28.3 per cent male probation staff. The percentage of senior probation staff is somewhat closer, with 56 per cent of women in senior positions compared to 44 per cent of men. Mawby and Worrell (2013) suggest that, notwithstanding the high proportion of women to men in the probation service, there remains a degree of ambivalence about the promotion of main-grade women. They also report that much remains in probation culture such as long working hours, compulsory socialising, and aggressive competitiveness of the new marketization that do little to accommodate women's caring responsibilities. Indeed neglect of family and stress on domestic relationships provides an added strain to working life. Mawby and Worrell found upwardly mobile women probation officers indicated they have to work harder to get where they are (similar to women police officers). Interestingly, Mawby and Worrell suggest that women may be promoted to precarious leadership positions, with men avoiding responsibility for failing departments or dysfunctional teams, i.e. the 'glass cliff' problem. This is defined by Ashby *et al.* (2007, p.778) as when women leaders 'are more likely than males to be appointed to leadership positions in problematic organisational circumstances'.

As shown above, the representation of women judges and prosecutors tends to decline with seniority. The roles they play are also gendered. Thus in England and Wales 52.29 per cent of magistrates are women (as are 9 per cent of those from an ethnic minority), whereas there are only 17.4 per cent of women serving as high court judges and no recorded members of an ethnic minority (MOJ, 2014). Belknap (2007) says that women in American law were more likely to accept placement in less prestigious positions and, like Westmarland (2001) for policing, the suggested reason for this lowering of ambitions is a combination of wanting to manage career and parenting, as well as potential discrimination. Ashby *et al.* (2007) report that only 17 per cent of women make partner in American law firms, whilst 78 per cent work as paralegals. Figure 16.2 summarises the percentage share by gender of the CJS workforce in England and Wales. This snapshot graphically demonstrates the remaining gender imbalance.

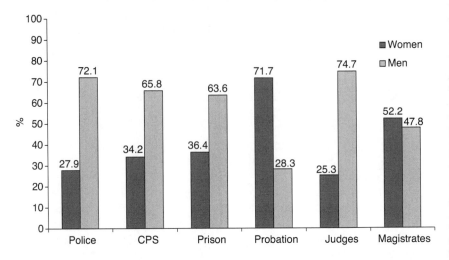

Figure 16.2 Percentage of women and men serving in different parts of the CJS in England and Wales, 2013–2014.

Under-recruitment of black minority ethnic (BME) police officers remains an 'obstinate' issue for the police service in England and Wales (Cashmore, 2001) and the number of officers employed lags behind the national average for the BME population. The Council of Canadian Academies (2014, p. 48) reported that although the police organizations in Canada have made attempts to increase the diversity of their workforce, the proportion of visible minorities employed by the police is significantly below that of the labour force's national average. Visible minorities are 20 per cent of the Canadian population yet only 8 per cent are employed as police officers.

Smith *et al.* (2012) undertook an analysis of disciplinary infractions within several British police forces. They found an over-representation of BME officers and staff in internally raised misconduct investigations. Qualitative data reported in their study revealed that BME officers believed there to be a dual system of misconduct operating in which they were subjected to unjust and punitive treatment compared to their white counterparts who were more likely to be dealt with informally. Their view was that supervisory officers preferred to ask their force's professional standards department to deal with issues involving black or Asian officers, possibly because of fears of being accused of racism. This is a pertinent observation, as Jay (2013) commented that a similar fear inhibited the investigation of extensive child abuse in Rotherham, UK because the perpetrators were from the Pakistani community.

The issue of racism is present in the prison service. Bhui and Fossi (2008), for example, observed that most studies show racism to occur not only between prisoners or between staff and prisoners, but also black members of staff were subject to racist comments from fellow prison officers. However, they point to anti-racist policies pursued by the Prison Service in Britain during the 1980s and 1990s that met with some success and when openly racist staff were dismissed. More stringent management and use of disciplinary procedures permitted further gains with the establishment of race relations committees, race relations officers, and sophisticated ethnic monitoring and complaints procedures. In more recent years the Prison Service has taken a more strategic approach. Two programmes were launched, RESPOND (Racial Equality for Staff and Prisoners) and RESPECT (Racial Equality for Staff), as well as the setting of key performance indicators to measure progress.

Bhui and Fossi (2008) commented that whilst there has undoubtedly been positive change, nevertheless the underlying culture in prisons has been less supportive and good intentions have been frustrated in fully implementing policies. Research suggests that the key ingredient to change was organisational commitment. Hogan *et al.* (2006) found that organisational stressors such as role ambiguity and role conflict were inversely related to commitment in a sample of British prison officers. As well as clarity of their role, the latter wanted clearer guidance and direction from their prison Governors. A particular difficulty in the prison environment is that equality policies tend to express the uniqueness and worth of individuals, whereas security needs encourage suspicion and defensiveness and discourage distinctiveness in the interests of maintaining order. This is especially true when the prison estate is under capacity pressures, and movements of prisoners within and between establishments may 'stifle' professional development by reducing time for staff training.

The percentages of BME probation officers (in England and Wales) is less than 10 per cent for those of Afro-Caribbean background and about 3 per cent for those of Asian background (Mawby and Worrel, 2013). Mawby and Worrel (2013, p. 128) suggest that efforts to recruit greater numbers of BME staff were hampered by:

- the perception that probation was part of the CJS that oppressed black people;
- cumulative educational disadvantage that rendered a disproportionate number of black people ineligible for training;
- unfair recruitment procedures and selection criteria.

Heer and Atherton (2008) note that diversity training with the Probation Service was geared more to how staff treated clients rather than colleagues. In their study of Asian probation officers, respondents often felt trainers did not necessarily deal adequately with racist comments or challenge stereotypic views. For Asian officers in particular there tended to be a failure to recognise the diversity within the Asian community. Recent terrorist activities may also have perpetuated negative feelings and suspicion.

There are also examples of age discrimination within the CJS. Redman and Snape (2006) provided evidence from their study of police personnel serving in a force in the north of England where 'officers experience a negative effect of perceived age discrimination on job and life satisfaction, perceived power and prestige of the job and affective commitment' (p. 173). Similarly, although great strides have been made in the employment and deployment of lesbian, gay, or bi-sexual (LGB) police officers, there remains evidence of discriminatory treatment (Bernstein and Swartwout, 2012; Jones, 2014; Miller and Lilley, 2014).

There is also the intersectionality problem. This refers to a person who is characterised by at least two protected categories, such as being black or Asian and a woman. Distinctive discriminatory experiences and particular forms of harassment are evident in policing (Brown and Harleston, 2003; Dodge and Pogrebin, 2001; Palmiottto *et al.*, 2005) and the law (Pratt, 2012), with black women at the intersection of both racial and sexual prejudice.

Evidence of positive outcomes

We have argued thus far the moral, ethical, and pragmatic case for increased diversity in criminal justice agencies, and that the absence of balanced workforces have negative impacts both on staff and communities. The data indicate a lack of diversity in the CJS. But is there evidence that having greater diversity achieves tangible benefits? Chrobot-Mason and Aramovich (2013) claimed that workforce diversity is a 'double-edged sword' having the potential for both positive and negative outcomes. What they suggest is that where diversity is managed effectively then the predicted gains of greater job satisfaction, more innovation, and higher productivity are realised. However, where the process is managed badly, this may actually create further discrimination and harassment and increase turnover of staff. They concluded from their review of the literature that the actual effects on workplace outcomes of greater diversity have been 'limited and inconsistent'. Their own study of public sector employees in the United States (50 per cent of whom were police officers) found that when diversity was managed well there were tangible benefits. Where diversity training is thought to be insincere or notional, marginalised groups tend to feel worse off. The practice implication of these findings is that organisations should deploy resources to impact employees' perceptions of the benefits of equal access and equal treatment to create a positive organisational climate.

Positive benefits of greater numbers of women in policing were reported by Dick *et al.* (2014) who indicated changes in the more problematic and troublesome aspects of a male-dominated occupational culture. Mawby and Worrell (2013) found from their study of probation that having women at senior level was associated with better administrative organisation, higher levels of computer literacy, greater victim focus, and more positive team playing.

Progress and barriers

Notwithstanding recognition of the problems, there are advantages to be had in a more diverse CJS workforce, but progress has been a case of 'one step forward and two steps back' (Belknap, 2007). Prenzler *et al.* (2010) say of policing in Australia and New Zealand that whilst the proportion of women police is increasing and women are moving up the ranks and across the organisation, levels of recruitment are stuck and resignation rates are above their representation in the ranks. From their international review, Brown *et al.* (2014, p. 5556) concluded that

> [in] Western democracies, all types of policing activity are open to women, but they are still likely to be a minority in specialist areas, such as those involving firearms, counterterrorism, traffic, and riot control duties. In practice, women are more likely to be present in general patrol duties and administrative and supportive functions, especially among non-sworn personnel.

In Canada women still only represent 20 per cent of all police officers and only 10 per cent occupy senior officer positions (Council of Canadian Academies, 2014).

This is not to say there has been an absence of successes. Prenzler and Sinclair (2013) indicated there have been 'enormous' improvements, especially in the recruitment of women to middle ranks in the Australian police service. Westmarland (2001) noted that women have achieved chief officer rank and migrated across into areas of specialism. However, a recent calculation revealed that 14 of the 43 police forces in England and Wales have no women at Chief Officer rank and women are still under represented in specialist areas (Independent Police Review, 2013). The Honourable Justice Ruth McColl (2014), whilst celebrating the success of women in the Australian judiciary, identified obstacles that might impede further progress. Malleson (2013, pp. 481–482) suggests that

> the lack of gender balance in the judiciary in England and Wales has attracted growing political attention over the last 20 years ... yet despite two decades of official activity, the pace of change has been far slower than anticipated ... and there remains little prospect of any significant shift in the composition of the bench in the near future.

A list of current barriers in achieving equity in criminal justice agencies was enumerated by Belknap (2007) and includes:

- perception of preferential treatment by men who think women are shielded from 'real' work, such as female police officers and prison guards not dealing with violent men (or women) and lawyers not handling high stress cases. Another version of this problem is paternalism or misplaced chivalry (although preferential and protective treatment is more likely available to white women than African American women);
- higher expectations, greater levels of scrutiny, and pressures of representing the competence of all women by their actions. So members of minorities

whether BME (see Rowe, 2014), non-heterosexual (see Bacon, 2014), or women (see Dick *et al.*, 2014) perceive that they have to work harder, smarter, and better than white, straight, or male colleagues. In addition there is the problem of the recruit or employee who holds 'token' status and is the pioneering first. In reference to a woman in policing, Heidensohn (1992) suggested she must represent a class action demonstrating the efficacy of all women;

• lack of access to male support networks and being presented with the horns of a dilemma: if women socialise with male co-workers it may be assumed that they are having sex with them, resulting in negative assessments of their moral (or indeed professional) worth, whereas desisting from fraternising may mean missing out on informal information about aspects of the job or promotion, as well as being labelled 'cold' or 'lesbians' with concomitant opprobrium;

• stereotyping, such that women prison workers are restricted to working with juveniles or incarcerated women, and women police officers are reluctant to take on duties such as specialist firearms officers.

In addition to Belknap's (2007) list, Silvestri *et al.* (2013) drew attention to organisational barriers in mainstreaming part-time working, and instigating accommodating shift patterns to manage caring responsibilities without which career progression may well be inhibited. They argued that 'premised on the "ideal" type of worker in which the possession of a full-time, long and uninterrupted career profile reigns, the impact of such a strict linear profile holds serious implications for some women wanting to progress in policing' (p. 66). They suggested that trying to balance family and career commitments creates an 'irresolvable' conflict, with women wishing to preserve time for caring responsibilities are less able to display the right amount or type of commitment and credibility necessary to attain higher rank. Belknap (2007, p. 449) discusses this concept of commitment in relation to lawyers where she describes the following double bind: if she is a good lawyer she must be a bad mother, i.e. she can only be a successful lawyer at the expense of her children. Dick and Cassell (2004) concluded from their qualitative analysis of British police that women officers who were mothers were seen as having greater commitment to childcaring; this was viewed as potentially compromising to their commitment to working long hours, responding to unpredictable call outs, and their deployability on potentially dangerous assignments (see further discussions about work–life balance in Chapter 12).

The negative attributes of the occupational culture (discussed in Chapter 2) of sexism, racism, and homophobia make it difficult for those who are 'other'. In other words being women, BME, or homosexual makes it more difficult to fit in and access the informal social support networks, as well as creating the climate of scrutiny and harassment alluded to above. Thus charges of institutional racism (and sexism) have been levelled at the police culture (Grieve and French, 2000) in the form of unintended discrimination outcomes brought about by the structures and procedures embedded in an organisation.

Belknap (2007) also refers to the effects of the 'glass ceiling' (mentioned previously) which blocks women lawyers from partnership and high-income elites. The Council of Canadian Academies (2014) makes a similar observation with respect to women police officers. Another proffered reason is that women simply do not put themselves forward, the 'sticky floor' explanation of self-imposed limitations. Brown *et al.* (2014) suggested that disadvantaged groups such as women may 'self-select' out of applying for employment, promotion, or specialist roles because of career expectations generated in childhood, the potential conflict between work and caring responsibilities, and, as Heidensohn (1992), suggested expectations of discrimination, especially being the first in post. Just as many women police become highly skilled and eligible for promotion, caring commitments often mean they drop out of policing and do not return – even when maternity leave is available (Prenzler *et al.* 2010).

Ashby *et al.* (2007, p. 778) suggest that 'women end up in leadership roles that are more risky and precarious than those of their male counterparts, and are more likely to attract unfair criticism'. They undertook a classroom-based experimental study with law students in which they had to assign a male or female leading counsel to run a case. Consistently, the woman lawyer was seen as more appointable to be lead counsel in a high-risk case associated with negative publicity and criticism than an equivalently qualified male. Gender did not feature in a decision to appoint counsel to a low-risk, trouble-free case. They concluded that selection of the women in the high-risk case was less risky for women than men because they had more to gain and less to lose. Heidensohn (1992) reports a variant of this in policing when she talks about women being appointed as 'a desperate measure' to deal with problematic or crisis situations.

Legislation and codes of practice provide the means of making reasonable adjustments in recruitment, accessing promotion or areas of specialism, but as Lee (2005) showed there is not only a resistance to these but also a lack of enforcement of affirmative action plans and initiatives. Malleson (2013) observed, in respect of the judiciary, that the legal profession believed women would naturally 'trickle up' once the Judicial Appointments Commission began its work in 2006. She concluded that the view dominating debates in England and Wales was that policies based on positive action were a threat to the merit principle and as such initiatives have been limited to 'road shows' and 'job shadowing'. There is strong resistance to the use of quotas as a way to enhance representation of minority groups.

Remedies

Standing and Baume (2001) in discussing some general lessons noted that:

- Policies must be accompanied by 'teeth', i.e. resources and commitment by senior staff.
- Implementation requires authentic training and development.

- There is evidence that flexible employment arrangements improve staff retention and reduce wastage of highly trained staff.
- Human resources remit should widen to include manifestations of indirect discrimination such as stereotyping and gender segregation.
- Monitoring, data collection, and evaluation to track differential recruitment, wastage, and patterns of entry and exit of staff is vital.
- Measurement should also be undertaken of the organisational climate to check if quality of work–life is equitable across groups, as well as examination of the links between specific diversity interventions and desired organisational outcome

More specifically, with respect to policing, Brown *et al.* (2014) proposed:

a   removing any female formal or informal quotas limiting the numbers of women in departments;
b   removing physical ability tests in recruitment – especially military-style obstacle course tests, replacing 'physical agility tests' with a general health test that assesses an applicant's ability to be trained in the basic physical requirements for general duty policing as demonstrated by research and case law (Lonsway, 2003);
c   giving a higher profile to educational qualifications in selection criteria;
d   including female representation on recruitment and promotion panels may guard against bias in selection;
e   introducing enforceable policies against sexual harassment and sex discrimination, with an internal unit responsible for their implementation.

The use of more formal, legalistic interventions can be exemplified in the United States by the imposition of quotas on the recruitment of women (and other minority groups), often through court-ordered consent decrees and class actions (Palmiottto *et al.*, 2005). In Northern Ireland, the 50:50 quota policy was a mechanism which mandated that the number of Protestant recruits be matched by an equivalent number of Catholics, in order to increase the latter's representation in the newly formed Policing Service of Northern Ireland (PSNI). This form of positive discrimination certainly brought about change much faster than any 'trickle up' approach (Malleson, 2013). Malleson (2013) also noted that there are many different models of quotas which could be adapted to meet the needs of different stages of the selection process (e.g. application and/or appointment). Furthermore, quotas can be set differently. For example, in Austria the gender quota for selection to the High Court is 30 per cent. The other variable in setting quotas is time-scale, which can be time-limited as in the PSNI 50:50 case. Tyler (2010) proposed that in respect to corrections four issues need to be addressed to redesign institutions:

1   voice: providing opportunities for inmates to participate in decision-making, especially routines affecting their daily lives;

2   neutrality: consistent application of the rules rather than on the whim or prejudices of officers or the authorities;
3   treatment: dealing with inmates with respect and dignity;
4   trust: authorities acting with a sincere desire to do what is right and fair.

Conclusions

We can reasonably conclude that diversity adds value to a workforce by drawing in a wider range of perspectives and experiences, that is, enhancing the available human capital. There is also a legitimacy argument which is especially pertinent to agencies of criminal justice. Treating people fairly and justly is likely to foster greater engagement and reduce antagonism, and is premised on profound ethical and human rights principles. More pragmatically, greater diversity is likely to provide a wider pool from which to appoint the best person for the job. Discriminatory treatment can have adverse impacts both on individuals and also the reputation and capacity of organisations. There are larger policy questions to consider, for example, Tyler (2010) suggested that incarceration is generally a delegitimating experience and we should consider more resources be directed at prevention and alternatives to prison. The more radical transformational intervention requires a 'paradigm' shift and wholesale rethinking of the organisational culture discussed in Chapters 2 and 12.

References

ACPO, APA, and the Home Office (2001) *Equality, diversity and human rights strategy for the police service*.

Ashby, J., Ryan, M., and Haslam, A. (2007) Legal work and the glass cliff: evidence that women are preferentially selected to lead problematic cases. *William and Mary Journal of Women and the Law*, 13: 775–793.

Australian Women Lawyers (2013) Media release: gender in the Australian judiciary.

Bacon, M. (2014) Police culture and the new policing context. In Brown, J. (ed.) *The future of policing*. Abingdon, UK: Routledge (pp. 103–119).

Belknap, J. (2007) *The invisible woman: gender, crime and justice*, 3rd edn. Belmont CA: Thompson Wadsworth.

Bernstein, M., and Swartwout, P. (2012) Gay officers in their midst: heterosexual police employees' anticipation of the consequences for co-workers who come out. *Journal of Homosexuality*, 59: 1145–1166.

Bhui, H. Singh, and Fossi, J. (2008) The experience of black and minority ethnic prison staff. In Bennett, J., Crewe, B, and Wahidin, A. (eds) *Understanding prison staff*. Cullompton, UK: Willan (pp. 49–64).

Brown, J., and Harleston, D. (2003) Being black or Asian and a woman in the police service. *Policing Futures*, 1: 19–32.

Brown, J., Prenzler, T., and Van Ewjk, A. (2014) Women in policing. In Bruinsma, G. and Weisburd, D. (eds) *Encyclopedia of Criminology and Criminal Justice*. Springer (pp. 5548–5560).

Cashmore, E. (2001) The experiences of ethnic minority police officers in Britain: underrecruitment and racial profiling in a performance culture. *Ethnic and Racial Studies*, 24: 642–659.

Chrobot-Mason, D., and Aramovich, N. (2013) The psychological benefits of creating an affirming climate for workplace diversity. *Group and Organisational Management*, 38: 659–689.

Cockburn, C. (1989) Equal opportunities; the short and the long agenda. *Industrial Relations Journal*, 20: 213–225.

Council of Canadian Academies (2014) *Policing Canada in the 21st century: new policing for new challenges.* Ottawa: Expert Panel on the Future of Canadian Policing Models, Council of Canadian Academies.

Council of Europe (2012) *Report on European Judiciaries.* www.coe.int/t/dghl/cooperation/cepej/evaluation/2012/Rapport_en.pdf.

Davenport, S. (2006) *Developing a diverse representative police force.* Unpublished ACPO discussion paper.

Dick, P., and Cassell, C. (2004) The position of policewomen: a discourse analytic study. *Work, Employment and Society*, 18: 51–72.

Dick, P., Silvestri, M., and Westmarland, L. (2014) Women police: potential and possibilities for police reform. In Brown, J. (ed.) *The future of policing.* Abingdon, UK: Routledge (pp. 134–148).

Dodge, M., and Pogrebin, M. (2001) African-American policewomen: an exploration of professional relationships. *Policing: An International Journal of Police Strategies and Management*, 24: 550–62.

Dowler, K., and Arai, B. (2008) Stress, gender and policing: the impact of perceived discrimination on symptoms of stress. *International Journal of Police Science and Management*, 10: 123–135.

Grieve, J., and French, J. (2000) Does institutional racism exist in the Metropolitan Police Service? In Green, D. (ed.) *Institutional racism and the police: fact or fiction?* London: Institute for the Study of Civil Society (pp. 7–19).

Heer, G., and Atherton, S. (2008) (In)visible barriers: the experience of Asian employees in the probation service. *Howard Journal*, 47: 1–17.

Heidensohn, F.F. (1992) *Women in control.* Oxford: Clarendon.

Hogan, N.L., Lambert, E.G., Jenkins, M. and Wambold, S. (2006) The impact of occupational stressors on correctional staff organisational commitment: a preliminary study. *Journal of Contemporary Criminal Justice*, 22: 44–62.

Independent Police Commission (2013) *Policing for a better Britain.* London: The Commission.

Jackson, S., Joshi, A., and Erhardt, N. (20033) Recent research on team and organisational diversity: SWOT analysis and implications. *Journal of Management*, 29: 801–830.

Jay, A. (2013) *Independent inquiry into child exploitation in Rotherham 1997–2013.* www.rotherham.gov.uk/downloads/file/1407/independent_inquiry_cse_in_rotherham.

Jones, M. (2014) A diversity stone left unturned? Exploring the occupational complexities surrounding lesbian, gay and bi-sexual police officers. In Brown, J. (ed.) *The future of policing.* Abingdon, UK: Routledge (pp. 149–161).

Kandola, E.S., and Fullerton, J. (1998) *Diversity in action: managing the mosaic.* London: CIPD Publishing.

Lee, T. (2005) The myth and reality of affirmative action: a study using the perceptions of female police officers. *Race, Gender and Class*, 12: 56–72.

Loader, I. (2014) Why do the police matter? Beyond the myth of crime fighting. In Brown, J. (ed.) *The future of policing.* Abingdon, UK: Routledge (pp. 40–51).

Lonsway, K.A. (2003) Tearing down the wall: problems with consistency, validity, and adverse impact of physical agility testing on police selection. *Police Quarterly*, 6: 237–277.

Malleson, K. (2013) Gender quota for the judiciary in England and Wales. In Schultz, U. and Shaw, G. (eds) *Gender and judging*. Oxford: Hart (pp. 481–499).

Mawby, R.C., and Worrell, A. (2013) *Doing probation work: identity in a criminal justice occupation*. London/New York: Routledge.

McColl, R. (2014) *Celebrating women in the judiciary 2014*. Address to New South Wales Women Lawyers, 27 February.

Miller, S.L., and Lilley, T.G. (2014) Proving themselves: the status of LGBQ police officers. *Sociology Compass*, 8: 121–149.

MOJ (Ministry of Justice) (2014) *Statistics on women and the CJS 2013*. www.gov.uk/government/uploads/system/uploads/attachment_data/file/380090/women-cjs-2013.pdf

Palmiottto, M., Birzer, M., and Smith-Mahdi, J. (2005) An analysis of discrimination between African-American and women police officers: are there differences? Similarities? *Criminal Justice Studies*, 18: 347–364.

Pratt, C. (2012) Sisters in law: black women lawyers' struggle for advancement. *Michigan State Law Review*, 1777–1795.

Prenzler, T., Fleming, J., and King, A. (2010) Gender equity in Australian and New Zealand policing: a five year review. *International Journal of Police Science and Management*, 12: 584–595.

Prenzler, T., and Sinclair, G. (2013) The status of women police officers: an international review. *International Journal of Law, Crime and Justice*, 41: 115–131.

Rabe-Hemp, C. (2008) Survival in an 'All Boys Club': policewomen and their fight for acceptance. *Policing: An International Journal of Police Strategies and Management*, 31: 251–270.

Rackley, E. (2013) Rethinking judicial diversity. In Schultz, U. and Shaw, G. (eds) *Gender and judging*. Oxford: Hart (pp. 501–519).

Redman, T., and Snape, E. (2006) The consequences of perceived age discrimination amongst older police officers: is social support a buffer? *British Journal of Management*, 17: 167–175.

Robinson, G., and Dechant, K. (1997) Building a business case for diversity. *Academy of Management*, 11: 21–31.

Rowe, M. (2013) Race and policing. In Brown, J. (ed.) *The future of policing*. Abingdon, UK: Routledge (pp. 120–133).

Silvestri, M., Tong, S., and Brown, J. (2013) Gender and police leadership: time for a paradigm shift. *International Journal of Police Science and Management*, 15: 61–73.

Smith, G., Hagger Johnson, H., and Roberts, C. (2012) *Disproportionality in Police Professional Standards*. Greater Manchester Police. www.gmp.police.uk/mainsite/pages/2073C1C52A9FABB880257A800044A656.htm. eScholarID: 170650.

Standing, H., and Baume, E. (2001) *Equity, equal opportunities, gender and organisational performance*. Geneva: WHO Department of Organisation of Health and Social Delivery.

Tait, S. (2008) Prison officers and gender. In Bennett, J., Crewe, B., and Wahidin, A. (eds) *Understanding prison staff*. Cullompton, UK: Willan (pp. 65–91).

Tyler, T. (2010) Legitimacy in corrections: policy implications. *Criminology and Public Policy*, 9: 127–134.

UN Women (2012) *Progress of the world's women: in pursuit of justice, 2011–2012*. United Nations Entity for Gender Equality and the Empowerment of Women

Van Ewijk, A. (2011) Diversity with police forces in Europe: a case for the comprehensive view. *Policing*, 6: 76–92.

Westmarland, L. (2001) *Gender and policing: sex, power and police culture*. Cullompton, UK: Willan.

17 Conclusions

Final thoughts, emerging issues and next steps

In this book we have identified the conceptual underpinnings that contribute to common problems within the criminal justice sector. We have also discussed how these conceptual underpinnings are also the solutions to optimising working environments within this sector. We believe we have succeeded in collating research evidence and best-practice examples of the key issues facing managers and employees working within the global criminal justice community. In Chapter 1 we discussed reasons why external factors of politics, IT, economics, and changes in the types and levels of crime have significantly impacted criminal justice services. Fulfilling the dual demands of modern employment requirements and providing just and fair operational services, all whilst performing on a reduced budget, is one of the greatest challenges our criminal justice services has encountered.

Our aim with this book was to review the pertinent evidence relating to current employment practices and the organisational behaviours of criminal justice workers. Chapters 2 to 6 in Part I and Chapters 12 to 16 in Part III each successfully achieved this aim. These chapters discussed the perennial impact of inadequate communication processes, impaired staff management practices, experiences of bullying, harassment and discrimination, and other issues occurring within the criminal justice agencies. We acknowledge that these issues are also experienced in all other employment sectors, but their occurrence within the criminal justice sector is particularly noticeable, as we described in each individual chapter. In these chapters, we also provided practice examples of criminal justice agencies from around the world who had directly addressed these issues, often through some quite innovative methods.

In Part II of the book, consisting of Chapters 7 to 11, we presented the common tools by which organisations address key psychosocial workplace issues. These five chapters described how criminal justice agencies often use methods of evaluation, focus groups, consultation, surveys, and the Delphi technique to both assess and attempt to remedy problematic organisational behaviours. The chapters in Part II were designed to contribute to organisational knowledge about the most appropriate techniques involved in the use and administration of each of these tools. Our discussion of these techniques was elementary but effective and these chapters were designed to inform organisations of the key necessities required to successfully perform assessments of employees.

These chapters also highlighted the advantages for criminal justice organisations of forming collaborative partnerships with university researchers. From our own experiences, and from many of the examples cited within these chapters, it is clear that research collaborations with academic researchers provide a number of advantages for criminal justice agencies, including:

- access to up-to-date expertise;
- the administration of objective methods that are bound by ethical guidelines;
- cost-effective projects that form the basis of research projects and/or research theses;
- detailed analyses including complex quantitative and qualitative techniques;
- international dissemination of the work in academic research outputs.

We consider this last point of international dissemination to be particularly important and criminal justice agencies are encouraged to overcome their natural reticence at being identified in research articles. The showcasing of 'best-practice' organisational initiatives to an international audience offers positive publicity and is associated with 'leading the field' in organisational learning endeavours (e.g. Brown and Campbell, 2010; Kalliath *et al.*, 2014).

Emerging issues for criminal justice organisations

The conclusions discussed within each chapter of this book and current discussions within the broad academic fields of criminal justice, suggest that over the next decade some critical human resource issues will have an increasing traction for criminal justice organisations. To conclude this book and to inform further research we briefly highlight some of these most important issues.

Retaining skilled employees is a growing concern for many criminal justice organisations, certainly most of those within the Western world. We discussed the changing nature of criminal justice employment conditions in Chapter 1. The use of technology (for both the conduct and detection of crime), increasing levels of employee diversity (including an increase in part-time employment), and the increasing public accountability of criminal justice organisations (in terms of financial performance and the just treatment of both employees and offenders) have changed the composition and working styles of the policing, corrections, and other criminal justice workforces. Similar patterns are also noted within the general workforce. The transition from traditional blue-collar workers employed primarily for their physical strength (i.e. mostly male) to knowledge-based workers employed primarily for their cognitive skills, has been observed in many Western countries (O'Driscoll and Brough, 2010). Thus a reliance on the recruitment of physically strong male police and prison officers, for example, is diminishing. The increased recruitment of female employees also brings a greater focus on work–life balance employment options, including part-time work, which, as we discussed in Chapter 12, is an increasingly pressing issue for many criminal justice organisations.

Increasing levels of employee diversity also impact on the organisational culture. While we discussed organisational culture within criminal justice organisations in detail in Chapter 2, we also identified its contributing factor to the occurrence of occupational stress (Chapter 13), experiences of bullying and harassment (Chapter 15), and leadership styles (Chapters 4 and 14). Increasing employee diversity, especially the employment of greater numbers of female police and prison officers, generally serves to weaken the 'traditional macho' culture commonly existing within these services. A more diverse employee pool requires different leadership styles, that is, a reduced focus on task-based supervision and an increase in supportive (or transformative) management skills (Biggs *et al.*, 2014).

A diverse employee pool with more skills-based workers also requires a **different work culture in terms of motivation and performance criteria**. Thus the traditional quasi-military culture inherent within many police and prison services, based on strict hierarchical chains of command and following orders, and regulated by a powerful disciplinary culture, is often inconsistent with the primary needs and motivators of skills-based work. Instead, we find that work cultures based on support, engagement, opportunities for individual autonomy, organisational justice, and positive recognition, for example, have a greater impact on the levels of motivation and performance for these workers (Brough and O'Driscoll, 2015; Dollard *et al.*, 2014). Certainly an emerging problem identified within many criminal justice organisations (and other similar agencies such as the Fire Services) is the clash between these two markedly different cultures and the difficulties of transforming a quasi-military, disciplinary-focused culture into a supportive and engaging culture for employees.

It is apparent that the **political climate of austerity** continues to constrain the budgets and operations of most public sector services, including those of the criminal justice services. The United Kingdom, Europe, the USA and Australia continue to forecast increased economic constrictions within the near future. Successfully managing organisational growth and development, retaining and improving operational services, addressing public demands and averting unrest, and satisfying employee requirements, all performed on constrained budgets is a considerable challenge for senior managers of our criminal justice services, as we discussed in Chapters 4 and 14. We also noted in Chapter 1: 'Cuts are likely to be a continual feature of the criminal justice system for the foreseeable future and so efforts to improve organisational functioning are going to have to be cost-neutral at a minimum and cost-saving at best' (p. 7).

Successfully operating within these budget constrains is particularly worrying when combined with the developments in crime we noted previously. It is increasingly difficult (and unpopular) to attempt to constrain, for example, current demands for increased resources to address issues of international organised crimes, the monitoring of domestic terrorism threats, and the evolutions in drug-based criminal activities.

Similarly, in times of economic austerity the **work demands placed upon employees traditionally increase**: staff positions are not filled, resources are not updated or are withdrawn, staff development activities are reduced, and 'soft' services including staff support programmes maybe limited or with-drawn. The willingness for organisations and their employees to participate in surveys, focus groups, or other research activities has also been noted to be significantly reduced when economic climates are contracting (Brough *et al.*, 2014). The consequences for employees, of course, include increased work demands and stress, increased job insecurity, increased instances of interper-sonal work conflicts including bullying and harassment, and reduced volun-tary turnover (less employment choices in an unstable job market). These issues were discussed in detail in Chapters 13, 15, and 16. So ironically, at a time when occupational stress management support for employees is most needed, organisations typically have less ability to offer such services and certainly less inclination to trial new programmes. Constraints placed upon union activities, employment tribunals, and judicial reviews currently occur-ring within many Western countries, also impacts adversely on the health, well-being, and performance of the workforce. The skills of senior managers to 'ride out' these economic conditions and lead an effective organisation with adequate levels of engaged and productive workers are extremely challenging.

Underlying most organisational changes, as well as operational practices for criminal justice organisations, is an increased reliance on **evidenced-based knowledge**. This is a refreshing focus and reflects in part the increased inter-nationalisation of both criminal acts and co-operations between international agencies. We discussed aspects of this topic in Chapter 6 with its focus on the movement towards professionalisation of criminal justice organisations. Thus the seeking of external advice for both specialised operational requirements and organisational management issues is now becoming more selective, as indeed it should. Interventions and organisational changes, which have a track record of success in similar agencies, are increasingly being called for. This reflects the comments we made above, in that long-term research collaborations between criminal justice agencies and university researchers are increasingly being recog-nised for their value and contribution. We certainly encourage each agency to establish the empirical success of any organisational programme prior to its administration to employees.

Next steps

In Chapter 1 we overlaid the current challenges being experienced by inter-national criminal justice organisations onto a six-steps *strategic foresight frame-work* (Hines and Bishop, 2006). We employed this framework, consisting of *framing, scanning, forecasting, visioning, planning, and action,* to inform both the structure and contents of this book. In closing, it is pertinent to emphasise the impact of considering potential alternative scenarios (i.e. forecasting), in order to improve the organisational performance of our criminal justice services and by which they can attempt to address the future issues identified above. From our discussions within this book it is apparent that management options which purport to provide rational choice solutions to employees (such as introducing penalties for periods of sickness absence, or performance-related pay incentives) remain popular with many governments and private-sector organisations. However, these employment conditions are commonly mismanaged to focus instead on the micro-management of work performance, including, for example, a rigid adherence to performance indicators, meeting targets, and the 'payment by results regime'. Such employment conditions are now common in many public sector industries including the criminal justices.

The ability of these rational choice employment conditions to be successfully maintained over the long term, given the future challenges facing criminal justice services discussed above, is however extremely unlikely. Certainly in times of economic austerity, these employment conditions tend to *increase* the work demands and occupational stress experienced by workers, primarily due to their inherent unfairness of administration, eventually producing disengaged and 'toxic' employees. A more meaningful approach is ensuring criminal justice services retain and improve their focus on **procedural justice** people management practices. Thus organisations which demonstrate consistency, clarity, and truthfulness in their decision-making and communication processes for employees at all levels and which enable these employees to have a voice in these processes will retain engaged and motivated staff. These organisations will, therefore, be better equipped to respond to future economic and political turbulence. The vital importance of procedural justice processes for the future of policing, corrections, and other criminal justice services has already been identified (Bradford *et al.*, 2013; Tyler, 2013).

Successfully leading and working within criminal justice organisations is increasingly requiring a creative focus, to enable agencies to adequately address future crimes and technologies that have yet to be fully developed. Effective managers must also keep abreast of changing employment issues concerning their staff. Current discussions concur that the status quo cannot be retained and instead criminal justice organisations do need to prepare themselves for dynamic changes. We also acknowledge that this is a challenging viewpoint for the more traditional members of our criminal justice services. We trust our discussions within this book have informed readers of the key changes ahead and highlighted critical points for further consideration and improvements within our criminal justice services.

References

Biggs, A., Brough, P., and Barbour, J.P. (2014) Enhancing work-related attitudes and work engagement: a quasi-experimental study of the impact of an organizational intervention. *International Journal of Stress Management*, 21: 43–68.

Bradford, B., Jackson, J., and Hough, M. (2013) Police futures and legitimacy: redefining 'good policing'. In Brown, J. (ed.) *The future of policing*. Abingdon, UK: Routledge (pp. 79–99).

Brough, P., and O'Driscoll, M.P. (2015) Integrating work and personal life. In Burke, R.J., Page, K.M., and Cooper, C.L. (eds) *Flourishing in life, work, and careers: individual wellbeing and career experiences*. Cheltenham, UK: Edward Elgar Publishing (pp. 377–394).

Brough, P., Timms, C., O'Driscoll, M., Kalliath, T., Siu, O.L, Sit, C., and Lo, D. (2014) Work–life balance: a longitudinal evaluation of a new measure across Australia and New Zealand workers. *International Journal of Human Resource Management*, 25(19): 2724–2744.

Brown, J., and Campbell, E. (2010) *The Cambridge handbook of forensic psychology*. Cambridge: Cambridge University Press.

Dollard, M., Shimazu, A., Bin Nordin, R., Brough, P., and Tuckey, M. (2014) *Psychosocial factors at work in the Asia Pacific*. London: Springer.

Hines, A., and Bishop, P. (eds) (2006) *Thinking about the future: guidelines for strategic foresight*. Washington, D.C.: Social Technologies.

Kalliath, T., Brough, P., O'Driscoll, M., Manimala, M., Siu, O.L., and Parker, S. (2014) *Organisational behaviour: a psychological perspective for the Asia-Pacific*, 2nd edn. Melbourne: McGraw-Hill Publishers.

O'Driscoll, M., and Brough, P. (2010) Work organisation and health. In Leka, S. and Houdmont, J. (eds) *Occupational health psychology*. Chichester: Wiley-Blackwell (pp. 57–87).

Tyler, T., and Jackson, J. (2013) *Future challenges in the study of legitimacy and criminal justice*. Yale Law School, Public Law Working Paper 264.

Index

Page numbers in *italics* denote tables, those in **bold** denote figures.